Driving
Peak Sales Performance
in Call Centers

Mary Murcott

What Others Are Saying about this Book

"Loaded with practical, compelling ideas about how to improve sales performance and increase the bottom line. The book is about people, profits and winning!"
Linda Nowlin, Enterprise Services Senior Program Manager, Dell, Inc.

"This book should be essential reading for everyone in the call center world. Mary Murcott has done her homework and has delivered a revolutionary book on driving sales in a call center. This is a must-read that is destined to become a call center management classic."
Stacy Smith, Vice President, Direct Bank Manager, Hibernia Bank

"I wish I had this book 12 years ago. It provides a concise, yet powerful perspective that will help any call center sales professional achieve top performance."
Roger K. LaGrone, Vice President, Reservations & Customer Care, Travel Impressions/An American Express Company

"Mary Murcott's comprehensive and practical approach to managing the ever-complex world of call centers is right on target... a must-read for any professional wanting to maximize the potential of his or her customer service and sales organization."
Russ Olivier, Senior Vice President, North American Operations and IT, Hilton Reservations Worldwide

"Mary has presented her hard-won insights in a manner that will be immediately actionable to every level within the contact center—from the COO right through to the first line. Everyone who reads this book will know exactly what to do when they get into the office tomorrow! You don't have to suffer through a lot of difficult trial and error—Mary has already done that for you. Her insights form the platform of the action plan she presents so clearly in this volume. Understand her experiences, follow her advice, and see immediate, positive results!"
Dennis Morgan, Principal–Contact Center Optimization Group, eLoyalty

"...Educational, insightful and well-written. This book is a significant business tool for all call center leaders who are interested in driving improved sales performance. It encompasses all of the key elements for driving positive outcomes: strategy, people and the use of appropriate metrics. It provides the critical foundational steps for successfully moving your call center organization to its maximum level of sales performance."
Joy I. Labadie, Vice President, Customer Service Support, Budco–The Dialogue Company

"Anyone who is involved in the recruiting arena will benefit from *Driving Peak Sales Performance in Call Centers*. The strategies outlined in "Sourcing, Selecting and Retaining the *Right* People" [Chapter 7] work... I know because I have successfully implemented many of these strategies and have seen the results firsthand."
Debbie Harding, Employment & Recruiting Manager, Televista

"Mary proves that the call center environment is not just about technology—it is about people, processes, information management and decision science. She takes a holistic, general management approach to the call center environment, and strikes the optimum balance between sales, service and costs."
Vic Macchio, President, Windward Marketing Group

"No matter what the size of the call center or how many years of leadership experience one may possess, the practical wisdom in *Driving Peak Sales Performance in Call Centers* can be applied. This book is an excellent roadmap for positively improving sales and impacting the total customer experience."
Tracy Romano, Director of Customer Satisfaction and Continuous Improvement, DHL Express

"...A must-have resource for any organization that is serious about generating revenue from its call center operations. Mary Murcott has written a truly groundbreaking book; it is the first to address this important topic in depth. This book presents not only a strategic view of driving call center sales performance, but also includes a multitude of practical tips, advice and case studies."
Brent J. Carstensen, Principal, Customer-Focused Solutions

Published by:
Call Center Press
A Division of ICMI, Inc.
Post Office Box 6177
Annapolis, Maryland 21401 USA
www.icmi.com

Printed in the United States of America

ISBN 1-932558-05-5

Driving
Peak Sales Performance
in Call Centers

Mary Murcott

Call Center Press™
A Division of ICMI, Inc.

Acknowledgements

I didn't realize it until a couple of years ago, but this book has been formulating in my head for at least 10 years. There were some things that needed to be said, and I appreciate my friend and colleague Brad Cleveland, president of ICMI, for his encouragement to go ahead and say them.

There are so many people to thank, as we surely never accomplish anything alone. I want to thank a number of colleagues, bosses and members of my management teams who have influenced my thinking on leadership, focus and performance management, including Margaret Brownlee, Linda Schaffer, Mark Sotir, Judy Versteeg, Cynthia Valles, Abhay Padgaonkar and Denise Karki.

Many thanks to Carol Trimmer, Dr. Mark Haug and Dr. Wendell Williams for providing absolute clarity regarding the mathematics and science behind performance management, incentive and selection systems. Thanks also to Ziad Khoury who reminded me to search for performance potential using gap analysis. Without Mary Lou Johnson, the project management forms and sections would not have been as robust. The CRM expertise of Bruce Daley provided a concise overview of a complex topic that was truly invaluable.

Kudos to those who pointed me in the right direction to find those managers and executives with great sales results, subject-matter expertise and real-life success stories from which we could learn, including Rosemary Wilkie, Skip Haislip, Antonio Maia, Brent Carstensen, Allen Boehme, Ron Dull, Jack Schiefer, Jeff Brown, Jeff Howard and Nick Covelli. Also, my thanks to additional subject-matter experts Joan Sims for training and coaching and Stacy Smith for performance metrics in the financial industry.

I especially want to thank the following executives—those who spend time in the trenches driving superior sales performance every day—for their time. Jud Linville from American Express; Nelson Elmore and Nancy

Peinado from Cox Communications; Susan Searle from Best Software; Georgia Eddleman, Denis Honan with Lands' End; Denise Cooper and Mike Kennedy from Wasatch Solutions Group; Tim Cook and Sam Perry from Hilton Reservations; Diana Kempf from Convergys; and Tom Morrisroe from RMH. Their insights, which are based on actual examples in their organizations, bring the book to life. This book is respectfully dedicated to them and their management teams.

Gratitude and admiration goes to the stellar group of editors, graphics managers and publishers at ICMI and Call Center Press, including Greg Levin, creative projects specialist; Rebecca Gibson, manager of educational services; Ellen Herndon, graphic designer; Susan Hash, editor-in-chief; and Brad Cleveland, publisher and thought leader.

A tremendous debt of gratitude to my best friend, spouse and editor extraordinaire, Brian Murcott, who brought wit, hope, resolve, emotional support and love for the proper use of the English language to my work; and to my mother, Barbara Brennan, a writer and author, who instilled in me the confidence to write about what I know with clarity and conviction. To all, my utmost appreciation.

Foreword

As a pioneering author in the call center field, I'm often approached to provide an endorsement or make some contribution to a new entry in the field. Usually, I decline gracefully. Occasionally, I write one as a favor for colleague. This time, though, it's my absolute joy to provide a ringing endorsement for Mary Murcott's indispensable *Driving Peak Sales Performance in Call Centers.*

If you're in any way connected with the call center world, you simply *must* own and digest the abundant wisdom and frontline experience that Mary provides in this invaluable volume. You're going to enjoy reading it the first time, and your neck will get sore from nodding, "Yes, she's right about that!" This book will gather no dust on your reference shelf.

Managing a call center has become such a science. You need to sit at the foot of a seasoned practitioner who knows what works… and what doesn't. That's Mary.

First, there is the constant technological innovation to consider. It now seems so funny to reread my book, *Phone Power,* which was published in 1986, and see my bold prediction that "no office technology has a more promising growth outlook than voice mail." I'll say! Today, just a couple of decades later, it's imperative that every manager have a fundamental grasp of extremely complex, rapidly evolving technological solutions to real-world issues. Mary manages to demystify even the most complex technical matters. Heck, she even makes such concepts as "standard deviation calculations" comprehensible in less than a page!

Driving Peak Sales Performance in Call Centers begins with a qualitative observation that's hard to quantify or put into words. Mary refers to "the Hum and the Buzz" of an optimally performing center. She has picked up the vibe when walking through centers representing diverse industries—and more often, she *hasn't* picked it up, because most centers just aren't run well.

You know that sensation of being in a call center environment where you intuitively know that things are working optimally. People are happy and enthusiastic. The stats are good. Revenues are healthy and growing. Staff turnover is minimal. When team members walk out at the end of their shifts, they don't look weary and spent—they look like they've enjoyed their hours of helping customers.

But how does a call center get that way? It's certainly not the result of good luck or fortunate circumstances. A well-executed formula is what creates that Hum and Buzz. It's like a three-legged stool that must have all three legs firmly positioned to create stable success. One crucial component—the foundation—is sound strategy. You'll read how to build a profit-oriented business case for your center's key role as a strategic element in your business plan.

Another leg of the stool is great people—and that requires sound recruiting, well-crafted incentive and compensation programs, and ongoing exciting training and motivation.

Still another critical element is the technical and technological support platform. All three of these elements—strategy, people and technology—must be in balance. If any one leg of the three-legged stool is weak, the call center will not Hum nor Buzz—it might not topple, but it certainly won't experience peak sales performance.

Mary brings to this volume an extremely rare, triple-whammy combination: 1) real-world, practical, in-the-trenches personal experience; 2) a superb ability to comprehensibly communicate complex strategic issues; and 3) a just plain fun-to-read writing style.

Personally, I'm proud to lend my name and support to this book. Its value is beyond estimation. All of what you find here will strike you as logical and reasonable. You'll also find that it's thoroughly researched and empirically based. And some of it will surprise you.

I always love those rare instances when you encounter an author who writes conversationally and with all-too-rare candor. Isn't it true in call center management—and in life—that our most profound and valuable lessons result not just when things go just right, but when the learning curve has some dips or even chasms? Mary shares some of the disastrous mistakes made by call centers, not just those glowing successes we all like to crow about. She's not afraid to say: "Quite frankly, we mucked it up!" And when she reveals the shortcomings of half-baked or ill-conceived programs that simply did not achieve their lofty goals, she saves you from having to make those same mistakes in your own call center.

I could conclude by calling this book "required reading," but I won't. There is no burden, no onerous imposition, no dry academic treatise in these pages. You're about to enjoy this expansive and entertaining guide to the profitable management of your call center. And as soon as you implement its principles, you'll begin to hear that Hum and Buzz.

George R. Walther
Professional speaker and author of *Heat Up Your Cold Calls*

Table of Contents

Driving
Peak Sales Performance
in Call Centers

Mary Murcott

Preface: "The Hum" and "the Buzz"

Recently I called my friend and colleague Brad Cleveland—president and "guru" of the call center consulting and training firm Incoming Calls Management Institute (ICMI)—for what I call a "Brad Fix." Brad is the kind of friend who challenges you intellectually and doesn't buy into all your precious theories too readily. It had been two years since I had spoken with him last—a year longer than my regular dosage interval—so we were ready to talk about the continuing evolution of call centers.

I was really excited to tell him that, after 30 years in the call center business, I finally had heard "the Buzz" in my centers. Let me explain.

A number of years ago, I consulted with a large, well-known company that ran large sophisticated contact centers in several of their divisions. One division had recently grown astronomically through the consolidation and acquisition of many smaller companies. Although they had a collection of business offices with 10,000 service reps answering phones, they had not realized that they were really a virtual call center.

In a company well-known for its service, this particular division was a service disaster. Phone reps were often "missing in action." The organization had ACD systems, but, in order to hit service levels, supervisors frequently "stripped" calls by physically answering the phone and taking a callback request. The answer to their problems—and, really, to the survival of their business—lay in the discovery that they were, indeed, a call center operation. Once that fact became clear, they realized that running their operation like a call center instead of separate offices with a lot of phones would enable them to optimize the workload to consistently hit good service levels at reduced costs. Management eventually became well-versed in concepts like forecasting, workforce management, scheduled occupancy, adherence, service level and average handling time.

An influx of capital, technology, training and new processes, as well as a significant amount of resilient leadership, eventually brought about a cultural revolution—turning a large organization of independent offices with a lot of phones into a virtual call center network. After two years of administering call center processes and training at all organizational levels, I received an excited call from one of the call center managers who had been challenged to oversee all of the changes necessary in a recent implementation of call center management practices. She called to tell me that she had finally heard "the Hum!" She was thrilled—she "got it."

"The Hum," as I had described it to the organization earlier, is *the actual sound* you hear when you enter a well-run call center. The Hum is *not* the sound of managers screaming across a center demanding that their people get "plugged in" or searching for "warm bodies" in the break room, or worse, the bathrooms. It is not phone reps wandering the floor looking for management to answer their questions. And it is not seeing paper airplanes flying across the call center because there are too few calls for the number of reps on the phones. Believe it or not, these conditions still exist in some call centers today. Rather, it is the low-key sound—*a real hum*—which occurs when service levels are being hit and employees are being very productive but not overworked. A nice balance. A wonderful sound—like a distant beehive where everyone knows what their job is and does it well.

Years later, after many false starts and myriad incremental sales improvement successes, I heard a new sound in my centers: I heard "the Buzz." The Buzz is an actual sound one hears in call centers that are driving sales at a peak performance level. It's similar to the Hum, but its energy level is higher—so pronounced that you think something might explode.

Peak-performing sales centers are rare, elusive creatures. In fact, I had rarely seen one. It is a call center where sales ratios and revenues are being driven at levels far beyond anyone's expectations. While most call centers take orders and only occasionally try to cross-sell or upsell, this particular center's reps not only sold better than the competition, they personally called their competitors to understand how to sell against them. The top reps held training classes on how to sell, tracked lost sales to identify new packages or promotions, and made recommendations at corporate meetings.

The sales managers looked forward to monitoring and development time with their reps because they knew that the reps were making a huge impact on the company's goals. This was a peak-performing call center.

Optimizing operations has been the trend in call centers over the last few years. However, when many consultants and vendors pitched *optimization*, they really meant finding ways to pull more costs out; to drive customers to less expensive distribution channels, such as the Internet or an IVR with natural language recognition; and to reduce human contact with the customer. This is all wrong. This is not optimization; this is driving a distorted view of efficiency even further down the current wayward road.

Optimizing a call center is about optimizing real business outcomes, like customer loyalty and revenue per call. If we want *spectacular* sales performance improvement, we cannot keep focusing on ancillary measurements, such as the cost of a call. We need new metrics like channel profitability. We may need to consider strategies that move some customers back to live agents for service. Why? To create an opportunity to offer exceptional products or services that reinforce our brands and strengthen our relationships with our customers.

Over the last 30 years, during the course of personally managing both service and sales centers, as well as consulting with hundreds of others, I've had the opportunity to review a great number of operationally efficient centers. I've met many call center managers who "get it right" every day. They hit their service levels and budgets without fail, which is no small feat. Nevertheless, I've seen only a few companies that understand true call center optimization—what it takes to drive peak sales performance or foster exceptional customer loyalty—and I've met only a few executives who are seriously focused on sales and who have devised ways to sustain centerwide and individual performance at consistently high levels.

After two decades of tweaking a lot of moving parts and getting it wrong plenty of times, my management teams and I have identified a few secrets about optimizing performance—particularly sales. While researching this book, I discovered that a number of these "hidden opportunities" also had been discovered by some of my colleagues at leading companies. They, too, were quietly driving sales to new performance levels in their call centers. I have spoken with managers and executives at companies such as Hilton Hotels, Lands' End, American Express, RMH Teleservices, Convergys, Cox Communications and many others—all of whom were willing to share their successes in driving large-scale sales improvements in sales and service call centers. A manager from one well-known company described how they achieved a 12-point increase in sales close ratios over a three-year period, which resulted in more than $200 million in additional profit each year. Another brought its small-market direct-sales function into an outsourced call center and reduced the company's cost-per-sale by 93 percent. However, changes of such magnitude do not happen overnight. They sometimes require rethinking *who* is selling and what the *rules* are for selling.

Whether your focus is on inbound sales, outbound sales or service calls in your center (or if you are like many of us—you manage it all), this book will stimulate your thinking about your center's potential. Although the performance management examples used throughout are primarily found in the call center industry, many of the guiding principles, processes and best practices that are outlined can be utilized in non-contact center support organizations, such as database groups or financial/IT shared service organizations, as well as other channels like the Internet.

In his book, *Call Center Management On Fast Forward,* Brad defines one of the basic call center management challenges as "getting the right people and supporting resources in the right places at the right times, doing the right things." This book is about getting the right sales people, the right sales training and the right sales management practices operating in an environment conducive to breakthrough performance levels. It examines the specific issues facing call centers that are aiming to boost revenue by improving sales performance, including:

- Finding the right people—50 percent of all sales people have absolutely no ability to sell,[ii] yet 70 percent of our call centers are attempting to sell.

- Training reps in sales skills—the best sales people rarely make good sales coaches.

- Identifying and recruiting top producers—the top sales producers in sales organizations are typically twice as productive at generating sales as low producers;[iii] however, in call centers, the spread between top and low producers falls in the range of 100 to 300 percent.

This book is not about *how* to sell, it is about discovering and unlocking unique opportunities for sales and additional revenues that are currently residing in your center. It concentrates on eliminating the restrictions we have placed on ourselves that limit the call center's potential—for instance, not selling on any service call, automating as many service calls as possible, and hiring sales staff who lack the ability to sell no matter how hard they try or how much training they receive.

This book will share with you the sales philosophies of some of the industry's leaders. You'll learn how to create new performance reporting tools; design new hiring, training, performance management and coaching processes; and introduce incentive programs that truly matter to high performers as well as the average sales staff.

Once you begin to hear "the Buzz" in your call center, you'll find that the profit from increased sales potential is so compelling, all cost-cutting initiatives pale in comparison.

Section 1:
The Case for Peak Sales Performance

Chapter 1: Identifying New Revenue Opportunities

"People can't do what they can't imagine."
THE CLEMMER GROUP

Call centers have matured tremendously over the last 30 years, improving upon operational basics and more. In the last decade, call center budgets were slashed to the core and managers faced the challenges of dealing with new contact channels, new technologies and the exportation of jobs offshore. We must ask ourselves, "What else is there?" When there is little cost left to cut, how else can we contribute to the company's profitability? We must look to our existing assets: our people, our processes and our customers. If we look hard enough, we can discover untapped revenue in structural issues with respect to who is allowed to sell, systemic issues highlighting how and what we sell, and individual sales or service representatives' performance gaps.

The revenue improvement opportunities found in today's call centers typically can be categorized into three areas of focus—structural, systemic and rep performance—which are represented in the schematic on the following page.

CALL CENTER REVENUE OPPORTUNITIES

Structural Factors	Systemic Factors	Rep Performance Factors
• Who is allowed to sell • On which calls can they sell • Automated calls that could be redirected to a sales rep • Organizational structure • Acquisition potential of a sales affiliate or a company that could provide requested products where products are missing	• Selling policies and procedures • Product availability • CRM capabilities • System limitations or problems • Service delivery issues • Closing tools	• Right person in inbound sales • Right person in outbound sales • Right person in service with sales capabilities • Right training • Right script outlines • Right performance standards • Right sales coaches • Right environment

---

As you can see, there are many places to look for missing revenue. It is a hunt. The items listed under *structural factors* will help you to seek opportunities that often can be missed if you've been looking at the *organizational role* of your call center, department or company in the same way for a long time. Questioning some of your long-held assumptions about who should be allowed to sell and on which types of calls can result in dramatic revenue gains, as you'll see in some of the interesting success stories in this book.

The *systemic factors* address systemwide processes, information or policy limitations in place that restrict the conversion of calls into sales transactions. However, the primary focus of this book involves the third category: *rep performance factors.* While tapping structural and systemic revenue opportunities can yield significant revenue gains (and you will be shown where to look), once an organization is aware of where those opportunities may be found, it rarely needs much assistance mining the missing revenue. While we will highlight methodologies to address structural and systemic factors, figuring out how to close the performance gap between high and low performers is not so apparent. Learning about the practices and guiding principles prevalent among top-selling call centers will save you from numerous pitfalls that endanger superior performance management. Think of structural factors as the "*who* sells" and "*to whom* we sell," and the systemic factors as the "*how* we sell." Let's look at one example.

Hilton Hotels' Structural Revenue Opportunities

Hilton Reservations is an outstanding example of an organization that has successfully tapped into all three revenue opportunities—structural and systemic factors, as well as individual rep performance. The operation is comprised of five domestic contact centers and 14 international centers staffed by more than 2,000 reps. Over the past three years, it has improved its close ratio (gross reservation transactions divided by calls handled) by almost 12 percentage points—moving from a close ratio of 29.9 percent to 41.9 percent—an amazing accomplishment when one considers that most call centers fight to gain a .25- to .5-point improvement year over year.

Sam Perry, president of Hilton Reservations, credits their remarkable sales improvement to three factors. First, he acknowledges that the acquisition of Promus Group hotels (which included Doubletree, Embassy Suites, Homewood Suites and Hampton Inns) enabled a cross-selling initiative that accounted for about half of its close-ratio improvement. The acquisition (a structural factor) essentially eliminated the major obstacles that frequently prevented reps from closing a sale. Instead of denying a caller's request for a reservation because a hotel was sold out or because there wasn't a Hilton hotel in the city which the caller requested, reps were able to cross-sell the other brands. Additionally, if a rate was too high or a room type was unavailable at one property or brand, the rep could cross-sell the customer to another brand more suitable to his or her requirements.

In 2003, cross-selling brands resulted in $337 million in incremental gross revenue—revenue that was simply not there before the merger, according to Perry.

Perry credits his management team (rep performance factor) as the second factor in increasing revenue. Over a two-year period, the team, led by Tim Cook, vice president of North American operations, implemented a performance management database; restructured the contact centers' incentive, recognition, monitoring, coaching, evaluation and feedback systems; and revised rep training. Cook points out that the key to this incredible movement in performance improvement "was the team's ability to pull together, take the best practices from both companies and get extremely focused, which allowed us to achieve outstanding results."

Finally, a move to consolidate sales calls into the call centers from the local hotel properties further increased close-ratio performance (both a structural and systemic factor). Previously, inbound calls were routed to the hotels or the network contact center, depending on which phone number the customer dialed. Today, almost 70 percent of the full-service properties' calls are routed to a central reservations group. Because reps at the central reservations center can access all of the hotel brands' pricing and availability through their centralized reservations system, they're able to cross-sell the brands, which has increased their close ratios 10 to 15 percent over those of the local properties. Additionally, the call centers can maintain significantly lower abandonment rates due to staff pooling capabilities. Perry estimates that, for every hotel property that consolidates its sales calls into the centralized reservations center, an additional revenue of $120,000 is generated annually.

Evaluate Your Need to Change

What can you expect when you embark upon this journey called "Peak Performance"? You may be asking yourself: Is "the Buzz" worth it? What must be changed? How long will it take? Is it painful? What does it take to see it through? Can it be institutionalized? Is the call center organization and, more importantly, the enterprise ready for a major change? What if we fail? What's in it for my reps, my management, my company and for me? I have a well-run organization, I sleep well at night, and I hit my objectives and my budget... why should I bother?

These are all concerns that I pondered as I considered what I could do in my call centers to drive breakthrough sales performance. They are all appropriate questions that must be asked and answered before expending significant time, effort and money to make the necessary changes. Let's take a brief look at some of these concerns to give you a preview of what is involved in moving forward. All of these topics are covered in depth later in the book.

WHAT CAN YOU EXPECT IF YOU EMBARK UPON A PEAK SALES PERFORMANCE INITIATIVE?

Expect to come up against a multitude of reasons (and myths) why sustained peak performance is impossible. Objections will be vigorously raised by your frontline staff as well as management. For example, sales reps might tell you that the competitors have different or better products, or that their price is lower, or that the service is not as good as it used to be, or that a new competitor is making it more difficult, or that they are getting more shopping calls. The list goes on and on. To overcome resistance, you must get to the root of the fear. People fear both success and failure.[i] Failure is easy to understand. But success? Success is sometimes feared for many reasons, including the fact that new expectations have been set and now the new level of performance or lifestyle, etc., must be maintained. Fear of standing out and jealousy are among other factors. Be prepared for dissimilar rationale among individuals. Fighting this type of resistance is difficult because it requires individual attention. Your job as a leader is to dispel the performance myths every day.

IS "THE BUZZ" WORTH IT?

You can determine the answer to this question by running your own numbers through the business case presented in Chapter 3. The results will vary depending on whether you're in a service or sales environment; whether you're addressing structural, systemic or individual performance gaps, or all three; and depending upon the service or product. A small operation (fewer than 50 reps) might find an additional annual revenue opportunity of $100,000 to $4 million, while a large organization (2,000-plus reps) might identify a revenue opportunity of $20 million to $500 million a year or more. These numbers are only estimates based upon my experience and interviews with numerous U.S. companies, but they are derived from *real* results.

It takes some time and effort to determine the sales potential of your call center. Here's a quick way to get an idea of how much potential exists: Calculate the revenue-per-phone hour or close ratio (total sales transactions or units sold by each rep divided by the total calls taken by each rep). Then calculate the difference between the results of the lowest producer and those of the highest producer as a percentage. If the difference between the revenue productivity of your lowest- and highest-producing tenured rep is only about 30 percent (e.g., close ratio of 30 percent vs. 39 percent equals a 30 percent difference), then you are one of the few call center managers who is getting it right. If your call center is like the majority that are leaving an incredible amount of revenue on the table, the difference will probably be around 100 percent (e.g., a close ratio of 20 percent vs. 40 percent equals a 100 percent difference). If you calculated the difference based on revenue-per-hour on the phones, the difference could be far greater—as much as 300 percent or more! Don't panic, just don't tell anyone how bad it is until you've read further and figured out what you are going to do about it!

WHAT MUST CHANGE?

Generally, almost everything changes—recruiting and hiring processes; training, evaluation and coaching processes; compensation and incentives; quality assessments; and standards, goals and targets. In addition, the call center may initially experience higher turnover, the number of calls that default to an IVR may decrease, new positions may need to be created, and skills-based routing may need to be revised. And, in most cases, more robust levels of integrated performance reporting are required. The biggest and most difficult change for many managers is moving people who lack selling ability out of sales positions, and moving those who cannot coach reps on selling skills out of supervisory positions.

Yes, this amount of change is considerable. Don't attempt it unless you have some level of stability in your current performance (e.g., service level, attrition, quality). It's not wise to try to walk the high-wire if you keep falling off the balance beam. This is high-wire management—it requires a relatively stable operation and strong change-management skills.

HOW LONG WILL IT TAKE?

Some changes will result in quick wins, others will take time. Some structural changes (who sells and to whom they sell) can yield improvements within months. For instance, a company that previously had not been selling to callers with service requests can implement a program in less than three months.

Systemic changes can also result in quick improvement. These include changes made to business rules, processes or systems that have been hindering the performance of your sales people. It may be as simple as changing a restrictive credit policy or an exclusion policy. For example, a change to your credit policy might involve adding the ability to approve and process checks over the phone to allow those customers without credit cards to purchase products. Or let's say a hotel company has an exclusionary policy that they won't rent rooms to individuals who are under 21 due to a history of room damage with this customer segment. While there may be very good reasons for this policy, like minimizing unprofitable revenue, there also may be ways to minimize that risk, such as creating insurance surcharges to cover it. In both of these examples, once restrictions are removed and the system modified to enable a new capability, the revenue increase is immediate and usually significant because the previous system hindered the performance of *all* performers.

Individual sales rep performance improves over time. If you replace your poor performers with higher-level performers, it will take at least a year to see the results. Implementing new hiring techniques will require about six months, and most new-hires will need approximately six months to reach their full sales potential. Overall, the initiative will require a minimum of two years to stabilize to the point where it is considered institutionalized and runs on its own cultural momentum.

IS IT PAINFUL?

Yes, of course—but it's a good pain. You know that it is good for your company. Embarking upon a journey like this involves change, sacrifice and a few battles. Probably the biggest gut-wrencher for managers is making tough decisions on what to do with their current poor performers.

Initially, turnover will be higher as you work to get people in the jobs that match their skills and personalities. But attrition typically can be reduced 25 to 50 percent simply by hiring the right people for the positions and effectively training and coaching them.[ii] When predictive hiring assessments are used in conjunction with an expertly implemented performance analysis and reporting system, attrition can be reduced by an additional 15 percent.[iii] Most executives or managers at the peak-performing sales centers that I spoke with reported remarkably low attrition rates, many of them in single digits annually (yes, they were counting all types of attrition).

Although the journey may be hard at times, the good news is you don't have to reach the final destination to reap the rewards; there are plenty of wins along the way.

CAN IT BE INSTITUTIONALIZED?

Yes, but it will take at least two to three years to complete the implementation, including two budgeting and performance review cycles to ensure that the success you are seeing is sustainable. Once the support structure is in place and the new levels of performance expectations are being met, the process and pride become self-sustaining. The call center organization may then be asked to assist other functions in performance optimization. The "learners" move past the "contributors" stage and become "teachers."

WHAT IF WE FAIL?

There are four main reasons why good call center managers may fail to deliver truly optimized call center operations:

First, in the daily challenge of running a call center, they forget that the internal measures of success (e.g., service levels, quality scores, AHT) are not the ultimate goal. The true purpose of the call center should be focused on the business outcomes, like profitable revenue and the loyalty of profitable customers. The internal process measures are important, but they're only the means to an end. If they're not driving additional sales or loyalty, then they need to be re-examined.

Being too task-driven is a second reason for failure. Obviously, managers need to be somewhat task-driven to fulfill the intense demands of the job. However, optimizing sales performance and finding opportunities for revenue requires the ability to periodically step back and broadly evaluate the call center's role in the company.

> **The true purpose of the call center should be focused on the business outcomes, like profitable revenue and the loyalty of profitable customers. The internal process measures are important, but they're only the means to an end. If they're not driving additional sales or loyalty, then they need to be re-examined.**

Third, managers are often unable to acquire and retain the necessary resources from their organizations. The call center often has to compete with other "good causes" within the enterprise. If you manage a call center, you already know how to make a compelling business case for ordinary expenditures, such as the right number of reps, workstations, and quality and workforce management systems. Implementing the changes necessary to optimize call center sales performance requires an airtight business case that justifies resources that are typically harder to obtain, such as sales training, new-hire assessment testing, organizational design consultants, performance databases and compelling incentives.

Finally, inaccurately assessing your organization's readiness for change will set you up for failure. Before tackling a venture like this, it's essential to obtain the support of your staff, upper-level management and the human resources department.

WHAT IS IN IT FOR MY REPS, MY MANAGEMENT, THE COMPANY AND ME?

Happier staff. Reduced attrition. Higher profitability. You will be able to pay your frontline reps a decent wage. One of the things that has bothered me over the years is that we in management speak of people as our greatest assets, and toss about sayings like: "The people who speak with our customers are critical," and "Our frontline reps provide the first impression of the company." Paradoxically, our "critical assets" are generally the lowest paid in the company and often work under somewhat inhumane conditions. Paying frontline reps slightly more than minimum wage to do a job with such high expectations is unreasonable. I'm not necessarily recommending raising base wages, particularly in a sales environment, but rather paying substantially more for dramatically better sales performance. If we don't change the way we pay, manage and respect our employees, then we should be more realistic and lower our standards and expectations. Doing the latter, however, will keep you on the attrition hamster wheel—which is not an acceptable alternative.

My experience has been that implementing peak performance sales practices and incentives benefit both the frontline and the company. In these call centers, many of the reps could finally afford to buy reliable transportation (thus, our attendance increased substantially), some went back to school part-time, and some could afford their first vacation ever. In management, we no longer felt like we were running a white-collar sweatshop. We felt better about the type of employers we were, and we attracted better workers once the word spread about how much our top performers could earn.

In addition to better compensation, the attention reps received from increased training and coaching raised their self-esteem and job satisfaction. They began to feel like a critical part of the company as their visibility increased and they participated in marketing, revenue management and advertising meetings. Their ideas mattered—they saw system and policy obstacles melt away, and watched their new product ideas get implemented.

I also found that, as the middle to top sales reps' performance improved and the lower performers self-selected out of the organization, the retained reps became more demanding. However, this was anticipated because peak performers have higher expectations of their managers and of their company.

I HAVE A WELL-RUN ORGANIZATION. I HIT MY CURRENT OBJECTIVES AND MY BUDGET, AND I SLEEP WELL AT NIGHT. WHY SHOULD I BOTHER?

Great question. Implementing a peak-performing sales center is a lot of work and carries some risk. Your organization believes you run a strong department now. Why risk your reputation by turning everything upside-down? Because if you don't, eventually, a consultant—or the competition—will. As organizations find it increasingly difficult to cut costs (many have already cut to the core), they are looking for ways to generate more revenue. Companies are searching everywhere for that next great idea. At some point, an internal auditor or a financial analyst will undertake a performance gap analysis and find this "gold" in your operation. Wouldn't you rather find it yourself and be in charge of your future?

Moreover, it's the right thing to do. It's that simple. Despite all the technological innovations, many companies today are just breaking even and some are failing. If you can generate a 20 percent improvement in your sales ratios or cost structure, your initiative could make the difference between profitability or loss—and ultimately, in some cases, solvency.

Key Organizational Considerations

If your organization is like most, it is attempting to shift more business to less expensive channels like the Internet or IVR systems. When a center gets into a peak performance mode, and sales conversion rates significantly improve, some organizational backlash can occur. In some cases, sales shifts in the channel mix go backward, which leads the organization to think there is a problem with the pricing, since more of the revenue mix is returning to the call center. Invariably, the immediate reaction is to decrease the price or rate structure of the Internet channel. But since research shows that nearly half of all consumer attempts to make an online purchase are abandoned, with a loss of $25 billion annually,[iv] it's critical for the organization to understand that the Web site must have its own peak performance process that focuses on higher "look-to-book" or "click-through" ratios, and not on just reducing price. It's too easy to sell on price; we must sell on value. We must solve a customer's problem.

Expect increased integration with and attention from other departments in the enterprise. Many call centers are viewed as only a support organization, or may operate very much as a standalone entity. Little important feedback takes place between these call centers and their corporate or field operation, marketing or revenue management departments. To be completely successful in this venture, you will probably need to assign accountability for many call-types to other areas within the enterprise. Unproductive calls or contacts will need to be eliminated or automated. New products or affiliates may need to be created for calls your center cannot currently satisfy. You may need to ask other departments or vendors to provide better information to your sales reps. Policies may need to be changed to enable reps to close customer sales. You may already consider these tasks as part of your regular management responsibilities, but often they aren't quantified or measured, or responsibility isn't formally assigned. Once that happens, the numbers will change dramatically.

Remember that when you begin to demand more from the company, the organizational dynamics will be affected. Make sure that other departments get all of the accolades they deserve for taking on additional work. Giving recognition where it's due will help strengthen relationships with your colleagues outside of the call center. You may even be offered a seat at the executive table. Managers who drive performance outside of their own department are always welcome at this table.

What Happens if We Do Nothing?

If I have not yet presented a solid business case for moving toward peak-performing sales centers, let me recap some of the implications associated with running merely "good" call centers:

MISSED OPPORTUNITIES FOR IMPROVEMENTS

Many call centers currently run on averages. Reality, however, is not an average. The individual customer's experience is not an average. For instance, most callers experience an actual speed of answer, and rarely the average speed of answer. Many call centers set annual objectives or have bonus programs in place that measure service level goals by weighted quarterly or even annual averages. This is not how the customer experiences service. Call centers that pay bonuses based on the number of days per month that service level ranges are attained are kidding themselves. If the calls are distributed in a certain way, an 80 percent service level can be achieved if 40 half-hour increments hit 100 percent and eight hit zero percent. This is not good service nor good cost control. (Note: actual results would depend on specific ACD calculations of service level, as well as on unique traffic patterns—but you get the idea!)

The same holds true for individual performance and call center averages. At the executive level, call center leaders have so much to oversee that most tend to manage by watching daily, weekly and monthly scorecards—looking for statistically significant variances and attempting high-level interventions to influence the numbers. But the gold is in the individual team and rep numbers. Look at the disparity of performance numbers. You will, of course, see a bell curve—if the curve is too wide at the base, an opportunity exists for improvement in either service or sales metrics (see page 18).

LOSING RESOURCES TO OTHER CHANNELS

Some businesses provide more sophisticated tools and better information on their Web sites than to call center reps. Not surprisingly, their call centers decline into abandoned distribution channels. Internet channels get more attention and capital resources from the organization for many reasons, both valid and invalid. If you're simply maintaining status quo with an average-performing call center, expect your resources to continue to diminish. But increasing service or sales throughput in the call center demands capabilities at least equal to what's offered on the Web site. Customers expect all channels to have similar capabilities, if not prices.

PERCEIVED VALUE OF THE CALL CENTER DWINDLES

In some organizations, the perceived value of the call center has begun to deteriorate somewhat as other departments have access to immediate customer data from other channels. Marketing and revenue management can go through other means to get data about customer buying habits and service issues. However, what these other channels cannot yet reliably offer is qualitative feedback and solid customer-focused conclusions. For instance, customers in focus groups are notorious for saying one thing but behaving in a different manner. That can be dangerous for the organization if actions are taken on single data points. Also, customer focus groups can be very expensive. On the other hand, an internal weekly focus group with 10 top reps, each of whom speaks with 20,000 customers a year, is invaluable. Opening the lines of communication throughout the company reinforces the value of real dialogue with the customer.

AVERAGE PERFORMANCE ATTRACTS MEDIOCRITY

If your training is merely adequate, the compensation low to average, and the performance standards not aggressive, how can you expect to attract and breed anything other than mediocrity? How hard is it to rise above mediocrity? Not very. Change everything ever so slightly, and you will have an organization that is slightly above average. But who wants to be only slightly above average?

Getting Started: An Overview of the Phases

For peak performance a lot must change, and some of the changes are fairly radical. Section 1 will give you the tools and rationale for the three major phases involved in peak performance call center transformation. Subsequent chapters will offer sample reports and project plans to get you there. But first, a brief description of the three phases:

PHASE 1: VISION, STRATEGY AND THE BUSINESS CASE

To effect the necessary changes, you need a business case. The business case is driven by a gap analysis, which helps your organization understand what is possible, given the right supporting structures (resources) and processes. The gap analysis allows for a quantifiable projection of the financial return expected by closing the gap between the low and medium performers, between the medium and high performers, and between the high performers and the highest performer. The objective is not to get everyone to the top performance level; that would be unrealistic. What happens is the lowest-level performers are completely eliminated, the "performance mean" moves higher, the bell curve moves to the right and narrows at the base (as illustrated in the box on page 18).

Besides analyzing the individual sales reps' performance gap through micro-gap analysis (which will be explained in Chapter 9), another analysis, called the "funnel exercise" (see page 24 in Chapter 2), allows you to visualize your center's "throughput potential" performance. It basically uses call-typing in a whole new way. Reframing your center's potential using this view of "throughput" can reduce resource demands or help you convert more service and sales calls into actual sales. It uses the concept of a funnel to show executives in other departments what happens to all of the calls coming into the call center, and how many customer calls that make it through the funnel culminate in sales (the resulting drop). What happens to the calls that do not result in sales opens up a lively discussion with all departments as to why we let them "get away," why we tell the customer we do not want their business, or why we have made a decision not to sell to a service call.

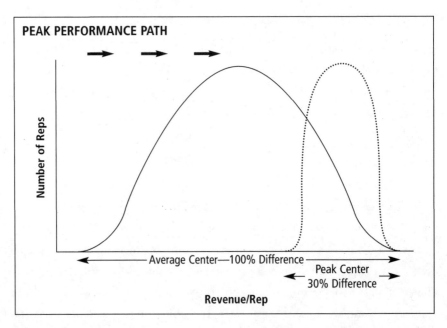

Once you have the quantifiable data and the financial projections, the fun part begins. There will be many ancillary benefits—over and above additional revenues—that are real and quantifiable, including reduced attrition, increased attendance and higher morale. Your description of the benefits resulting from the investments and process changes solidifies the vision. It states that the vision is possible provided the right changes and resources are applied, as outlined in your strategy. It lays the groundwork for the deliverables and milestones of a project plan.

PHASE 2: CREATING THE PROGRAM TO CLOSE THE GAP

The deliverables, which you outline in your vision in Phase 1, become the Peak Sales Performance Program's major projects with designated project managers. Project managers, together with project teams, have the task of creating a project agreement and plan with detailed tasks, deliverables and dates assigned. The program will most likely consist of the following projects and project teams:

- Performance Standards and Key Performance Indicators

- Sales Recruiting and Selection
- Sales Training
- Sales Coaching
- Environmental Assessment and Issue Management
- Building Incentives that Matter
- Performance Database
- Structural Factor Improvements
- Systemic Factor Improvements

These teams will likely include individuals who may not reside in your department or be under your supervision. It is doubtful that you will have all the resources or skills to create or implement all of these deliverables. Your organization will need to use matrix management to drive results. Matrix management is an often-used term that describes an organizational structure which is permanently or temporarily created to address complex issues or projects. Often, functional managers report to functional department heads on a straight line on the organization chart, but are "matrixed" to another department or project director through a dotted-line relationship. The department head with the straight-line relationship typically has the responsibility for formal reviews and merit increases, but the dotted-line director sets priorities and direction for the project the manager is involved in and has input into the manager's review. (Note: This is a classic, simplified example of matrix management. Two good sources of definition and debate on the topic include the article "Matrix Management: Method Not Magic," by Ronald Gunn, managing director of Strategic Futures, www.strategicfutures.com, and *The Wideman Glossary* on The Project Management Forum's Web site at www.pmforum.org.)

The project is not over when the tool is delivered, but when the tool is delivering the desired results. It is quite possible that some of these teams will exist for the entire two years. If something isn't working, the operation will look to the team to assist in changing the tool or instrument until it achieves the desired result.

PHASE 3: SUSTAINING AND INSTITUTIONALIZING

A significant portion of Phase 3 consists of communication: celebrating the successes and debunking the myths around performance management. It is ensuring that other departments know their efforts are appreciated and that there are meaningful and quantifiable performance results. At some point, the rest of the organization may realize that there appears to be an inequitable amount of dollars being spent on training or incentives in the call center organization. Around budgeting time in the second year, executives will question whether your organization is getting a disproportionate amount of training resources. There may be a perceived fairness issue. It's critical that the heads of the departments competing for resources understand your performance successes throughout the year. The best way to demonstrate this is to commit in the budgeting process for the revenue improvements you promised in the business case. The protests will virtually disappear when you put your track record on the financial line. In other words, put your money where your mouth is.

Institutionalization results from a combination of two things: time and consistency. Enough time has to pass to build a tradition with its own lexicon, rhythm and forms; and enough time has to pass to "get rid of the old," so that there is nothing to which one can revert. You'll know that you're there when sales reps stop talking about "the way it used to be," and when managers start teaching their peak performance methodology to others in the organization—and they become your disciples.

Points to Remember

- Powerful revenue opportunities are discovered in structural, systemic and employee performance gaps.
- If the difference in performance between the top and bottom tenured rep is more than 30 percent (best in class), performance potential still exists in your center.
- Look to individual rep statistical analysis for opportunities. Do not manage call center performance on averages.

Chapter 2: Estimating Your Center's Revenue Potential

"Pearls are formed around points of irritation."
UNKNOWN

The cost of launching a new brand in the crowded U.S. marketplace averages $30 million.[i] Clearly, it is hard to get noticed today. Add to that the annual amount of image and "call to action" advertising generated by a typical Fortune 1000 company, which could cost anywhere from $10 million to $1 billion, and we can see why the call center is so important. It takes that much money to get the phone to ring–to get someone to care enough about your company to pick up the phone and ask you something about your product.

Wouldn't it be helpful to know the actual value of your call center? If your company spent all that money in branding, advertising and promotions, wouldn't it be helpful to know how many sales you are producing, at what cost, and what your center is actually capable of when all of the obstacles are removed? Wouldn't it be helpful to express the *real* revenue potential of the call center if your reps could stop saying "no" to customers who ask you for a product? Inevitably, all reps must sometimes decline sales due to lack of inventory, inability to deliver, lack of location representation or lack of product line. In this chapter, we'll look at a few methods to help you estimate your center's potential sales contribution when structural and system limitations are lifted.

The following model, in the form of a funnel, can best demonstrate to your COO or CEO what happens to those branding and advertising dollars that the company spends every year—the ones that make the phone ring. Your 800 number has huge intrinsic value. The funnel example below represents the sales throughput of a hotel company's call centers. Look at the funnel as energy expended, with a goal of attempting maximum throughput. The drop of water at the bottom of the funnel represents the sales output from all the calls presented to the call center.

This particular company spends $150 million annually getting its customers to call and visit its Web site. It receives 100 million calls annually, but for the sake of simplicity and ease of percentage calculations, the illustration shows what happens to 100 representative sales calls.

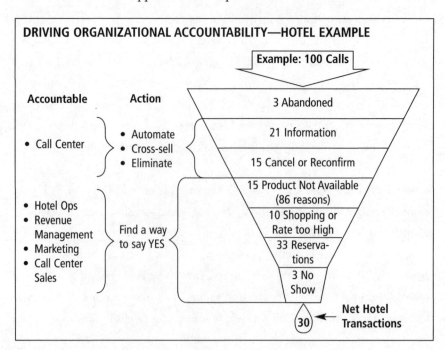

At this point, you may be thinking: "This is just a variation of basic call-typing." Granted, but rarely has anyone walked senior management through where their money goes and why you can't convert all calls to sales. The funnel also serves a different purpose: To place a value on each call in terms of revenue generated or potential revenue lost, and to eventually calculate the cost of each call-type. To determine the value of your call center, you must calculate how much hypothetical revenue could be generated if you could say "yes" to all customer sales requests.

The Value of Call-Typing

I hear frequently that call-typing costs too much money (additional handle time) or is unreliable. Consequently, it isn't done at all, it's done at such a high level that it's not actionable, or it's done sporadically (quarterly). This book is about sales effectiveness. When one pushes productivity of any kind, even sales productivity, there is an inherent danger that quality might suffer. If you have not already done so, I recommend instituting a very small Quality Assurance group (e.g., one QA specialist for every 125 reps, assuming an AHT of 180 seconds) that can monitor and review a small sampling of calls across centers and across all reps. While the QA specialists are monitoring for an outside view of quality and calibration among supervisors, they can call-type at a very reliable, detailed level. This monitoring does not replace supervisory monitoring; it just minimizes the rating inflation that occurs when incentive performance plans require minimum quality scores for payout. Additionally, the QA group can provide insights into competitive problems and identify techniques used by high-tier performers that might be useful for medium-tier performers to learn.

Finding Structural and Systemic Revenue Opportunities

The **abandoned call-type** in the illustration on page 24, derived from an abandonment rate target, is the combined responsibility of the marketing department, call center operations and finance. In this example of a sales environment, we'll use a service level of 85 percent of calls answered in 20 seconds (85/20), which correlates to a typical 3 percent abandonment rate for this company.

Each company has its own loyalty profile. Several years ago, it was possible to get "retry studies" from the phone companies. These studies allowed companies to understand their callers' brand loyalty and willingness to call a company again within set trial increments like one hour, 24 hours or 48 hours. Such studies revealed the percentage of abandoned callers who chose to call competitor A, B or C. By understanding the customer's disposition to call again, you could back into a target service level and abandonment rate through a break-even analysis—in other words, abandonment rate return on a staffing investment (ROI). If you have one of these studies from several years ago (before the phone companies began cost-cutting and stopped providing them), then refer to the last study.

Clearly, delivery on the target abandonment rate is the responsibility of call center management. Marketing will be able to contribute to the assumptions around demand management and call distribution, which will determine if these targets are reasonable.

Informational calls, when unnecessary, can drive huge costs in an operation—or they can be an untapped wealth of sales in disguise. Further call-type breakdown is required to determine the action plan in terms of how to process these calls. Call centers typically have a high volume of informational calls, but since the handle time is relatively short, they don't get a lot of attention. Do the math anyway. That will determine the priority of working a plan to reduce such call-types, or to offer products during these calls. Many informational calls result from unclear marketing tactics. This can be corrected. Sometimes merely reformatting the information on promotional literature or a Web site, or making the terms and conditions larger or clearer, can alleviate the problem.

Cancellations and reconfirmation calls are in the same category as transferred calls, only because they have some similar solutions sets.

Cancellations should be broken down into categories, as there will be a number of action plans for each category. Some should be automated, while others should be transferred to skilled sales reps to "save" the sale. Cancellation reasons should always be tracked and reported down to the smallest category so that you can take action to reduce further cancellations.

Incidentally, all of this tracking should generate action. I have encountered call centers that appear to be running well, gathering extensive data and doing all sorts of analyses—but while they can tell you everything about anything, they have not positively moved their numbers in years! This is not about record-keeping. It's not about analytics. It's about action and accountability.

Reconfirmations frequently reflect bad experiences that customers have had in the past, although not necessarily with your company or even in your industry. Such calls can also occur because customers are so overloaded with information that they're not organized. Sometimes the reconfirmation occurs because the rep lacked

> **"Never confuse movement with action."**
> **—*Ernest Hemingway***

confidence when confirming the sale. The best way to eliminate these types of calls is to email a confirmation immediately upon receipt of the order, followed by an automated phone call or a second email reconfirming the product or service ordered just prior to shipping. Always include a way for customers to get back to you. It's better to have a cancellation than to have a scheduled resource go unused.

No product or service available in our hotel funnel example might be the result of either no available hotel in the vicinity that the caller is requesting, no rooms available in a particular hotel, or because the caller has requested a particular room type but none are available. For the most part, this situation cannot be resolved by the rep—it represents a short- or long-term problem that must be addressed by management in other departments.

Frequently, these are structural or systemic opportunities (as discussed in Chapter 1), but finding and acting on them requires facilitation, communication, quantifiable reports and diligent follow-up by call center management. There also may be other alternatives used by better-performing reps that result in a sale or a satisfied customer (e.g., offering an upgrade to a suite if the room type is sold out). If a company has enough information on lost business, it might acquire another company that complements its product mix and distribution points. A great example of this is Hilton Hotels, which was mentioned earlier. Hilton found more than $100 million in annual margin by implementing this strategy.

With this call-type, conducting a focus group with reps can generate a list of obstacles or barriers to the sale of products or services. It has been my experience that rep focus groups can quickly identify numerous obstacles that the company has created due to lack of product, old business rules or complex procedures or processes. Collectively, reps often can identify 50 to 100 reasons why they are unable to serve or sell a product. Many of these reasons may be valid while others are not. The marketplace and competitors change very quickly, and what might have made sense two years ago may no longer apply. The company needs to periodically reassess its position. As a call center manager or executive, it is your obligation to highlight these issues, provide visibility at a senior level, and create a forum to reaffirm or modify the company's position. Quantifying the issue through analysis and providing "next steps" will break through some of the organizational inertia.

Our hotel funnel example is based on a real company with whom I consulted. With the help of the sales reps, we identified more than 80 reasons why they were unable to sell product. We tried to estimate the magnitude of the problem by having them identify the top 20 obstacles to sales, and then rank those obstacles in terms of frequency of occurrence. The ranking then became the target issues on which we worked with other departments. Our objective was to evaluate, through analysis and discussion, whether or not we could justify the loss of $100 million in revenue to maintain a particular policy or a "lack of product" condition. We had to decide whether we wanted to "pass" on an estimated $80 million in profit due to the lack of seasonal availability of the product. In about 40 percent of the cases, we revalidated our marketplace assumptions and no further action was taken. For the remaining obstacles, however, we created specific second-close tools for the sales reps, resolved pricing issues by creating new packages, crafted new sales dialogue, removed overly onerous customer qualification rules and created new information database capabilities that allowed reps to improve their sales.

I urge you to understand and define your reps' sales obstacles in a tangible and quantifiable way, and communicate those obstacles to the organization. You may need to add a project manager or a revenue manager who can quantify the obstacles and help to drive the projects necessary to close the gap. This is crucial because if you can fix several of these problems, *you will significantly increase the sales productivity of all reps*, not just that of the low or medium performers.

> **TIP: Make it your mission to reduce the times a sales rep must say "no" to a sale!**

Shopping or rate too high is a call-type caused by lack of a sale due to the inability to satisfy the customer because of a rep's sales ability, product or rate. Calls in this category also stem from the customer's inability to commit to the reservation sale due to the lack of a credit card, needing permission from a boss, needing to consult with a spouse or simply not being ready to commit to the trip in general. If you look deeply into this category, you will find a wealth of revenue opportunities. This category is so large and general, it must often be broken down into more finite call-types to be actionable.

Reserved business—asking for the sale or recommending a service solution that results in a hotel room reservation (in our example)—is something that many passive reps don't do. Generally, these reps should not be in a sales job. In addition, because of poor hiring profiles and lack of training, many reps don't know how to close a sale. Management often assumes that a sale is the natural conclusion of a call, but time after time, through monitoring, we don't see it happening. We hear "dead air" until the customer asks another question. Your supervisors or team leaders may not realize it's happening, but check it for yourself. As a call center manager or executive, you should personally silent-monitor at least five random calls a day.

No-shows are not call-types, they result simply because customers changed their minds about what they wanted or found something better later. If this statistic were not controllable, then all reps would have similar "no-show" statistics, but they rarely do. Generally, there is something inherently different in what some sales reps do that produces consistently lower no-show or cancellation statistics and, therefore, better revenue throughput. You can close the performance gap by understanding the tactics that your best reps use to achieve higher show rates, and by teaching those tactics to other reps in the call center.

Sales Accountability Model

Company executives should be educated with respect to the cost of various call-types, the lost revenue by call-type and the related obstacles that have been identified. The objective is to generate more revenue throughput from your call center. The model on the facing page represents a possible call-type accountability matrix that might be shared with executive management.

MANAGING WHAT IS NOT IN YOUR CONTROL

As a call center manager, you know only too well that you are not in complete control of all things that happen in your call center. Nevertheless, you cannot abdicate responsibility merely due to the lack of control. It is essential that you get buy-in at the highest levels in the organization as to the ownership of the problem or opportunity (call-type). This will require some matrix management and "influence leadership." Influence leadership is a

CALL-TYPE ACCOUNTABILITY MODEL				
Call-Type	**Owner**	**Team**	**Deliverable**	**How**
Abandoned	CCM*	• CCM • Finance • Marketing • Operations	• Correct seasonal abandoned target	• Break-even analysis
Informational	CCM	• CCM • Marketing	• A plan to reduce, automate or cross-sell • New target percentage budgeted	• Automation • Cross-sell • Elimination
Transfers	Marketing	• CCM • Telecom • Marketing	• A plan to reduce, automate or cross-sell • New target percentage budgeted	• Retraining • Call-routing review • Marketing material review
Cancel/ Reconfirm	CCM	• CCM • Revenue Management • Training	• A plan to reduce • New target percentage budgeted	• Automate through IVR • Reiterate through email confirmation
No Hotel in Vicinity	Distribution	• Marketing • Distribution	• Set acceptable target metric	• Brand distribution analysis
No Room Available	Revenue Management	• Revenue management • Marketing	• Set new percentage sold-out targets as goals for revenue managers	• Create metrics to match "closed out to the call center" with actual occupancy rates for those days
Room Type Not Available	CCM	• CCM • Marketing • Revenue Management	• New training materials • New dialogue	• Upgrade or cross-sell promotions
Rate Shopping	CCM	• CCM • Marketing • Revenue Management	• New training materials • New dialogue • Second close tools	• Analyze "rate shop" call-type by rep • This is an indication that individual performance management plan is required
Reserve a Room	CCM	• CCM • Supervisors	• Performance management tools	• Micro-gap analysis
No-Show	CCM	• Operations • CCM	• Review policy on no-shows and email • Policy confirmation • Review reps' dialogue	• Micro-gap analysis
* Call Center Management (CCM)				

term used to describe leaders whose influence extends beyond those whose livelihood depends on them. For example, it's not hard to influence direct reports, or even your direct reports' subordinates. It is infinitely more diffi-cult to influence peers, your peers' subordinates or your boss' peers. (If you want to learn more about this fascinating topic, there are two excellent books by John C. Maxwell, *Developing the Leaders around You* and *Becoming a Person of Influence*. Also, Stephan J. Zaccaro has a section on influence lead-ership in his book, *The Nature of Organizational Leadership: Understanding the Performance Imperatives Confronting Today's Leaders*.[ii])

Ownership and accountability mean more than just a name on a plan; responsibility must be taken at a senior level for writing tangible objectives into the bonus plans of management outside your organization.

Frequently, activities outlined in the matrix on the previous page are del-egated to low-level managers in other departments. Do not let this happen. If the obstacles are not being appropriately resolved, escalate them to the senior management team. Often, problems can be overcome and opportuni-ties pursued if you can garner enough resources to focus on them. It is for senior management to determine those priorities and perhaps add resources, if necessary. Developing this type of meaningful dialogue with other departments will get them integrated and involved, and will help them to discover the power and value of the call center.

Using Call-Typing to Identify Structural and Systemic Revenue Opportunities

The point of call-typing and assigning accountability for call-types is to find revenue opportunities that exist in structural factors and systemic fac-tors. The following two checklists (on pages 33 and 38) illustrate areas in which peak-performing sales centers find revenue. They are examples of how several companies are driving new revenue streams or reducing the cost of sales.

Structural Performance Factor Checklist

Structural improvements—such as requiring service reps to begin cross-

or upselling on service calls or creating a lead-generation revenue stream by referring customers to another company when you do not have a product available—must be prioritized against both the systemic and individual sales rep projects that you want to implement. Question all of your company's assumptions regarding who is allowed to sell to which customers, on which calls and at what hours.

Review the following checklist to validate that no revenue or sales opportunities are missed in any one of the following areas:

- Call-types to cross-sell
- Call-types to upsell
- Customers or market segments to cross-sell
- Customers or market segments to upsell
- Which call center departments are allowed to sell
- Sales staff's hours of operations
- Fullfillment hours of operations
- Direct selling vs. call center selling for key products or customer segments
- IVR calls with revenue opportunities
- Call-referral or lead-generation opportunities
- Synergy opportunities with an alliance or company acquisition

CHANGING THE SALES VS. SERVICE CULTURE

If your service organization is not selling, you're missing opportunities. Even though reps who work in a primarily service-oriented environment may not be the best at selling, they can still find opportunities to cross-sell products that customers lack, offer a product or service to solve a customer's problem or sell a product when a sales rep is not available. Sometimes the paradigm of who is allowed to sell to the customer simply must change. It may be a cultural issue. Consider the following example involving a television shopping channel.

Georgia Eddleman finds sales everywhere. Although currently a vice president and general manager of service for a large call center in the healthcare industry, Eddleman described her experience as a service executive at a television shopping channel. The company's selling philosophy was based on the tenet that their target customer was an impulse buyer. Therefore, the company never allowed their customer service reps access to item numbers. When customers called to request items that were shown on the shopping channel earlier in the day, no one could help them. The sales staff was only available during the hours that the show was broadcast. The sales and order-entry management were committed to their limited market niche of impulse buyers. Of course, there was wisdom in creating a "call to action" and a buying frenzy with a "limited-time only" offering, but they were missing a major market niche.

Customer television viewing behavior created a natural "non-impulse" market that did not dilute the impulse market. The two markets were completely separate. Many customers were video-taping the shopping channel while at work, and would call in the evening when the item was off the channel or the sales/order-entry group was closed.

Eddleman did the math. She easily convinced the "powers that be" that their deeply held belief in catering only to an impulse-buy market consumer was costing $60 million in revenue per year.

Soon thereafter, Eddleman's service reps began selling as well as servicing. Also, because customers who called for products after programming hours were not impulse buyers, merchandise returns dropped and net profits rose. The program was so successful, Eddleman's team implemented an upsell program designed with their service customers in mind. It consisted of a "feature of the day" that wasn't advertised on television but that had been successful in the sales group. The upsell program netted the company significantly more revenue.

Performing a "back-of-envelope" ROI exercise on structural performance factors will allow you to prioritize them among themselves, and against reps' performance improvement opportunities. The following case studies represent examples of the revenue that can be generated rather quickly when outdated systemic and structural factors are questioned and exploited.

USING A CONSULTATIVE SALES APPROACH

Convergys is a large outsourcer of customer service, sales and process management. Convergys' Director of Operations Diana Kempf relates the following experiences of two of her clients and how they were able to deliver increased sales at dramatically reduced costs.

Convergys works with a leading national equipment manufacturer that sells to repair shops, dealers, industry organizations and consumers. Kempf's team of 30 reps handles approximately 24,000 inbound and outbound customer calls each month from small businesses and consumers for this client. Inbound service calls from consumers are typically orders for parts, dealer location referrals, literature requests and product issues. Outbound calls are made to small-business customers, small retailers and service dealers to educate them on new products, rebuilt products and parts. The client still maintains a direct field-sales organization that personally calls on and manages larger accounts.

In a strategic move from a primarily service-focused cost center to a revenue-generating service center, Convergys used a consultative sales approach to increase the annual revenue generated through service calls approximately tenfold within five years with a decreased call volume of 20 percent. How did they achieve an improvement of this magnitude? Kempf attributes the success to a number of factors, including a judicious use of IVR, very low attrition rates, a healthy incentive program, and most importantly, the role of the team leaders (supervisors) and their relationship with their reps.

Like several *best-of-breed*, sales-oriented contact centers, Convergys and its client do not send all IVR-eligible calls to the IVR. If they have a new product available, they may choose to route the call to a Convergys sales rep who services the call and then educates/sells the customer.

Approximately 60 percent of all calls for this client have potential for a sales offer. The close ratio (all service calls divided into all calls closed with a sales transaction) runs about 20 percent, which makes their conversion ratio (all sales-eligible calls divided into all calls closed by a sales transaction) around 33 percent. According to Kempf, the reps on this account are very tenured, with annual attrition at only 4 percent. They do not use screen pop-ups to help reps recommend products nor do they use scripts—partially due to the long rep tenure.

The sales productivity spread between high and low sales producers is only 60 percent, indicating that there is good sales performance management. (Remember, the average sales organization has an average spread of 100 percent, and sales contact centers traditionally experience even higher spreads due to lack of performance management.) Kempf attributes the very low attrition and stellar sales results mainly to the relationship that Convergys reps enjoy with their team leaders. The team leaders consistently record and coach two calls per rep every week. Team leaders frequently show the reps how the business is doing and how the sales reps' performance metrics directly affect the clients' overall business and that of Convergys. In essence, the team leaders "connect the dots," and show a concern for their reps' welfare and an interest in their lives.

The incentive program allows the average sales rep to earn approximately 10 percent of his or her base pay; a very high producer can earn as much as 20 percent of base pay per year in incentives. In addition, the client kicks in for additional contest money and prizes throughout the year. At the top level, and even at the average payout, these are incentives that can change lifestyles.

MOVING FULL ACCOUNT MANAGEMENT TO A SALES CONTACT CENTER

Convergys also has been successful at increasing sales by transferring full account management for business-to-business customers into a sales contact center. Kempf has a group of reps who provide full account management services to the smaller accounts of a provider of consumer package goods. Today, the client's cost of sales for its small-market segment is 93 percent less than when the direct sales force staff managed the account. Moreover, this measure allowed the client to further reduce its wholesale costs and gain market share.

In a true spirit of partnership and trust, the client has given Convergys sales reps full access to its internal systems. On average, the reps sell at least at the same levels as the direct sales force did in the past, but because of contact center productivity tools and processes, and the lack of travel downtime, they're more productive. The sales reps are considered to be fully equivalent to the client's field account managers, who are responsible for maintaining the account base, including new product presentations and maintenance of more than 500 product types. The Convergys sales reps are proficient in all of the customers' processes and have access to all of the client's departments. A customer business plan is jointly developed between the client and the Convergys sales rep, with growth rates projected for upcoming quarters. The plan can be viewed via a Web-based "customer portal."

Kempf notes that running a full account management organization is somewhat different. She will only hire internal or direct sales people from the same industry because the learning curve is much too long, and as an outsourcer of full account management, one cannot afford to make a mistake. "It can be a cultural challenge to properly recruit someone from direct sales into a phone sales position," Kempf acknowledges. But, she explains, "it's all about connecting those dots; once reps understand that every second counts to their paycheck and our bottom line, they get it. We explain that AHT or schedule adherence is only a means to an end—higher sales for them, for Convergys and the client."

Clearly, one should only move those small accounts that cannot receive frequent enough face-to-face contacts into a centralized contact center environment. Too many direct sales reps still attempt to reach all their customers, even those with low volume or low margins, thereby reducing their overall sales productivity. By segmenting the market and allowing a lower-cost channel like a contact center to sell and service the account, the direct sales staff can concentrate on higher-value customers.

The economics seem evident, so why don't all companies centralize their small account management into the contact center? In many cases, there may be an issue with organizational control, a lack of capacity or skills, or union/pay issues. Additionally, many centralized call centers have not had the most stellar track record for sales proficiency. Quite a few are operationally efficient centers, but have not mastered sales performance management. For these reasons, some companies have chosen to outsource full account management to companies with demonstrated capabilities instead of bringing it inhouse.

Systemic Performance Factor Checklist

Systemic performance factors are those that apply to all reps, regardless of skill; for instance, product availability, product quality and computer response time. All of these factors, if wrong, inappropriate or suboptimized for a sales environment, could impact the performance of all reps. Fix one of these, and you will realize performance improvement not just in the bottom third or bottom two-thirds, but across your entire center's population.

Reviewing the items on the following checklist (which is not intended to be exhaustive) can help to reveal whether revenue or sales productivity is affected by any one of these factors in your call center:

- Product availability
- Product quality
- Product information
- Computer response time
- Documentation rules
- Mandatory dialogue
- Business rules
- Policies
- Practices
- Processes

- Procedures
- Computer formats
- Software edit rules
- Access to customer information
- Complaint data
- Rates
- Close tools

FINDING SALES IN COMPLAINT DATA

There is real gold in your complaint data. Many executives look to the complaint data merely to find service and loyalty issues that need fixing. They are right to vigorously focus on eliminating these problems. Service problems cost money to fix, and they can adversely influence customer goodwill and loyalty, which can ultimately affect the lifetime value of a customer.

It is the rare executive who focuses on complaint data as a way to find new market niches, new product or lost revenue. Georgia Eddleman offers a lucrative example of using service data to generate more revenue from her days as VP of customer service at the television shopping network.

In reviewing complaint data from customers who had not received the merchandise they ordered, Eddleman noted that the problem was most prevalent among first-time customers, and most problem orders were cancelled by the system within 24 hours of the sale. Her research showed that the credit card approval process took place nightly, and that an auto-cancellation occurred if the addresses did not perfectly match. The management in charge of credit card fraud never followed up to correct the data and replace the order. When this process issue was brought to their attention, they indicated they did not have a follow-up process in place because they "did not think it was worth it."

It wasn't that the management didn't care about revenue, they just had not taken the time to do the math. Eddleman did, and found that a follow-up process would result in $9 million in additional sales annually. Although she worked in the service department, Eddleman probably brought in more sales that year than any one sales program or sales individual.

Points to Remember

• Use call-typing and revenue extrapolation to estimate your center's revenue potential if all structural and systemic factors were to be eliminated.

• Assign owners inside and outside your organization for every call-type.

• Prioritize and build action plans to address all systemic and structural limitations.

Chapter 3: Building Your Business Case

"There is one thing stronger than all the armies in the world, and that is an idea whose time has come."
VICTOR HUGO, POET AND NOVELIST

A peak sales performance initiative requires a significant commitment and allocation of resources on the part of your entire organization. The business case is developed from several simple gap analyses, which will project the incremental revenue and profit, and support the additional resources and new processes required to reach a radically new level of performance. Interestingly, the benefit numbers in the business case generally will show performance potential so high, your company's financial analysts may find it unbelievable. Try to be conservative, perhaps by using only the elimination of the lower performers' poor performance data to justify the expenditures, and choosing the structural and systemic projects with the highest ROI and least risk. Of course, you'll be hoping to deliver twice what you're *projecting* (read: promising).

A rule of thumb, learned over many successful and failed projects, is to halve the benefits and double the cost. If the business case still looks good, pitch it to senior management. Keep in mind that, in this business, credibility and integrity are everything—at the end of the day, it's all you really have.

With upward of 75 percent of projects failing to deliver on time, on budget or to yield the deliverables,[i] is there any wonder that executive management is skeptical of any lucrative business case? Your credibility is only as good as the results of your last project or your current operating results. So if your last project was a big yawn, or if you're not hitting your service levels or budget right now, the likelihood of getting management to invest in your business case is slim to none. What can you do?

Fix the basics first. If your last project failed, see if you can modify or re-implement it with better success. Much of the costs are probably expensed anyway. If your service level is broken, fix it. Then communicate your success to the organization and try to gain support next year for these new investments and strategies.

Managers often ask how to get unconventional resources. Getting them is the easy part—through a good business case. *Keeping* resources that you didn't have a year ago is the hard part. Sustaining resources, especially through difficult economic times, and maintaining senior management focus despite newer, more sexy ideas—now *that* takes real political acumen and absolute conviction to your cause. It must be backed by a stellar business case and tangible ongoing results.

In many companies, senior management suffers from a short attention span, which is fundamentally driven by an overemphasis on three issues: 1) quarterly earnings, 2) building short-term shareholder value, and 3) board pressure. Don't get me wrong. I'm all for excellent earnings, building share-holder value and strong boards, but it's the imbalanced focus that is the problem. If your organization is constantly in an earnings crisis, look for some of the "quick wins" that will deliver immediate results (see Chapter 12). The benefits will not be nearly as dramatic, but this might be all you can do, given your organization's current readiness. A wise mentor once told me, "A great idea before its time is not a great idea."

The WOW Business Case: Three Critical Steps

There are three major steps necessary to present an outstanding business case for major changes, as well as acquire the resources to drive them.

STEP 1: ESTABLISH YOUR CREDIBILITY

Gaining the resources to drive a major organizational initiative is all about credibility and integrity. It doesn't matter whether you or your boss believe that your center delivered on your budget or a major project. It's what the rest of the organization believes that matters—obtaining and retaining resources requires organizational buy-in.

The organization, your colleagues, your boss and other executives want to know two things: 1) Can your team deliver the goods?; and 2) Is your initiative a better use of company resources than the others presented or those that have not fully materialized?

As previously mentioned, if your call center is not very stable in terms of service level and basic process management, then attempting the changes required for peak sales performance isn't a feasible and appropriate use of your time. If your center is basically running well in terms of service but you are not delivering within 1 percent of your annual budget, or if your prior projects have not been considered successful by the organization at large, then save yourself and your team a lot of aggravation and concentrate on smaller projects first. Focus on some of the performance management techniques, quick-win strategies and coaching processes, as well as the deselection process. None of these process changes require additional money or resources.

If I haven't scared you yet, and you meet the minimum qualification standards, then you should begin discussing the performance potential that exists within your organization with your boss and your colleagues. Start planting the seeds months before your presentation. Begin by sharing with them any incremental improvements that have been made over the past months or years. Numbers speak volumes. Educate them on how much a 1 point improvement on close ratio would be worth to the bottom line. Emphasize the fact that, with the organization's resolution and resource commitment, your center could have a major impact on profits.

STEP 2: BUILD A COMPELLING BUSINESS CASE

If you're not really excited enough about your own business case to commit yourself and your team to a lot of work, risk and aggravation, then why would anyone else want to? You *must* complete the analysis and perhaps rework the resources, but you must be inspired by the possibility of peak sales performance. You must sustain the enthusiasm and focus on the endgame through a long, often difficult journey. Individuals and teams want to make a difference more than anything else. They want a difficult challenge and the possibility of achieving something remarkable. The end-game must be worth it—and the execution of the right business case will ensure that it is.

Your top-level business case should define both the vision and roadmap for success (see example on page 47). If you want to minimize risk, attempt the transformation to peak performance by starting with one major sales department (e.g., inbound sales). Use it as a pilot for the rest of the organization. The only downside to transforming one major department at a time is that a potential compensation inequity may result between the departments' staff.

Think through the pros and cons associated with revamping all the call center sales groups vs. just one. This doesn't mean that you cannot begin a number of improvements in other sales departments, but the resources you request may be staggered. However, a major project that is divided into phases is less daunting for executives to buy into. They may agree more readily to an entire program when their approval is required for each phase, and the success of the previous stages is proven.

Your management team will be an integral part of devising the business case. Encourage them to play the role of devil's advocate, questioning all the assumptions and flushing out all the risks. The decisions you'll have to make include:

- Will you initially address all operations or pilot one operation?
- Will you ask for approval on all resources, or take a phased approach?

TOP-LEVEL BUSINESS CASE (HYPOTHETICAL) **PROFIT**

Structural Improvements

Selling on 20 percent of calls previously sent to IVR
- 5 million IVR calls/year x 20 percent=1 million calls
- 1 million calls x 20 percent conversion ratio=200,000 orders
- 200,000 orders x $100/order= $20 million/year gross revenue
- $20 million/year-$1 million returned/canceled=$19 million/year net revenue
- $19 million/year-$3 million cost (60 reps+sups/mgr/equip/facilities/telecom)
- $16 million/year x 70 percent incremental margin= **$11.2 million/year**

Project risk: Low

Centralize to a call center and sell on targeted service calls in field offices
- 2 million field office service calls/year x 50 percent rerouted call types=1 million calls
- 1 million calls x 20 percent conversion ratio=200,000 orders
- 200,000 orders x $50/order=$10 million/year gross revenue
- $10 million/year-$0.5 million returned/canceled=$9.5 million/year net revenue
- $9.5 million/year-$3 million cost (60 reps+sups/mgr/equip/facilities/telecom)
- $6.5 million/year x 70 percent incremental margin= **$4.55 million/year**

Project risk: Low

Systemic Improvements

Change computer system to allow personal checks as well as credit cards
- 20,000 sales orders lost/year due to lack of customer credit card (from call-type study)
- 20,000 orders x $100/order=$2 million/year gross revenue
- $2 million/year-($300,000 incremental cost of AHT)=$1.7 million/year
- $1.7 million-$100,000 cost of returned/cancelled goods= $1.6 million/year net revenue
- $1.6 million net revenue x 70 percent incremental margin= **$1.12 million/year**

Project Risk: Low

Reduce product availability problems by 50 percent
- 40,000 sales orders lost/year due to lack product availability
- 40,000 orders x $100/order=$4 million/year gross revenue
- $4 million/year-($600,000 incremental cost of AHT)=$ 3.4 million/year
- $3.4 million-$200,000 cost of returned/cancelled goods= $3.2 million/year net revenue
- $3.2 million net revenue x 70 percent incremental margin= **$2.24 million/year**

Project Risk: Medium

Rep Performance Improvements

Move lower third performing reps to middle third levels (see Chapter 6)
- $650 revenue average/hour/med-tier rep-$450 revenue average/hour/lowest tier rep=$200/hour
- $200/phone hour difference x 1,500 productive phone hour/rep/year=$300,000/year revenue increase
- 600 sales reps x 33.3 percent low performers=200 bottom third performers

(continued next page)

TOP-LEVEL BUSINESS CASE *(continued)*   **PROFIT**

- 200 bottom third performers x $300,000/year revenue increase
                                              =$60 million/year revenue increase
- $60 million/year net revenue x 70 percent gross margin on all products=$42 million/year
- $42 million/year-$2.5 million call center expenses (training, incentives, performance
  dbase, etc.)=   **$39.5 million/year**
Project Risk: Medium

Total Incremental Profit   **$58.61 million/year**

STEP 3: CREATE A PRESENTATION THAT DOES NOT REQUIRE SELLING

A strong business case budget presentation does not need to be sold. It commands attention because the presenter has clearly made the case for pain, and with that, opportunity. The path to success is concise and clear, and the ROI impressive, yet conservative. Risks have been mitigated by a plan that is largely self-funding, and includes a phased approach to spending, ability to back out of the program if the results are not positive, and the focus of the right dedicated resources.

In your business case for peak sales performance, most of the additional expenditures do not require capital investment, but you'll likely be competing with other proposed initiatives that are funded from operating revenue. To get your proposal approved, you need to make a stronger business case presentation than the others.

A superior business case presentation generally has the following attributes:

- Validated, quantifiable assumptions.
- A structured approach to discovery, design, development, deployment and documentation.
- A competitive advantage—oftentimes previously hidden—which needs exploiting.
- Contingencies in the budget.
- A high-level project plan.
- A high-level risk-assessment and mitigation plan.

- An ROI that meets the company's minimum returns, even with the costs doubled and the benefits halved.
- Delivered by someone with credibility who will be executing the plan.
- Self-funding, if possible, with the results built into the budget.
- A "back-pocket" slide with lower-end expense alternatives, if necessary.

Assessing your constituencies

Business cases that get approved and earn the organization's commitment also address unspoken or undocumented issues that are in the minds of the approving executives. Therefore, it's essential to understand your audience. Knowing who will be attending the presentation and what business issues keep them up at night, can give you insight into how to craft the presentation. If the CFO has not seen the organization deliver results on past projects involving performance, you may want to give him or her some industry examples which indicate that they are doable or show him the new talent you will be bringing in to augment the company's skill deficiency. If technology projects never seem to get off the ground or gain traction, alleviate concerns with a short bullet-point summary, indicating that the database deliverable will be performed by a contractor who has successfully integrated and constructed many performance databases in the past.

Once you have assessed each participant's potential reaction to the final presentation, it's often helpful to begin informally walking each participant through your business case a month or two prior to the final presentation. Gauge their reactions and determine if you need to make any adjustments.

In addition, consider whether some of your colleagues should attend the presentation(s)—those who are held in high esteem and who might assist you in providing support for the business case. Also, think about how you might handle the objections of those who oppose the project. Take these individuals through the business case well before the presentation. Try to understand what their issues are and counter them at that time. If you're at a standoff, at least you'll know what the objections will be prior to the presentation, and you can be prepared to respond.

Every so often, a viable presentation will go awry. Sometimes the organization likes the improvements, but wants you to achieve them without spending any money. While I encourage you to go into the presentation process with a fall-back slide showing reduced resources and a reduced return, do not commit to deliver significant improvements without the necessary resources. If you do not win the major resource battle, then retreat and commit in the budgeting process to deliver incremental improvements by implementing skills-based routing, improved coaching methods and tools, and a deselection process. If you implement these processes with success, perhaps the following year you can pursue the next level of improvement.

The Presentation

Your presentation should be clear and concise. Use whichever application your company prefers for assimilating information (in most cases, it will be PowerPoint).

The presentation slides should loosely follow this format:
1. Title Page
2. Opportunity statement
3. Assumptions
4. KPI and supporting driver analysis
5. Macro-gap analysis
6. Strategies and tactics to close the gap (repeat, as needed)
7. Strategies and tactics to close the gap
8. Strategies and tactics to close the gap
9. Micro-gap analysis example
10. Deliverables (repeat, as needed)
11. Deliverables
12. Resource requirements
13. ROI and NPV analysis
14. Financial investment timing

15. High-level project plan

16. High-level risk mitigation plan

17. Discussion and next steps

Any further detailed analysis should not be attached; instead, hand it out separately at the end of the presentation.

Send copies of your slides to all attendees approximately 48 hours prior to the presentation. It won't be a surprise, since you already will have shared much of it with all the constituents. Most participants appreciate advance copies—it gives them time to consider your ideas and develop appropriate questions. If they see the presentation for the first time while you're presenting it, you'll likely lose their attention. They'll be reading or skimming through it, instead of focusing on you.

The real presentation is your dialogue with the audience, augmented with interesting and brief supporting comments. The slides merely provide the outline. Ideally, you'd like to walk away with an answer like, "Yes, it's approved with these modifications…"; however, we rarely get everything we ask for. If participants haven't had the time to contemplate the right questions, the best you can hope for is, "We'll think about it and get back to you with our questions." Ask for a timeframe, and schedule the next meeting while everyone is in the room.

PRESENTATION TIPS

• Practice it. Know it without notes.

• Present it in less than 30 minutes.

• Discuss and gain commitment within the next 30 minutes.

• Assess the commitment level by asking questions.

Validate the Organizational Commitment

After the requested resources are approved, there is another step—assessing the organization's level of commitment. Do not start committing resources or communicating your plan until the final budget is approved by the board of directors and you're positive that you have the unequivocal financial and mindset commitment of the enterprise.

Employees have long-lasting, negative memories of cultural changes that fail. In my experience, it generally takes an organization at least seven years to recover from a derailed attempt at a major cultural change. Why? On average, at that point, the majority of employees will have left the department or the company. So you only have one chance every seven years or so

---

THE WOW BUSINESS CASE: THREE CRITICAL STEPS
Note: The details on how to accomplish these steps are provided in the following chapters.

Step 1: Establish Your Credibility
Deliver what you have already promised:
• Budget.
• Service levels.
• Projects on time and on budget with deliverables met.
Begin to build interest in the opportunity within the corporate organization.

Step 2: Build a Compelling Business Case
Review the systemic and structural opportunities:
• Perform the revenue analysis on each.
• Determine the opportunity priorities.
• Choose a few that have high return and low risk.
• On a high level, determine the resources and costs necessary to close structural and systemic performance gaps.

Perform a macro-gap analysis on sales rep performance:
• Define your one sales Key Performance Indicator (KPI).
• Divide the line performers into three groups and compare their average sales KPI. Quantify the opportunity by extrapolating the average gaps between the low and medium producers, and between the medium and high producers.
• Validate that there is enough of a gap between either pair of performers to justify a major overhaul of your operation.
• Extrapolate the annual financial results that would be realized if either of the gaps were closed.

Determine the resources required to close the gap(s):
• Choose the key performance drivers that support the KPI.
• Validate via regression analysis that those performance drivers are accurate.
• Conduct an environmental analysis.
• Create a plan to close the gaps:
    • New predictive hiring assessments
    • New rep, supervisor and manager competencies

- New minimum performance standards
- New deselection processes
- New sales training
- Incentive program redesign and investment
- New closing tools or new customer resolution practices
- New processes for eliminating obstacles
- Resources required from other departments
- Development of a performance database
- New coaching and feedback requirements and processes
- Consulting or executive coaching assistance
- Revenue manager, project manager(s)

Determine financial impact of this resource commitment:
- Create the ideal resource package that delivers the most revenue.
- Then create a resource package at a lower scale that delivers the best ROI. This is your "fall-back plan."

Step 3: Create a Financial Presentation that Does Not Require Selling

Determine the audience and approval requirements:
- Who must approve?
- What is the minimum ROI threshold for investment?
- Who can derail the approval?
- At a minimum, attendance at the presentation should include the president, your boss and the CFO. Add HR if your relationship is strong.
- If your company operates on a "limited pie" theory of expenditure budgeting, have the departments that compete for resources also attend.

Time ahead of the budgeting calendar:
- Begin showing the business case and presentation outline to all non-CFO constituents— at least one or two months before the final budget presentation—to ferret out any problems.
- Put up or shut up: Commit to YOUR operating budget, the conservative rampup schedule of revenue, and the productivity targets imbedded in the sales performance improvement initiative.
- Gain tentative resource commitment at this time, or reduce sales productivity commitment.

Create a powerful presentation:
- Keep it simple: PowerPoint, less than 20 pages.
- Keep it clean: Four points down, six words across.
- Summarize the organizational commitment required, with strategies, tactics, financial expenses and benefits.
- Add a 10 percent expense contingency for the unexpected.
- Use an actual macro-gap analysis.
- Make the ROI work on the premise of only improving the bottom 30 percent of performers.

to make this kind of cultural and structural change in your organization—don't blow it by jumping the gun.

Points to Remember

- Build a WOW business case that doesn't need selling.
- Carefully assess your constituencies' biases, concerns and own self-interests.
- Presell the business case to the major stakeholders.
- Underpromise and overdeliver.
- Build in a 10 percent contingency.
- Keep the presentation simple, using an addendum for all the detailed analysis and supporting spreadsheets.
- Prior to your presentation, get Finance's buy-in to your financial analysis, assumptions and methodology.
- Do not sign up for the revenue improvements without the necessary corresponding investment in people or resources.

Section 2: The Path to Peak Sales

Chapter 4: Selecting the Right Performance Criteria

"If you pick the right people and give them the opportunity to spread their wings, and put compensation as a carrier behind it, you almost don't have to manage them."
JACK WELCH, FORMER CEO OF GENERAL ELECTRIC

Before getting into the process of determining which key performance indicators will drive peak sales performance in your call center, it's important for you to understand the terms that will be used throughout the book. Some of them already have been introduced informally in the previous chapter, but now it's time to become more formally acquainted with them.

GARFIELD © 2003 Paws, Inc. Reprinted with permission of UNIVERSAL PRESS SYNDICATE.

Performance Management Terminology

Action plan. A list of tactics or activities that the supervisor and rep believe will help bring about a measurable performance improvement. For instance, if a rep's close ratio is only 20 percent, three items in the action plan might include: 1) attending a refresher class on the required dialogue points; 2) utilizing additional sales close tools; and 3) additional commitment to monitoring by the supervisor to determine other root causes.

Conversion ratio. The ratio of closed sales transactions to sales-eligible calls (closeable calls). Generally not recommended as either a KPI or a performance driver (see the following definitions) since it is too difficult to track accurately on a real-time basis, and is normally extrapolated from sample call-typing. Usually, you would not use a conversion ratio as a KPI because there are a lot of non-sales potential calls in any call-answering group. If this is not the case, and all calls have sales potential, conversion ratio and close ratio mean the same thing, and could be used as a performance driver.

Correlation and regression analysis. Correlation analysis is concerned with the degree to which one variable is related to another; for example, whether the high or low AHT has any effect on the close ratio. Regression analysis concerns itself with predicting one variable from the knowledge of independent variables.

Goal. The point of arrival (POA). It's the quantifiable and qualified tangible component of the performance objective (e.g., increase close ratio to 25 percent within the next 12 months: 25 percent close ratio is the goal).

Key performance indicator (KPI). The single, most important "business outcome" performance measure of the effectiveness of a call center's or department's mission. For example, if the mission is sales, the sales KPI might be "net revenue per phone hour (NRPH)," or net sales units/rep/month. If the center's or department's mission is service, the service KPI might be "service inquiries/complaints as a percentage of total transactions," "percent perfect orders" or "first-point-of-contact close." A center may have multiple KPIs, but generally only one KPI per skill or per group. A service group that sells would have two KPIs—one for service and one for sales.

For a call center sales department, regardless of whether it's an inbound or outbound sales center or a service center with cross- or upselling, the best KPI is generally a net revenue per phone hour (NRPH) metric. By focusing on this one business outcome metric as the most critical in the metric hierarchy, a number of root-cause metrics can be generated to help coaches and reps create effective action plans. Seen in a more positive light, the performance-driver metrics related to the KPI can provide leverage points for performance change. Many well-performing call centers do use other metrics for their sales KPI, and continue to rely on close ratio, conversion ratio or net sales per rep per month. In some of these cases, the sale is relatively straightforward. The variables that may exist in the previously mentioned hotel model may not exist in other businesses (e.g., if it is not possible to cancel an order once it is placed or if there is only one product to offer).

Measurement. A quantifiable unit. In call centers, this is generally *time* (handle time, after-call work time) or an *input* (a call, an email, a customer), an *output* (e.g., a sales unit, a proposal, a completed problem resolution) or a *ratio* derived from a dividend and a divisor (e.g., hours worked/hours scheduled, revenue/hour, absenteeism percentage, close ratio, first-call resolution percentage, reopened complaint percentage).

Performance driver. A previously "suspect" performance driver that has been validated to drive the business outcome KPI through statistically sound correlation and regression analysis. When used in sales call centers, a performance driver typically falls into one of three categories: 1) a skill or personality factor; 2) a sales approach or element of a script outline; or 3) any one of a few metrics that has been scientifically shown to affect the corresponding KPI (e.g., revenue per hour). Call center sales examples include extraverted rep personalities, a script outline that requires a rep to ask for the sale under certain circumstances, or a metric like AHT—all of which, we know through analysis, correlate to higher sales.

Performance objective. Usually stated as a quantifiable goal that must be accomplished within a given set of constraints, within a specified period of time or by a given date (e.g., increase close ratio to 25 percent within two weeks). A good objective or target generally follows the design guidelines of the S.M.A.R.T. acronym (Specific, Measurable, Attainable, Realistic and Time-bound).

Personal best. The best measurement over a cyclical period—such as, one month—actually achieved by an individual in any one area. Sustaining a personal best on a daily basis, and surpassing it consistently to a new sustainable performance level, is known as *peak individual performance*.

Standard. A quantifiable acceptable level or range of performance. Performance below or outside the standard range should not be acceptable or tolerated for very long. Frequently, in call centers, the standard is expressed as an acceptable range of tolerance (e.g., an AHT standard over a 30-day rolling average period might be expressed as 240 to 300 seconds.) Times below and above that standard would indicate that something is wrong, and it would show up in variances in other standards. If the AHT is 200 seconds, customers are likely to complain about the quality of service received. In addition, reps' sales will likely not be as high as they could be. If neither is the case, you may have a best-demonstrated practice that should be duplicated across the center—but this would be a rarity. Most likely, another standard is also not being hit. Look for it.

Note: You need to know your business and determine if the standard is reasonable. In other words, are most individuals currently accomplishing it? Do not set standards that cannot be attained by most of your staff. If a rep is not meeting a standard, it means that person should no longer be in that job after an acceptable retraining time. Do not set standards if you do not follow through with consequence management by setting positive consequences for exceeding the standard (e.g., continued employment and a shot at incentives), and negative consequences for consistently failing to meet the standard (termination of employment). Otherwise, the standards will be meaningless and will undermine your credibility.

Suspected performance driver. One of a large number of qualitative or quantitative purported performance drivers that, over the years, have been attributed to driving the major departmental KPI, referring to increased revenue or better service. Every rep, supervisor, manager or even a department head from another division probably has his or her own ideas about what drives sales. Predictive hiring assessments will validate the right technical capabilities and personality attributes. Focus groups or informal interviews will generate the list of other suspected performance drivers, such as the use of a second close tool. Each of the rational suspects must be tested through correlation and regression analysis to determine if it is a true performance driver of the KPI.

Target. A short-term or interim improvement level required at a specific future point in time. It is a "checkpoint" to reassess progress and correct action, as necessary, to reach the final point of arrival (e.g., decrease cancellation rates to 5 percent by the end of the month).

Choosing the Right Performance Indicators for Your Business

How do you know which sales rep attributes, scripts, tools and metrics are the most important drivers of performance for your call center?

As a call center manager or executive, you may have several KPIs because you probably manage multiple functions; e.g., a sales KPI (e.g., NRPH), a service KPI (e.g., complaints as a percentage of orders), a budget KPI (e.g., cost per sale variance to budget), service level KPI for operations management (e.g., percentage of half-hours in which 70 to 90 percent of calls are answered within 20 seconds). Each function or area will have one skills-based KPI in addition to a quality indicator. They should not be weighted; they stand separately.

Reps and supervisors will probably only have one KPI with a number of

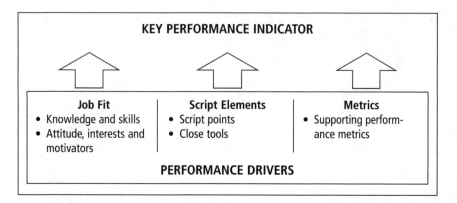

supporting performance metric drivers and supporting performance script drivers. Performance metric drivers—typically, no more than six—drive the movement of the KPI; these drivers are leverage points that a rep can improve to move the KPI in a positive direction.

In performance management, not all drivers are created equally. Weighting them for the rep can appear overly complex, so I recommend using a "what-if" gap analysis automated spreadsheet. The spreadsheet, when tied in with your performance database, will allow coaches and reps to include interim targets in the performance driver "what-if" analyses, enabling them to see what effect the change in the driver would have on the KPI.

The template allows the rep and the supervisor to imagine the KPI outcome for the rep, and the business outcome's influence on future incentives. In Chapter 9, we will walk through setting up a micro-gap analysis template and performance improvement plan for the individual rep.

Evolving the Call Center KPI: From Suspects to Prospects to Real Performance Drivers

Many call centers measure everything, and in an effort to be open with reps and drive performance, show them *all their statistics*. This typically overloads reps, and they get confused about what the manager wants. On their end, supervisors and managers often disagree as to what drives overall performance. This often occurs because they have not defined the one ultimate measure of performance (the skills KPI), or they simply don't know which conditions and statistics truly drive performance.

Earlier, we looked at how to define your call center KPI, and how to find the suspected drivers of the KPI, by interviewing leaders, managers and supervisors of medium, high and peak performers, and holding focus groups with low, medium and high producers. Be sure not to limit your interviews and focus groups to just the high performers. You also need to know what the low performers are doing that is driving low performance. What are you looking for? Closing techniques, tools or script points that do and do not work. The point of gathering metrics, script elements, tools and techniques is to formally test all these variables using correlation and regression analysis. You want to establish, once and for all, the most important elements that drive your ultimate business objective—sales.

You'll end up with at least 15 to 30 suspect drivers of performance. If you have fewer than 15, you may need to look harder. If you have more than 30, you probably have duplicates that are just a matter of semantics.

Next, you or your financial staff will need to perform a correlation and regression analysis (which will be discussed later in this chapter) to determine if there is a statistical or factual correlation between the suspected performance driver—e.g., higher handle time and shown revenue.

Once you have all of the proven and validated performance drivers, you can build detailed resource and tactical plans for closing the performance gap among individuals.

What Really Drives Sales?

Good business outcomes, like increased revenues, start with an understanding of what is really driving sales. Chapter 2 examined the structural issues that can affect sales—policies, procedures and pricing that do not make sense in the current marketplace—as well as operational issues that should be fixed, such as lack of product types or product availability. In addition, methods for getting quick structural wins were pointed out, such as separating sales calls from the service mix through an IVR, and using skills-based routing to deliver the customer to a rep who has a proven track record for strong sales.

Now it's time to focus on the individual sales reps. To choose those who have a natural affinity for the sales process, you'll need sound hiring criteria that allow you to identify the relevant personality traits, motivators and skills necessary to perform a sales job. You're not just looking for someone who can do the job; you want to improve your chances of hiring more superstars and fewer low performers.

You'll also need effective evaluation criteria to determine whether or not rep job performance is actually driving anything important. Focus on flushing out the true performance drivers. Performance drivers are proven criteria that, when properly executed, will drive top sales performance. The only way to know for sure if you're selecting the right individuals, and evaluating and coaching them on the right performance drivers, is to use some of the great hard data available within the contact center to choose the hiring criteria and performance drivers.

Finally, you will want to reward your sales reps' performance with what is important to them; therefore, you'll need to create incentive systems that reward the right people based on the right evaluation criteria.

Common Performance Measurement Mistakes

The most common performance management mistake made in many organizations, both inside and outside the call center, is equating a performance standard with a performance driver, a KPI or a performance measure. This is not a matter of semantics. Each should be used for its intended purpose. A performance measure is any of a number of interesting pieces of data information that can be trended and benchmarked. It may relate to a process, financial marker or customer segment. Performance measures are interesting and are generally watched to stay within a range in order to hit a budget, but unless they move out of a normal range, they are usually not critical to the outcome of the business. Performance standards are minimum levels of certain performance measures that are essential to maintain in order to hit the business goals. They always include the KPI for the skill set or department, and frequently include several other performance measures (e.g., attendance, quality) that are not accounted for in the KPI. Performance drivers are those few metrics, script points or job-fit criteria that, when properly leveraged, can really affect the KPI.

It's important that your performance drivers are clear and measurable. According to Mark Haug, Ph.D., J.D., "Many performance management systems that use scorecards with several performance measures have redundant elements and vague categories. They give the appearance of science without being actual science." Dr. Haug teaches graduate and undergraduate courses in operations management, business law, statistics and leadership at the University of Kansas School of Business, and is a partner with and general counsel to Oread Consulting Group, LLC.

He points out that even focused scorecards (those containing fewer measures) are useful only if the proper correlation and regression analytics have been performed using hard data, which ensures that measures are not double-counted and that they positively affect the desired business outcome (e.g., sales or customer satisfaction) in a statistically significant way. Hard data is defined as clearly quantifiable data, such as a close ratio, AHT or whether or not a rep uses a certain script or close tool. Monitoring criteria that are based on opinion—such as a supervisor's opinion of a rep's professionalism or voice tone—are considered "fuzzy or flaky data." It's not that you shouldn't coach reps on them; you just don't want to evaluate job performance using fuzzy data. It's just too difficult to prove that such elements drive results.

Validating Performance Drivers Using Correlation Analysis

Few call centers have rigorously validated any of their performance measurement systems. Most rely on a common sense, "it just feels right" approach, using anecdotal evidence or flaky data-points to determine what makes a great sales person perform well.

You should use correlation and regression analysis to help you select criteria throughout all hiring, monitoring and evaluation processes that will predict, direct and support job performance (see table on page 69). Although all criteria may not be resident in all instruments, they should not be in conflict with each other.

In correlation analysis, if two performance criteria both show a linear correlation with, for example, revenue per hour (see box, below), then they cannot show a relatively strong correlation with each other. In this case, it's acceptable to use both measures as separate performance criteria that affect the final business outcome. But if both of the performance drivers show a substantial correlation with each other, and you use both as performance criteria, you would be double-counting the metrics. For instance, close ratio and revenue per hour should not both be used to evaluate reps. A correlation analysis of those two variables would show a strong positive correlation with each other—i.e., when one measure increases, so does the other. Therefore, using both to evaluate for merit or incentive purposes results in double-counting.

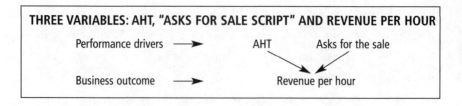

You must rigorously test all performance management variables to confirm that you're selecting and leveraging the right criteria for recruiting strategies, hiring, monitoring and scripting. How? By subjecting all variables to correlation and regression analysis to ensure that there is a direct correlation between that variable and the desired business outcome. For example, all points of a monitoring form should be validated to make certain that everything you're requiring a rep to say—which is not compliance-related from a regulatory viewpoint—will drive the desired business outcome. (See "Examples of Correlation Scattergrams," on page 73.)

In addition to monitoring forms, evaluation form criteria should also be subjected to similar analysis. You'll quickly learn that there are relatively few variables in monitoring or evaluation forms that really make a difference in moving sales. Keep in mind that you're looking for fewer measures—only those that really matter. Likewise, your hiring assessment criteria must go through the same thorough statistical analysis process. I highly recommend hiring a professional firm with industrial psychologists to do this work for you.

You may be surprised to discover that some "common sense" probing questions typically required in a sales call can actually have a reverse and negative effect on sales. For example, in order to offer the right car category to customers, a rep with a rental car agency might be required to ask customers how many people will be traveling with them, how much luggage they'll be carrying and how many miles they'll be traveling. This simply sounds like customer-focused selling. However, if consultative selling creates a much longer call for customers and annoys them, then the correlation and regression analysis would show an inverse correlation—revealing that these questions both cost more in additional handle time and reduce the prospect of a sale. A better tactic would be to first ask customers what type of car they desire; they probably know. It is a bit scary to think that your reps are taking 1 million, 10 million or 300 million calls a year, and are faithfully following your scripts and "best practices"—and realize that you have

Validated Variables	Predictive Instrument
• Hiring criteria—traits, skills or motivators ———▶	Hiring assessments
• Script points ———▶	Monitoring assessments
• Deselection criteria • Performance drivers of the KPI ———▶	Performance evaluations

not done the statistical analysis to know that they are "proven practices."

Performing a correlation analysis on every script element of your monitoring form and every criterion on your performance evaluation form may sound like a daunting task. But a good MBA-level operations analyst or HR analyst should be able to complete the analysis (and spreadsheet programs like Excel have built-in tools to handle the tough math). If you don't have the talent inhouse to perform the analysis, look for a consultant who can provide the service. If you do not perform the analysis yourself, you should understand the methodology completely. Getting this right is one of the most important things you can do to improve sales performance or, for that matter, any performance area in your center.

Correlation Analysis in Predictive Hiring Assessments

A predictive hiring assessment is more than simply an evaluation of a social style or personality profile. It is composed of numerous sophisticated testing instruments, usually including a behavioral interview, validated personality profiles and competency tests that predict the degree to which an individual is likely to succeed or fail in a given position. The testing instruments are not sophisticated because they are inherently complicated; they are sophisticated because they have undergone rigorous testing.

In a predictive-designed assessment, all applicants in a job category (e.g., sales) over the course of, say, one year, are given a test. At the end of the year, all tests are scored and compared with the actual job performance of the corresponding employee for that year. A correlation and a regression analysis is performed, the outcome of which provides a set of traits, attributes, motivators and competencies that will comprise a final predictive hiring assessment. The assessment sets the hiring criteria and creates the behavioral questions that a hiring team will use to assess the probability of success of a given candidate. *Note:* A good predictive hiring assessment should predict high job performance potential as well as low performance potential.

Do not attempt to build your own predictive hiring assessment tool. While assessments are highly effective in helping you to recruit, promote and select the right individuals, they rightfully come under the scrutiny of the U.S. Equal Employment Opportunity Commission (EEOC) if the use of them causes discrimination and the hiring criteria do not show a high correlation to a critical business outcome. There are several commercially designed assessment tools already on the market for the job (e.g., inside sales), as well as several good consultants and products from which to choose (e.g., ScientificSelection.com, FurstPerson and others).

The Correlation and Regression Analysis Process

Now that we've considered common performance measurement mistakes, as well as where and why you should use correlation and regression analysis, let's look at the process itself. First, however, let's take a quick refresher of business statistics: A *correlation analysis* is concerned with the degree to which one variable is related to another; for example, whether high or low AHT has any effect on close ratio. *Regression analysis* concerns itself with predicting one variable from knowledge of independent variables. A linear correlation coefficient is the measure of the linear relationship between two random variables; for example, the *extent* to which AHT or key script elements affect the close ratio.

You can validate your performance measurement system using the following eight-step correlation and regression analysis process.

CORRELATION AND REGRESSION ANALYSIS PROCESS

1. Data cleanup:
   - Obtain a large sample of observations of reps who have taken the same call-types during the same shift.
   - Remove data on all reps who were not there for the last year.
   - Eliminate the outlying anomalies from the sample.
2. Plot the data using two variables (e.g., X and Y).
3. Determine what you are trying to predict.

4. Plot the variable that you propose might be affecting the business outcome statistic.

5. Run a correlation coefficient using a formula function in Excel spreadsheet tools:

- Type in the formula and highlight.
- Or type in the names of the rows of data (e.g., A1-A20).

6. Interpretation—extent to which one variable correlates with another:

- Look at the correlation scattergram (similar to those on page 73) to see what is happening. Does it make sense? Is it what you expected?

- Correlation varies from -1 when both variables are headed in opposite directions (e.g., AHT goes up when net revenue/hour goes down) to +1 when both variables are headed in the same direction (e.g., net revenue/hour goes up when AHT goes up).

- If the results show a correlation coefficient of +.3, this is considered a low positive correlation.

- A correlation coefficient of zero shows no correlation.

- A negative number indicates that the variable is having an inverse effect.

- Square the correlation number to get a variance (.3 x .3 = .9 = 9 percent variance).

- This means that 9 percent of the business outcome (e.g., sales units, net revenue) can be explained by that variable (e.g., script point on the monitor form; a performance driver like AHT or tenure; a personality motivator; or a skills competency).

7. Repeat steps 1 through 6 for all possible variables.

8. Regression analysis:

- Pick out the variables that have a strongly positive or strongly negative correlation and input them into Excel.

- Utilize a regression formula in Excel, the output of which will be the percent for which you can explain your business outcome based on your variables.

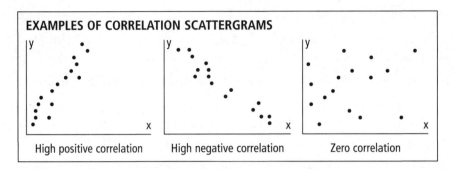

The equation below is the mathematical expression of the correlation coefficient, which is the a measure of the extent of the linear relationship between two variables. Like the Erlang C or Erlang B formulas that call centers use in calculating staff and trunking requirements, respectively, this is a complicated formula, but no less important. Similar to the Erlang formulas, it is important to know what they represent, but you will be using software with this tool embedded to do this work.

CORRELATION COEFFICIENT

The measure ρ of linear relationship between two variables X and Y is estimated by the sample coefficient r, where:

$$r = \frac{n \sum_{i=1}^{n} x_i y_i - \left(\sum_{i=1}^{n} x_i\right)\left(\sum_{i=1}^{n} y_i\right)}{\sqrt{\left[n \sum_{i=1}^{n} x_i^2 - \left(\sum_{i=1}^{n} x_i\right)^2\right]\left[n \sum_{i=1}^{n} y_i^2 - \left(\sum_{i=1}^{n} y_i\right)^2\right]}} = b\frac{s_x}{s_y}$$

A Word about False KPIs

A KPI is tied to the business outcome of a group with a common mission. A false KPI is really a measurement that has been inappropriately elevated to KPI status in the belief that it would drive improved results. In most cases, these types of measures simply require a minimum acceptable tolerance level, a minimum continued employment standard.

For instance, you're trying to measure the ability of your reps (in this case, sales reps) to drive sales. It is expected that they must drive sales with quality and that they must show up for work on time with a high degree of regularity. But all of these work attributes, while very important, have a level at which they are satisfactory. You don't want your reps trying to balance a theoretical quality measure vs. sales ratio. If they are good sales people, they know that service comes first—they cannot sell without solving the customer's problem, and if they create another problem due to poor quality, the sale will not stick. While, certainly, you want to measure the quality of your reps' work, I suggest measuring it separately and not indexing it against sales for purposes of incentive pay-outs. Attendance and quality measures are examples of false KPIs.

You can ensure quality by establishing a measurable minimum tolerance level. Those employees whose work consistently falls below the acceptable level are not eligible for incentives. Instead of creating another KPI, set a minimum standard and subject poor-quality performers to consequence management and possible termination.

Schedule adherence, attendance and, in some cases, AHT, should receive the same "minimum standard" attention. Perfect attendance is not as important as stellar sales productivity or, in the case of a service skill, a great call-resolution ratio. Set the minimum levels you think you can live with from a predictive scheduling and cost standpoint—and live with them. Wouldn't you hate to terminate a great sales person because you set an overly onerous attendance policy? By the same token, if a stellar sales rep is rarely at work, then his or her superior close ratio or NRPH is not contributing enough to your final business outcome.

Setting Performance Goals for Other "Work Input" Organizations

Clearly, some departments, like marketing and operations, will frequently drive work volume, both desirable and undesirable, into your call center operation. How can you work to eliminate the unnecessary non-sales calls coming into your center and, therefore, help your revenue to increase?

At budgeting time, it's helpful to confer with your colleagues in these other "work input" areas to establish a related performance objective for their areas. For example, one interdepartmental problem faced by many call center managers is dealing with the needless calls driven into the call center by the Internet. A performance objective that might be appropriate for a marketing department that wants to drive orders through the Internet due to the lower cost of sale might be:

Reduce the number of Internet-related calls to an annual run rate of 15 percent of all Internet product orders by the fourth quarter.

Take a collaborative approach to help each department craft a tactical *workplan* appropriate to the goal. It should be relatively easy to produce with all of the call-type statistics your call center has available. In many cases, the other department is simply unaware that there is a problem, or doesn't know how to fix it. If the financial impact is significant, the performance objective should be included in the incentive plans of relevant senior managers.

Selecting Management KPIs

The sales KPI you set for supervisors, managers and directors should be the same as the one set at the frontline level. Managers may have more than one KPI if they have multiple departments. Additionally, they may have a number of minimum standards that must be met, just like reps.

For example, a supervisor might have the same KPI as the department (e.g., net revenue per phone hour), but is also held accountable for 10 call evaluations delivered (and signed) for each rep every month. A manager of that same department might have the same KPI and call evaluation goal as his or her supervisors, as well as an absenteeism minimum standard percentage that must be met monthly. A director and VP would carry the common departmental KPIs and several more strategic objectives.

Points to Remember

> TIP: Include five to eight objectives per performance plan per management position, including the KPI metric.

- Choose one KPI per department skills set.
- If possible, make the KPI the business outcome (results).
- Statistically validate that all performance drivers, hiring criteria, script points and close tools actually drive a positive business result (KPI).
- Set minimum standards for attendance and quality, instead of creating a KPI or new evaluation criteria.

Chapter 5: Closing the Revenue Performance Gap

"What is the answer to 99 questions out of 100? Money."
REMARK MADE BY MALCOLM FORBES TO HIS SONS

If you've been in call center management for a while, you've probably seen a lot of initiatives launched over time, some several times. You've probably launched a few of your own, as well. In many companies, initiatives often don't stick and management stands accused of employing a "management du jour" or "flavor of the month" approach.

How can you ensure that your program for peak sales performance maintains the momentum and closes the revenue performance gap? The key is to institutionalize a few major areas of focus with new supporting strategies and resources, as well as the discipline, accountability and metrics to back them up. Let's look at the four main steps for closing the revenue performance gap.

Step 1: Determine the Single, Most Important KPI in Each Major Department

While there is no one KPI that is the universal measure for the call center industry, there is probably one best answer for your call center. The critical KPI for sales is the business outcome (sales productivity) that can easily be translated into bottomline impact, and which can be tied to the company's strategies and mission, as illustrated in the Performance Pyramid below. Sharing this pyramid with reps will help them to understand how their individual performance and success is tied to the company's performance and success.

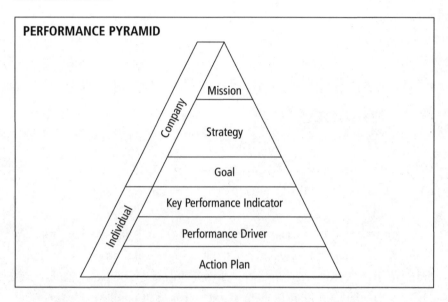

PERFORMANCE PYRAMID

Company

Mission

Strategy

Goal

Individual

Key Performance Indicator

Performance Driver

Action Plan

Step 2: Collect All "Suspected Performance Drivers"

In Chapter 4, "suspected performance drivers" were defined as qualitative or quantitative purported performance drivers that, over the years, have been attributed to driving the major departmental KPIs, usually increased revenue or better service. Also, it was pointed out that each of the rational suspects must be tested through correlation and regression analysis to determine if it is a true performance driver of the KPI.

Performance drivers come in three flavors:

1. The personality traits and skills that create "job fit" (which already have been validated through the creation of hiring assessments).

2. The elements of the reps' script dialogue.

3. The subordinate metrics that we collect.

At this point in the process, you have not yet validated the latter two with correlation analysis that will tell you whether the suspected metrics and script element performance drivers are, in fact, real drivers of your sales KPI.

Certainly, you want to validate that what you are *currently* doing is driving sales, but don't assume that all of the things you're measuring or requiring sales reps to say in mandatory scripting or script points are the only things driving the sales KPI. You'll probably discover that very few mandatory script elements really drive sales—and, in fact, one or two may even hurt sales.

There is always the possibility that one of your top performers is doing something that you have not identified which is driving sales, or that someone has a great idea for a way to drive sales. Try to capture all of these techniques and ideas, and put them to the test—literally. It's important to statistically validate whether or not these hidden techniques or script elements correlate to increased sales. It may take months of trial, error and analysis to get a handle on the right supporting behaviors and metrics, but it's a crucial step. Make sure that you get input from everyone involved before setting the measurements and metrics in semi-permanent concrete.

Step 3: Validate the Real Sales Performance Drivers

Having one common KPI upon which everyone—from VP to rep—is focused breeds tremendous camaraderie, clarity of mission, innovation and job satisfaction. It creates a daily dialectic in the organization in which the ideas get better and better because everyone speaks one common language. Through correlation and regression analysis, you will determine the drivers of individual sales rep performance; closing the gap will require developing meaningful, prioritized strategies and tactics.

Generally, individual performance drivers will fall into several quantifiable metrics, such as a cancellation rate or number of products sold per sales transaction, as well as key elements of your script outline for calls. Be careful that you don't end up with too many. It is not likely that there will be more than five to 10 total performance drivers over and above the sales rep's personality profile and the sales skills that really drive the sales KPI.

PERFORMANCE DRIVERS THAT MOVE THE KPI

To demonstrate the value of identifying true performance drivers that move the sales KPI, let's use our previous example of a hotel reservation call center. For this center, the final eight statistically *validated* performance driver metrics (really KPI diagnostics) and five performance driver dialogue elements that support the sales KPI are as follows:

Validated **performance driver metrics:**

1. AHT

2. Close ratio

3. Cancellation ratio

4. Show ratio

5. Length of stay

6. Room category or class of service

7. Number of rooms per reservation

8. Percentage of calls transferred

Validated **performance driver dialogue elements:**

1. Asks for the sale

2. Asks for the next destination on itinerary and recommends a hotel

3. Offers a room upgrade alternative

4. Suggests multiple rooms with connecting doors to families with children

5. Closes with a positive reaffirmation like: "We will see you in Seattle on Friday."

Let's take a closer look at each of the eight validated performance driver metrics to see how they support the sales KPI in a hotel reservations call center:

Average Handle Time (AHT). Remember: Be careful what you ask for—you may get it. Setting an AHT goal or range is always a slippery slope. It can and should be a type of target, but you should be very careful about using it as an end performance measure that directly impacts reps' merit increases. I've seen managers try to cope with poor service levels by forcing down the AHT across the board or with individuals who typically have high AHT. However, the problem is exacerbated when reps are challenged to bring their AHT within an average range by a certain period of time or suffer the consequences (i.e., less money, a poor performance review or disciplinary action). Such a challenge is unfair—it's built around the assumption that reps have direct control over AHT. In many cases, reps will simply try to talk faster or rush the customer through the call, which often causes customers to ask for things to be repeated—making AHT actually *increase*.

Instead of demanding a lower AHT or trying to set a different target, the best approach is to provide tangible suggestions on how to lower the AHT, or in some cases, increase it. The following are some examples of common AHT control metrics and techniques:

- Know the computer's short cuts and codes
- Know the product
- Memorize policies and procedures
- Minimize "after-call work" mode by talking and typing simultaneously
- Reduce hold-time percentage
- Ask closed-ended questions

Close Ratio. A close ratio is derived from the number of gross sales divided by the number of calls handled by a rep. It's interesting to note that reps who have the best close ratio generally have lower overall AHT than reps with an average close ratio, even though a closed sale inherently lengthens the handle time. I have found this to be true in the call centers I've worked with. At first it seemed counterintuitive until we realized that these reps had acquired a number of skills: They knew not to attempt a "third close"; they were confident and had a brilliant command of product and computer knowledge; and they exercised great call control. Customers appreciate it when a rep exercises professional (not bullying) call control. Customers want and expect reps to know their products, and to efficiently lead them through the call to its conclusion. Dreaded "dead air"—where the customer is waiting for the rep to do something—never occurs with peak performers. They ask for the sale, or reinforce the benefits of the product or service option they're recommending as they're working the keyboard or waiting for a computer response. Many also have great phone personalities so the sales effort is simply less work for them, and a pleasant experience for the customer.

Cancellation Ratio. Again and again, I hear reps and their supervisors say that a rep has no control over cancellations. They cite many valid reasons; e.g., customers must postpone trips due to deaths in families, changes of plans, etc. I usually counter by asking: Why do our peak-performing reps, over the course of a month or a quarter, tend to have lower cancellation rates? What are they doing right? Clearly, they, too, have these types of cancellations, but they avoid controllable cancellations. I've found that sales reps with low cancellation ratios tend to do the following:

• They reinforce the great value or special rate for that time of year.

• In the reconfirmation, they stress the quality, size and amenities of the room and hotel.

• They reinforce the hotel's proximity to the guest's ultimate destination (scenic attraction or business center).

• They do not force a confirmation or make a false sale.

• They obtain an email address to reconfirm all the details.

• They "fit" the customer with the right product and do not force an upgrade.

Show Ratio. The show ratio—or show factor—is the percentage of confirmed phone sales that actually turn into revenue. In other words, it's the customers who have not cancelled their orders and are not "no-shows." Cancellation percentage and "no-show" percentage are two derivative metrics that should be tracked to understand how to improve them. Reps with the best performance driver metrics in this category typically do two things:

1) They do not oversell; and 2) They reconfirm the value of the purchase at the end of the call.

Length of Stay. A longer length of stay would obviously increase the NRPH. Many reps think a metric like length of stay is really a random number and entirely up to the customer. They believe that they have no control over it. However, many customers are open to suggestions, and a good rep can often influence the length of stay. Customers might book for an extended stay if offered a lower rate for additional nights, especially on weekends. A customer who is inquiring about a longer stay might be given more attention and assistance on the call than someone booking for just one day (in which case, it's OK to have a longer AHT).

Reps must be taught how to practice *situational call handling* with customers (i.e., not treating all customers alike). Having one major KPI that really, truly matters will help to instill this practice and support the concept that it's OK to go longer than the AHT norm on certain calls because the ultimate goal is revenue productivity, not AHT. A business result KPI, such as Net Revenue per Phone Hour, makes reps feel like they are running their own business. They usually make excellent judgment calls when it comes to AHT vs. revenue trade-offs.

This change in how KPIs are viewed puts the power back with the rep. Empowerment was the big word in the 1980s, but few people really understood it. It was never about self-directed work teams, it was about doing what was right. It should have been about topics such as situational call-handling. With the proper performance metric system in place, the reps feel like they have much more control, they're servicing the customer more effectively, and the company gets more revenue. What could be better?

Room Category. The higher the room category, the higher the average daily rate, and therefore, the higher the NRPH. For many call centers, average daily rate would seem to be a natural performance driver metric. Although it is certainly measurable, there is a good possibility that reps who are measured by average daily rate would not offer or acknowledge possible discounts—a disservice to the customer. Also, if the customer is sold a room at a higher rate and subsequently finds a lower rate elsewhere, then the "no-show" factor will increase, reducing the net revenue. Instead, you can use a proxy for average daily rate and show reps that upselling a higher room category, if the customer sees the value, would increase overall revenue. A few of the supporting skills and tools for this performance driver include:

- Product and market knowledge
- Utilizing second close tools
- Command of sales dialogue skills

Number of Rooms per Reservation. Reps think they have no control over this metric. I'm sure you see a theme by now. After reviewing the previous scenarios, your staff—who may not have thought they had control—would probably admit otherwise. It's important to look for facts to ensure that you're not missing a component of performance potential—that is what peak potential is all about. Is someone, anyone, doing it without compromising quality? Then it must be doable. It's as simple as that. If you have reps who are not selling well, coach them to increase their command of second-room offer dialogue. In our hotel reservations center, we recognized this as an opportunity area and created a short upsell dialogue that reps could use for situations with two adults and two children.

Percentage of Calls Transferred. This might sound like a strange and seemingly unrelated performance driver because it appears completely unrelated to NRPH. However, many calls are inappropriately transferred (or dumped) to another department or a supervisor because the rep doesn't know how to handle them. Transferred calls also have a negative impact on customer satisfaction. In fact, industry surveys continue to show that multiple transferred calls are a strong source of customer dissatisfaction, along with busy signals and being put on hold.[i] There is frequently revenue potential in these calls, but the rep is giving it away to someone else. Coaching reps on call-handling skills and techniques can help to lower the percentage of calls being inappropriately transferred.

SAMPLE PERFORMANCE DRIVER METRICS FOR DIFFERENT INDUSTRIES

Travel/Reservations	Financial	Catalog	Software/Hardware
• AHT • Call-to-sale close ratio • Cancellation ratio • Show ratio • Length of stay • Room category or class of service • Number of rooms per reservation • Percentage of calls transferred	• AHT • Call-to-sale close ratio • Number of referrals • Approved loan/application ratio • Outbound calls/hour • Percentage of right-party contact • Sales/right-party contact • Customer account profitability/sale	• AHT • Incremental sales/call (gift wrap, express shipping, special offers) • Items sold/call • Revenue/call • Order-taking error rate • Backorder/sales call • Product return rate • Order cancellation ratio • Calls transferred to service • Number of calls per unique order	• AHT • Call-to-sale close ratio • Incremental sales (warranties, support contracts, report services) • Items per order • Cancellation ratio • Product return rate • Upgrades sold (premium goods or services) • Number of additional seats sold

Step 4: Design a Bold Plan to Close the Gap

To bring about real performance improvement, there are several critical disciplines that need to be revamped. These include: 1) recruiting and selection; 2) training and coaching; and 3) the environmental landscape. Let's examine each of these disciplines.

Recruitment and Selection. When I recall the call center selection processes that we used in the past, I'm amazed at how we got it so wrong. We magnanimously called our reps "sales associates." We advertised in newspapers, via the Internet and the radio, using phrases like: "$12 per hour plus great incentives, benefits and working environment," or "Seeking motivated individuals with one-year service and/or sales experience." We spent a lot of time on behavioral-style interviewing, looking for people with good attendance records in the hopes that they would actually show up.

I've heard that one definition of insanity is doing the same thing over and over again, and expecting different results. In fact, that is what we were doing in the call center industry. We wanted dramatically different results, but for years, we did nothing dramatically different. We thought the model was right, but we really needed to blow it up.

Attracting better quality staff requires a revamp of everything—from where you look for people, to the language used in recruiting campaigns and interviews, to the attributes that you require, to the type of compensation advertised. To transform into a peak sales environment, you'll have to look for new and different leaders, and train existing ones for their new roles and performance expectations.

> **TIP: It takes at least six months to properly implement Steps 1 through 3. Some of it will be trial and error, but if you don't get this part right, nothing else will work. Moving the KPI by using validated performance drivers is the key to coaching success.**

Training and Coaching. Improving sales performance in the call center often requires a radical makeover for training and coaching processes. In our call center, we decided to go with what we thought was the "high-tech" route—a program that was 50 percent computer-based training, spending a lot of time working with the computer, and perfecting the order-taking process and dialogue sequencing. Looking back, we found that we had spent very little time in the new-hire classes on real sales training, and virtually no sales "up-training" took place. (Up-training is a term used to describe any new skills training initiated subsequent to new-hire training. Usually a budget is developed for up-training so that tenured reps can learn advanced skills and stay current on product knowledge.)

Meanwhile, the monitoring responsibility fluctuated over the years between supervisors and a QA group. In a 10-year span, no fewer than 20 monitoring forms had been used. Although we thought we were practicing continuous process improvement, the changes were esoteric—alterations in the point system, the "look and feel" of the form, in dialogue requirements or in some complicated index or weighting system that we thought was particularly clever. Yet there was little effective change in actual coaching/training methods. Feedback to reps was generally composed of a few informal comments about what they did wrong or right, what process they missed or what dialogue point they should have included.

Sound familiar? Many of the call centers that I visit have standards in place for service level, training and the number of required monitors. However, a "hands-on" check of the monitor forms (by carefully reviewing them) usually shows that the full monitoring and feedback process is often accomplished by only 50 percent of the supervisors. And that's just the numbers—before even looking at the quality of the input or if the monitoring or coaching actually mattered (i.e., did it substantially improve any sales numbers?). These managers do not understand the power of proper monitoring and feedback. *Every time a call is monitored, even a good one, you can find five to 10 things that could be improved either by the rep, IT or Marketing.* How can that not be compelling?

The right coaching and training programs, with the right follow-up metrics to measure whether they are consistently being accomplished, and how effectively, are key to really moving the KPI.

Environmental Assessment. To achieve peak performance, you must rid your call center of all elements that distract employees from their focus on customer service and sales. These irritants may include unclear performance metrics, poorly conceived or articulated policies, procedures that aren't working, training/monitoring/evaluation criteria that send conflicting messages, and incentive programs that are perceived as unfair or that fail to motivate. They can also include such diverse issues as an uncomfortable physical environment, unclean restrooms or the lack of respect that a supervisor shows for frontline reps.

The environment includes incentives and recognition programs that truly reward performance and, in particular, high-level performers. I'm constantly amazed by highly paid senior executives who love to quote studies that say money ranks far down on the list of employee priorities. Generally, such quotes occur concurrently with the publishing of a competitive salary survey.

Let's get a few things straight:

- Money *does* matter—particularly if your position is one of the lowest paid in the company, and if you are single with children living just barely above the poverty level. This is often the case with many frontline employees.

- Recognition is necessary and it does make you feel good, but you can't take it home and feed the kids with it. Recognition is critical to sustain high performance, but it is not a substitute for money. You must do both to achieve high performance; one does not compensate for the other.

- Providing adequate training and frequent two-way communication in a pleasant working environment free from harassment are basic elements just to retain employees today.

The chapters that follow will demonstrate how a combination of the right incentives and supervisory recognition can work wonders in driving performance. The components of job satisfaction are the same for both frontline reps and senior executives: trust, respect, career opportunities and (surprise!) money. Contests can work well for a period of time and are great for short-term sales-blitzes, but the performance results are not permanent because contests don't have a long-term impact on the employees' lives or living conditions.

Points to Remember

- Use rep and management focus groups to collect all suspected performance drivers, including supporting metrics and all script elements.

- Validate and reduce the number of performance drivers by performing correlation and regression analysis.

- Identify three to five ways a rep can positively impact each performance driver metric.

Chapter 6: Sales Performance and Macro-Gap Analysis

"We divide business plans into three categories: candy, vitamins and painkillers. We throw away the candy. We look at vitamins. We really like painkillers. We especially like painkillers!"
K. FONG

Organizations typically don't make major cultural changes unless they're in some sort of "pain." Identifying the amount of revenue your call center is leaving on the table will create pain—and the momentum necessary to change the culture.

In this chapter, you'll learn how to utilize methods to find additional revenue in service and sales calls, and to perform a macro-gap analysis of the sales reps' productivity potential. The result will be a strong business case for the resources and process improvements necessary to improve individual rep and centerwide performance. In addition to macro-gap analyses, we'll begin to look at the *micro-gap* analysis necessary to improve individual employee performance.

Understanding Macro-Gap Analysis

Macro-gap analysis is a technique commonly used by consultants or investment firms to identify opportunities. From a performance standpoint, it really amounts to internal benchmarking—you look at a major key performance indicator for a rep (the larger, more encompassing the measurement is, the better), then benchmark those reps whose performance falls into the bottom third against the middle third and the highest third, and play out "what-if" scenarios, such as: "What if the bottom third were to perform at least as well as my medium-tier performers?" (This scenario is the easiest to imagine because it's the easiest to achieve.)

> **"What are the facts? Again and again and again—what are the facts? Shun wishful thinking, ignore divine revelation, forget what 'the stars foretell'—what are the facts and the decimal places?"**
> **—R.A. Heilein, Renowned Science Fiction Author**

Inevitably, there will always be a bottom third because the other tiers will naturally get better as they receive new training by better coaches. The point is that higher levels of performance already exist. True, those levels are not being attained by the bottom third of your reps, but that is where *micro*-gap analysis comes into play. Micro-gap analysis compares an *individual's* performance to the average of reps who receive calls in a similar skill set, and on a similar shift. (Chapter 9 discusses how to use micro-gap analysis.)

In sales, the preferred all-encompassing measurement for macro-gap analysis is net revenue per phone hour (NRPH). I like using this measurement because the divisor (phone hours) accounts for almost all conditions (e.g., part-time vs. full-time, absenteeism, holidays, schedule adherence). Using net revenue as the dividend allows you to analyze numerous performance driver metrics (e.g., cancellation rate, product mix and close ratio) that can be used as levers or root-cause attributes of the performance targeted for improvement. Many good companies still use only close ratio as their KPI to evaluate sales performance and productivity. Sometimes using only close ratio as the KPI for sales productivity suboptimizes sales by not accounting for all avenues of revenue. We'll look at the pros and cons of using that approach in more detail in Chapter 9.

Applying Macro-Gap Analysis: A Sample Case Study

Now let's apply macro-gap analysis to our hotel reservations call center example. In the example on page 96, the center is divided into thirds—the bottom third consists of tenured sales performers (those who have been in the center for at least six months) who contribute, on average, $400 to $500 per hour; the middle tier of tenured performers contribute about $500 to $800 per hour; and the top tier of tenured performers contribute $800 to $1,100 per hour. There will be some "outliers"—those producing below the low tier, say, $300 per hour, and those producing above the high tier, for instance, $1,700 per hour—but remember, this is a macro analysis. If the outliers are representing the productivity of real performers, then leave them in the analysis. In this particular case, we found that the $300/hour performers were real, so they were included. The $1,700/hour performers, on the other hand, had a lot of very short calls. We suspected that they were hanging up on calls with little sales potential, therefore, they were excluded from the analysis.

The difference between a low and medium performer in the same skill set, on the same shift, was a remarkable $200 per hour. With 1,500 "plugged-in" phone hours per year per rep (69 percent phone hours based on 2,080 hours full-time per year), and with a potential $200 per hour increase, we deduced that an overall revenue performance improvement of $300,000 per rep per year is attainable. Our hotel company had 600 skilled sales reps and, therefore, roughly 200 low performers (33.3 percent of 600).

UNDERSTANDING THE MACRO-GAP ANALYSIS TOOL:
THE BUSINESS CASE FOR SALES REP PERFORMANCE IMPROVEMENT

EXAMPLE: HOTEL INDUSTRY—SALES SKILL FIRST SHIFT

Key Performance Indicator: Shown Revenue Per Phone Hour

Low Tier	Medium Tier	High Tier
$400-500	$500-800	$800-1,100

$650/hour   Avg. medium performance
-$450/hour   Avg. low performance

$200/hour   Avg. difference

1,500 productive phone hours/year/rep x $200 difference = $300,000/rep/year revenue increase

600 Reps x 33.3 percent low performers = 200 low performers

200 low performers x $300,000/year/rep increase = $60,000,000 revenue increase/year

$60,000,000 x 80 percent incremental margin = $48,000,000 additional gross profit per year

Less additional expenses:
Training..$800,000
Incentives $1,000,000
Performance Database* $100,000
Hiring Assessments*..................$200,000
Consulting* $400,000

Sub total $2,500,000/year
Net profit/year $45,500,000/year

Note: This business case spends money on the whole group of performers, yet takes benefit credit for just the improved performance of the lower tier of performers. Additional benefits, hard and soft, for attrition reduction and AHT reduction should be identified but not committed to in the business case. This is, therefore, a conservative analysis of potential profitability improvement.

* Caution: Many call center consultants do not understand real performance optimization, especially around sales; and many general consultants who understand sales are not sufficiently trained in call center operations to be effective. If you use outside resources, be careful whom you choose.

If the performance of the bottom 200 was improved, the annual revenue increase for this company could be $60 million, or $48 million at, say, an 80 percent rooms departmental profit margin. Therein lies our business case;

therein also lies our "pain," if we do nothing about it.

You'll notice that the business case says nothing about the "upside" opportunity if the medium performers migrated to the current top-performer tier. Nor does it address the top performers reaching the individual peak performers' statistics. For the sake of the business case, and the ability to truly deliver on what you promise, leave those opportunities alone for now. True, those scenarios are possible, and you will pursue them in due course, but the numbers will seem unbelievable. So while your program will address all your staff, build your business case for the required resources solely on the migration or performance improvement of the lower third tier.

At the hotel company, the light bulb over management's head "lit up" at this point. This particular company entrusted 20,000 customers per year to each of their reps, yet the call center did not provide the reps with the level of sales training or coaching that the direct sales organization gave its field sales representatives.

Given the volume and the revenue potential, why are frontline rep positions not recognized as being among the most important in the company? They should certainly be worth more than four weeks of computer and dialogue training, and worth more than $12 an hour. But for the most part, not only do call centers not provide enough initial or advanced sales training, they also rarely terminate or discipline a rep for poor sales performance. Managers will terminate phone sales reps for hanging up on customers, for poor quality, for "hiding" in after-call work, and for poor attendance—but almost never for poor sales. Sales supervisors rarely receive real sales training by real sales professionals. While most call centers talk a lot about sales, and some may even do a little role-playing, if they knew what was really at stake—possibly millions in profit in certain situations—things would be handled very differently.

You've probably heard about the four levels of competency: 1) unconsciously incompetent, 2) consciously incompetent, 3) unconsciously competent, and 4) consciously competent. If you have just completed this exercise, you are now consciously incompetent. You know that your center is not performing at its peak sales potential, but you have not yet demonstrated the sales management competency to effect the change. Now, if you do nothing, you would be making a conscious decision to leave at least $48 million in profit on the table. That should be unacceptable to you and to your management staff.

At this point, you'll begin to view your call center world in a very different way: You're no longer just looking at what someone brings in (the sale), but also what they're leaving on the table. Similarly, at the hotel reservations center, the management team and, more importantly, the supervisory staff decided that they could not *afford* poor performers. In the past, management had, at times, pointed out to supervisors the individual poor sales performers and recommended considering them for different jobs. Perhaps they could be transferred to a service skill, or if they could not be retrained sufficiently to meet the minimum sales standard, they might be placed in another position outside the company. Frequently, the supervisor would point out all the other really great attributes the individual possessed and brought to the company in an attempt to "save" the rep. They weighted good performance on measures like attendance, average talk time, quality and schedule adherence equally with the bottomline KPI (NRPH).

This protective attitude, displayed by many supervisors, reveals a lack of understanding that effectiveness is more important than efficiency. In fact, effectiveness really takes efficiency into account. Once we show supervisors that the individual poor performers are leaving at least $240,000 in company profitability on the table, they will quickly realize they cannot afford to keep these employees in that position.

So now you have the business case and a real burning platform. You can see and clearly communicate the center's potential. You know your point of departure (POD)—or the baseline from which you are starting—and your point of arrival (POA) for the business case to be a success (i.e., $48 million in additional gross profit contribution).

Four Components
of a Peak Performance Management System

Now what? You need to build the plan for resources and the strategies to move the lower performers "up or out." You need to get smarter at hiring the right sales people in the first place. You need to figure out how to keep them engaged at the highest levels. There are four critical areas for which you must plan, budget and improve processes, as illustrated below:

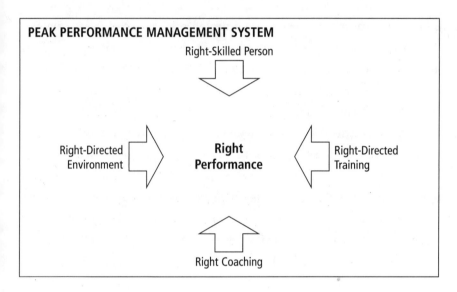

Let's take a brief look at the components of a peak performance management system. Section 3 will offer a detailed discussion on each area.

THE CASE FOR BETTER HIRING TOOLS

Numerous analytical studies by industrial psychologists indicate that thorough hiring tests and employment methodology consistently yields employees who out-produce low performers by at least 100 percent, train in half the time and have about 50 percent lower turnover. It is also worth noting that the more complex the job, the greater the gap between the highest and lowest performers.[i] It stands to reason then that someone who sells and services customers might see even greater gaps. In my experience in the call center industry (where sales performance management has not been a traditional focus in a truly technical sense), the gap between the highest and lowest performers is even greater than 100 percent—it is actually in the range of 100 to 300 percent or more if the sales function is not properly managed.

If sales consultants Jeanne and Herbert Greenberg's findings are correct, and 50 percent of all people in sales positions have little or no ability to sell, then what are the chances that we're selecting and hiring staff well? For those of us who are not using sophisticated predictive hiring assessments, the answer is "slim to none." Interviews alone will screen out only the most incompetent or unqualified people who obviously should not be in the job. And interviews, after an initial screening, are only about 50 percent accurate at predicting future performance.

Highly predictive hiring assessments, on the other hand, rely on validated tests for each critical aspect of the job—knowledge and skills, as well as personality traits like *attitudes, interests* and *motivators* or AIMs.[ii] The AIMs acronym was coined by Dr. Wendell Williams, Ph.D., an expert in the science of predictive assessments, and founder of the organizational consulting firm ScientificSelection.com. His extensive research on predictive hiring and organizational effectiveness led to the development of an inventory of specific personality attributes associated with job satisfaction and validated attitudes that predict job fit.

Organizational psychologists like to define the predictability of job performance using the following equation:

K&S (Knowledge & Skills) + AIM (Attitudes) = Job Performance

The most thorough hiring process presents the applicant with a realistic preview of the job, requires the successful completion of situational simulations of the job competencies, and includes written problem-solving and learning tests, as well as validated behavioral interview questions. This type of process has been used by many Fortune 500 companies since the 1950s.

DEVELOP RELEVANT TRAINING

Many managers believe that a good training program can help to bolster a weak hiring process. But as Dr. Williams points out, "Training can make people better, but it cannot fix hiring mistakes." The reality is that there are numerous behaviors and personality factors that simply cannot be taught. You cannot make people smarter or change their attitudes or make a rep more charismatic. While training can teach a prospective sales rep what not to say to irritate a customer or obstruct a sale, energy and a positive attitude cannot be taught.

Even with effective assessment and selection tools and processes in place, you won't retain new-hires if the training is not pertinent to their success on the job—in this case, training in the tactics and strategies that will help them to succeed in sales.

Many training programs teach new-hires how to do the job, but not how to do the job well. How do you ensure that your training is dynamic and effective? A sound approach is to perform statistical correlation analysis on each point on your monitoring form and script outline. The process is similar to the predictive hiring assessment analysis used to determine which technical competencies and personality factors are statistically correlated with the success or failure of an individual in a specific job position. In addition, you'll also need to create advanced sales training modules for your sales reps, sales coaches and supervisors. (These types of analyses will be discussed in more detail later in the book.)

COMPETENT COACHES ARE CRITICAL

So you've hired the right people and have provided the proper training to help them succeed in a sales position. But what will happen if you try to support them with supervisors who are not properly trained in sales coaching? You'll lose your valued new-hires and have to start the process all over again. Low performers may put up with incompetent coaches, but high performers will not do so for long.

Try to recall a time in your career when you had a truly top-performing supervisor or manager—someone who was a great coach and leader. It's hard, isn't it? If you can think of one or two, you've been lucky, because there are not many around. Studies show that only 30 to 40 percent of managers are considered competent.[iii] Dr. Williams estimates that only 10 percent of all managers can be considered good leaders (e.g., effectively coach subordinates, are trustworthy, plan and organize effectively, are intelligent enough for the job, are good communicators, provide clear direction, etc.).

Creating new predictive criteria for supervisors will ensure that you hire individuals who will be able to effectively coach sales reps and provide them with the support they need to perform and remain committed.

CREATE AN ENVIRONMENT THAT SUPPORTS TOP PERFORMERS

An environment that does not support high performers, that sends conflicting messages, that features irritants which distract staff from their sales mission, or that does not reward reps appropriately can torpedo all of your efforts. Peak sales performers thrive on competition, risk and rewards that are significant.

A good performance management system built on sound data analysis will ensure that the criteria used in hiring, training, monitoring, performance evaluations and incentives are aligned and are positively driving performance and business results. Periodic environmental assessments must be conducted that ask questions to get to the root of the elements that are either hindering or helping reps' sales performance. You must be prepared to act quickly if you discover an issue that negatively affects peak performance. Remember, peak performers are very demanding—they will deliver for you only if you deliver for them. Your job is to remove the roadblocks and get out of their way.

Points to Remember

- A great business case is so compelling that it creates pain if not acted upon.

- A Peak Performance Management System includes the right people, training, coaching and environment.

- Use new tools like predictive hiring assessments to dramatically improve your chances of hiring top performers and screening out poor performers.

- Develop new training that not only teaches how to do the job, but how to do it well.

- With 50 to 80 percent of people in the wrong job, and only 30 to 40 percent of managers generally competent, rethink who is coaching your reps.

- Creating an environment that supports top performers and not mediocrity is critical to retaining the best performers.

Section 3:
Placing Your People on the Path

Chapter 7: Sourcing, Selecting and Retaining the *Right* People

"Only the mediocre are always at their best."
JEAN GIRAUDOUX, FRENCH DIPLOMAT

In U.S. companies, failure in the hiring process is at epidemic levels. Some studies suggest that as many as 50 percent or more of U.S. workers are in the wrong job, or more accurately, not in the ideal job for their natural skills and personalities. Selecting the best sales reps is more of a science than you probably realize, and if you can do it better than the competition, you win.

The chart on the following page represents common selection methods and their ability to predict job performance. Think of these numbers as an "average of averages" (i.e., extracted from a significant number of controlled studies).

Why Traditional Hiring Practices Don't Help

Traditional job interviews will only screen out the obvious 10 percent of candidates who are not suitable for the job. But sales people, in particular, tend to excel at interviewing. They're notorious for their ability to use

Selection Method	% Predictability
Handwriting analysis	0
Age	0
Amount of education	0
Self awareness	3
Projective tests	3
Traditional interviews	4
Grade point average	4
Expert recommendations	4
Personality tests	4
Reference checks	6
Biographical data	9
Situational interviews	9
Behavioral event interviews	10
Mental-ability tests	25
Content-valid simulations	64

Adapted from a Meta analysis conducted by Hunter and Hunter, Psychological Bulletin, Volume 96, 1984. Percentages have been rounded. "Predictability" is an oversimplification of a statistical term that refers to the amount of explained variance.
Source: Chart adapted by Dr. Wendell Williams, Ph.D.

"impression management" to influence an interview outcome.[i] They consciously or unconsciously try to project themselves as being similar to the interviewer in outlook. (While many job-seekers use this technique, studies have shown that seekers of sales positions do this to a far greater extent.) In other words, they are born "schmoozers." They know how to make people like them, which does, in fact, have a positive influence on the interviewer.

However, just because they can sell *themselves*, does not mean they can sell *your product*. It's true that people tend to buy from people they like, but they don't buy because they like them. Potential sales reps must have more skills than impression management.

Single-dimension personality tests, likewise, are not good predictors of performance. Personality tests—which have only a 2 percent to 8 percent average correlation factor to job performance—aren't reliable enough when used alone. Personality can either help or hinder the application of skills and knowledge. What about educational level? Education seems to make no difference to the predictability of job performance and, at least in the case of sales, neither does job experience.[ii] Past experience (e.g., being No. 1 in sales) does not tell you how the job was accomplished. It doesn't tell you if the sales rep "overpromised and underdelivered" or if he "skimmed the cream." Did he leave a trail of disasters in his wake? We all know those types of sales people—you're better off without them.

So if traditional hiring practices are not effective, how do you select the right sales reps—those who have a better shot at being a top performer? Conversely, how do you avoid the reps who will be poor performers? Consider the selection methods listed at the bottom of the chart on the previous page. You'll find the answer in structured behavioral interviews, in mental-ability tests that analyze cognitive and interpersonal skills, as well as in tests to measure motivating factors. Add to those tests content-valid simulation exercises.

Almost all job competencies tend to cluster into four categories, represented by the chart below. A job discovery and validation process helps to develop a list of relevant skills, knowledge and personality attributes that fall into one of these four categories. Appropriate assessment tools are then designed to predict a candidate's success.

The table on page 110 lists competencies that describe the skills and motivators necessary for a general sales position. It demonstrates how the

---

JOB COMPETENCIES: THE FOUR-QUADRANT MODEL

Planning Competencies (Can do)	Cognitive Competencies (Can do)
Interpersonal Competencies (Can do)	Attitudes, Interest, Motivational (AIM) Requirements (Will do)

Source: Dr. Wendell Williams, Ph.D., www.ScientificSelection.com

right predictive hiring tool can be applied to categorize performers by their
productivity:

Productive Salesperson	Poor Salesperson	Tools to determine which is which
Cognitive: • Learns fast • Knows all about customer's market and problems • Solves problems	**Cognitive:** • Refuses to learn about product details • Thinks everything reduces to a sales pitch • Knows little about the customer's environment • Goes from sale to sale	• Mental-alertness tests (varies with product complexity) • Behavioral interviews • Attitudes, interests and motivations test
Interpersonal: • Develops trust • Uncovers needs • Recommends solutions to problems • Helps overcome hesitancy • Functions as a team member	**Interpersonal:** • Fast talker • Does not ask questions • Dismisses objections • Goes straight into a sales presentation • Functions as a loner	• Service simulations • Sales fact-finding simulations • Presentation simulations • Teamwork simulations • Behavioral interview • Attitudes, interests and motivations test
AIMs: • Welcomes challenges • Is proud of role as a salesperson	**AIMs:** • Secretly fears customers • Is ashamed of being a salesperson; prefers to be called an account representative	• Behavioral interviews • Attitudes, interests and motivations test
Planning: • Strong planner • Manages time • Manages territory • Tracks order status	**Planning:** • Thinks sale ends with the order • Seldom follows through • Misses details • Makes mistakes	• Low to complex planning skills test, depending on position • Behavioral interview • Attitude, interests and motivations test
Source: Dr. Wendell Williams, Ph.D. [iii]		

A best practice for hiring sales positions uses four types of predictive hiring tools (included in the following steps), which allow management to screen out 75 percent of all applicants.[iv] Using predictive assessment tools and processes brings the job offers to applicant ratio to 1:7. In spite of this great track record, the number of companies using these tools is fairly low.[v] Therefore, if using these tools can predict performance—which they do— then using them will give you a tremendous advantage over the competition. Dr. Williams recommends the following six steps for maximum hiring accuracy:

EMPLOYEE SELECTION STEPS

1. Offer a job preview early in the process.

Give applicants a chance to see the work environment and the job being done. Sitting side by side with a strong sales rep may sound like a good idea, but what if all the calls the rep takes that day are difficult? Or easy? A realistic job preview should be controlled, and it should include a proportion of both the best and the worst aspects of the job. The benefit of using this tool early is to give the applicant an opportunity to self-select out of the hiring game before he or she enters a time-consuming and resource-intensive process.

2. Use a prescreening behavioral interview.

Prescreening via a behavioral interview will eliminate the most blatantly unqualified applicants. Prescreen candidates via a phone interview or IVR system for reasons that will be detailed later.

3. Use a validated test to assess the attitudes, interests and motivations, then use a comprehensive behavioral interview.

The test(s) and the interview must be validated for the specific job for which you are hiring.

4. Use selected tests, cases and simulations.

Simulations can predict interpersonal skills, while cases measure cognitive abilities, and additional tests measure technical knowledge.

5. Confirm data and unclear information through another behavioral interview.

6. Select the most qualified person based on the measurable data. Or if the available selection of job applicants is slim, use the system to identify any applicants who would be the easiest to coach.

It takes about three to four hours for an applicant to complete this entire process, which may seem overly onerous. As you can imagine, the people responsible for hiring and prescreening complain that it's a lot of work; however, frontline managers consistently praise its effectiveness.

There are many ways to build in efficiencies. One way to reduce the amount of hiring time is to implement a "multiple-hurdle" approach—sequence the tests so that an applicant must successfully pass one phase of the hiring process before progressing to the next. Just remember, hiring high performers is a zero-sum game without shortcuts; if you don't weed out weak performers in the pre-screening phase, you'll end up doing it on the job.

NOTABLE ASSESSMENT FIRMS

Two of the more notable hiring assessment companies are ScientificSelection.com (www.scientificselection.com) and FurstPerson (www.furstperson.com). Furst-Person has tailored a number of solutions and services specifically for the call center industry. One product, CC Audition, is a job simulation application that can be used to assess rep applicants over the phone, via the Web or from a CD-ROM.

Tailoring Existing Assessment Programs

Best-of-breed companies strongly believe in detailed employee selection systems—so much so, many have tailored off-the-shelf assessment tools to account for variances inherent in their cultures or in specific types of sales positions (e.g., developing different hiring criteria based upon whether the individual is being recruited for an outside sales position, inbound sales position, outbound sales position, outbound sales position with cold calling, or a phone service position which requires sales skills). These companies assert that doing so has refined their success in selecting the right sales people with the right traits and competencies.

What should you consider when tailoring assessment programs for sales jobs? While 25 years of research regarding the correlation between job performance and personalities reveals that extroversion almost always accompanies the success of individuals in sales and management,[vi] one could not simply trust an extroversion test to predict sales performance. Sales reps need more than an outgoing personality—they need hard skills. Additionally, outbound sales reps should be tested for their ability to work under pressure, to learn quickly and to plan, while inbound sales reps should be evaluated more on persuasion skills. Customer service reps who are asked to sell should be assessed on their ability to learn. Outbound reps selling a very complex product or business solution might require a much higher level of intelligence and stronger planning skills than those selling a simple product

---

A SIX-STEP MODEL FOR ASSESSMENT PRACTICES

The right analysis and tools can help you to predict with a high degree of accuracy which candidates will be high performers and which will be low performers. Without predictive tests, your chances of hiring an above-average performer is about 50 percent, regardless of whether or not they pass an interview screening.[vii] Use the following six-step model as a guideline to develop your criteria for good assessment practices.

1. Define explicit job requirements (using the Four-Quadrant model as a guide).

2. Design a set of target simulations, tests and interview questions that you think will accurately measure an applicant's job skills (using the Four-Quadrant model as a guide).

3. Conduct a study (validation) to prove that each tentative hiring tool accurately predicts job performance.

4. Train people to use the system, and ensure that they are accurate and consistent.

5. Monitor adverse impact and seek alternative tests with less impact. Adverse impact exists if the selection ratio for a discriminated-against group is 80 percent of the selection ratio for the group with the highest selection ratio. This is also called the "Four-Fifths Rule."

6. Continually monitor and tweak the system to improve performance.

sold on a transaction basis in less than 10 minutes. A rep dedicated to service requires completely different skills, with customer focus as a main differentiator. Sales coaches should be assessed on judgment abilities, in addition to many other skills, such as planning and interpersonal strengths. Motivations for each of these sales persons would also vary by specific position.

"Hard-Skill Specific" Hiring	
Specific Job	Hard Skill
• Service Reps ⟶	Customer Focus
• Service/Sales Reps ⟶	Ability to Learn
• Inbound Sales Reps ⟶	Problem Solving
• Outbound Sales Reps ⟶	Problem Solving and Planning
• Outbound++Sales Reps ⟶	Problem Solving and Planning Intelligence

A helpful analogy might be the development of a driver's license test: Driving a car requires physical coordination, physical heath, good eyesight and knowledge of driving laws. To get a license, you're required to drive a car (a simulation), take a written test of driving laws (to prove that you know the basic rules) and take an eye test. Imagine what would happen to the road accident rate if these testing standards were loosened? Alternatively, what would happen if we added tests for addiction, coordination, stress reactions, road conditions and weather conditions? How far do we go? If we want to absolutely *minimize* accidents, we would give applicants every kind of test to cover every kind of driving condition.

To increase accuracy in your ability to identify the right person for the right sales job, be sure to carefully select the depth of your assessment

NOTE: The U.S. Department of Labor has prepared an excellent free source of information on legal and effective hiring practices. This 79-page PDF document, titled "DOL's Testing and Assessment: An Employer's Guide to Good Practices," can be downloaded at www.dol.gov. Outside the United States, check with your regulatory agency for information.

methodology and vendor partner. There are many predictive hiring assessment tools and systems on the market; even some developed by people who are not really qualified. And there is no shortage of fun but flaky personality tests on the Web. However, these "pseudo-scientific" tests generally have not been criteria- or content-validated ("chicken feather tests created by witch doctors," according to Dr. Williams).

There are, however, companies that create legitimate assessments, as well as organizations that tailor tests which focus on the individual job in specialized industries. There are also more full-service companies that integrate assessments with training, coaching and, eventually, the company and departmental environment. Choosing a provider with the fullest range of services will usually yield the best results.

So how do you decide which supplier would be your ideal partner? Asking the following five questions will help you to screen potential supplier/consultant candidates:

1. Is your system or test specifically designed for hiring?

2. Do you perform a legally credible job analysis that conforms to the Department of Labor's Uniform Guidelines on Employee Selection Procedures?

3. Do you use a multitrait and/or multimethod design to cover all critical skill elements?

4. Do you validate each hiring tool for use with my company and my job?

5. Do your consultants have specific degrees/certificates in the science of hiring, and do they belong to professional associations specializing in hiring and measurements?

If the answer to any of these questions is anything other than an unqualified "yes," you are probably dealing with the wrong company or consultant. At a minimum, you may get sued for hiring discrimination and spend hundreds of thousands of dollars in legal fees. (In 1998, the median damage award in cases involving hiring discrimination of this nature was $137,000.[viii]) Or worse, you'll hire an abundance of unqualified people and lose millions of dollars each year.

Hiring Assessment Costs and ROI

The costs for basic predictive hiring assessments generally run around $15 to $20 per applicant per test—assuming you're processing a fairly high volume of candidates. Based on typical call center turnover rates and the 7:1 "candidate-to-hire" ratios (see page 111), expect to test 1,000 candidates per year, if you have 1,000 employees, or 300, if you have 300 employees, and so on. Therefore, a call center with 300 employees and average turnover rates should budget $6,000 per year for a very basic assessment program. Surprisingly, the more unscientific, single-hurdle tests tend to cost more— $40 to $125 per applicant per test—since they're often developed by training-oriented individuals who typically operate on lower volumes. You'll need to plan for a bigger budget if you want to add multi-hurdle testing to improve predictive accuracy. For instance, if you choose a validated multi-hurdle approach and utilize a Web-based assessment, a phone assessment and a phone job simulation assessment, the costs per applicant can range from $150 to $200.

A comprehensive and accurately developed hiring assessment system delivers one of the best returns on investment—literally, in months. Integrating these hiring tools with your other performance management systems will provide you with sales reps who deliver twice the productivity of the low producers that you will be eliminating. Also, it will reduce your turnover by 25 to 50 percent, and reduce training time by 25 percent. On a properly validated and executed predictive hiring assessment program, the ROI is, realistically, 200 to 300 percent. Some companies suggest that the return on the right multi-hurdle assessments are as high as 500 to 1,000 percent.

The Recruiting Process, on the facing page, is one employed by RMH Teleservices. They use a psychometric profiling assessment tool provided by a qualified, third-party, predictive assessment partner.

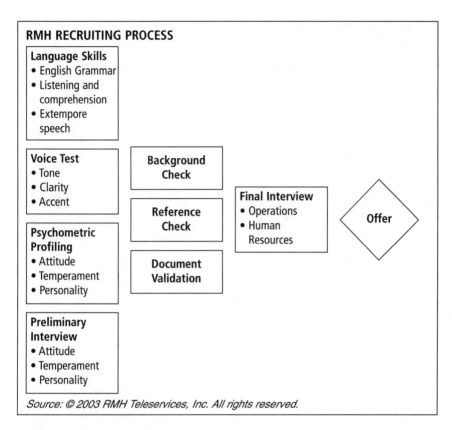

RMH RECRUITING PROCESS

Language Skills
- English Grammar
- Listening and comprehension
- Extempore speech

Voice Test
- Tone
- Clarity
- Accent

Psychometric Profiling
- Attitude
- Temperament
- Personality

Preliminary Interview
- Attitude
- Temperament
- Personality

Background Check

Reference Check

Document Validation

Final Interview
- Operations
- Human Resources

Offer

A Word about Deselection

Deselection is a friendly term for removing an individual from a job that they may or may not have once been qualified to do. Deselection can take numerous forms, including an employee quitting because he has determined that he can't or chooses not to do the job at the newly prescribed performance levels; a forced termination for the same reasons; or a movement to another position for which the individual is more qualified.

Deselection is not an evil concept. The truth is, it doesn't happen enough in call centers. Many centers will terminate employees for poor attendance, hanging up on customers or for high error rates, but rarely does the process go beyond that. Weak service or sales employees are seldom terminated because of poor service in a service environment or poor sales in a sales environment. Why? Because performance metrics and coaching processes are inadequate or virtually non-existent. Many managers are either unaware of how bad a rep is because they have not drawn a minimum acceptable line in the sand, or they feel bad because they have not helped the rep to improve performance.

The minimum line in the sand—the minimum standard below which performance is unacceptable and the point at which deselection must take place—has to be set for the sales KPI, as well as for attendance and quality. As an industry, we've done a stellar job setting minimum standards for attendance because we can clearly feel the pain when a rep doesn't consistently show up for work. Once you've done the gap analysis, you can understand the pain of the sales KPI that is well below average.

Many times, once the minimum standard is in place, deselection will not fall upon the supervisor's shoulders, but upon the employee himself. Poor performers will self-select out because the vision for performance is clear. They would rather leave on their own accord than have a supervisor terminate them or move them to a different job.

Some companies—and executives—are strong proponents of deselection. When Jack Welch ran G.E., he mandated that the bottom 10 percent of performers be terminated annually. Besides keeping everyone on their toes, the lowest performers are replaced, making room for a new and better-qualified candidate, or a promotion for those who have earned it.

Is 10 percent the "right" number? It's difficult to say for sure, but research and anecdotal evidence show that it probably is. Even in good sales organizations, Gallup studies show that at least 10 percent of a sales force is disengaged, and that that number is more in the neighborhood of 20 percent for the average sales organization.[ix] Let's say you have 100 sales reps, and terminate your bottom 10 percent, or 10 employees. Then you hire 10 new sales reps to replace them. Statistically, one of the new people you hire may not be any better than the one you just let go, but by the law of averages, the other nine you hire should be better than the other nine you let go. Also, by the law of averages, you are likely replacing the other nine with at least three "superstars" and three to four average performers. If I were the manager of a baseball team, that would sound like a great trade to me. But it gets better than that. By using predictive hiring assessments and validated behavioral interview and job simulations, you have a 75 percent better chance of selecting a higher-than-average producer, not just someone who is better than the bottom 10 percent!

What is the Right Attrition Rate?

Some sales executives boast about having very low turnover among their reps, others worry that their turnover is too high. What is the right number to ensure good productivity and to minimize the customer inconvenience associated with new reps? This question is frequently asked, but it's the wrong question. Instead, we should be asking: *Who* is turning over? And why?

In interviews with executives of peak-performing sales centers that have institutionalized their peak sales hiring, training and coaching processes, and have corrected their environmental problems, I have found that turnover is low or very low. These organizations usually have minimum standards in place for the sales KPI or offer low base pay and no incentives for the bottom 10 to 15 percent of the sales staff. Improving the performance management system has reduced attrition overall while the minimum standards and the incentive system have ensured that the bottom performers *will* turnover.

> **Some sales executives boast about having very low turnover among their reps, others worry that their turnover is too high. What is the right number? This question is frequently asked, but it's the wrong question. Instead, we should be asking: *Who* is turning over? And why?**

My suggestion would be to compare your reps by KPI sales performance tiers—dividing them into thirds, quartiles or quintiles—and then compare their sales productivity. Contrast that index with the turnover statistics for those same sales performance tiers. Who is leaving? If your new employees are leaving, re-examine your hiring and training practices. In many organizations, the worst managers have the highest turnover and are the ones hiring the most people. It can be a vicious cycle if not interrupted. If your bottom performers are the ones who are leaving most often, then your performance management and incentive systems are working. If your top performers are leaving, you'll definitely want to know why. Top-performer turnover can be an indication of a compensation or incentive plan that is no longer competitive, or more often, it can mean that there is a managerial problem. Top producers can be hard to manage, and only the most seasoned managers can coach them at a level that makes a difference. Because managers have traditionally spent most of their time and attention trying to develop poor performers, they often fail to look after their top-producers' concerns. Whatever the cause is, you need to fix it promptly—your lifeblood is draining away!

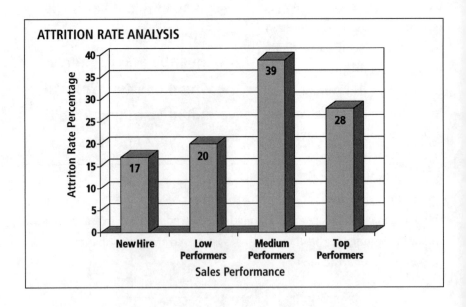

GOOD ATTRITION VS. BAD ATTRITION

One argument against deselection that I often hear is: "Our attrition rate will go up!" Yes, in the short term, deselection will increase attrition, but it is "good attrition." Not all types of attrition are bad. Let's examine the differences between good and bad attrition:

Good attrition includes internal promotion or lateral moves to other positions or departments (which is how general managers are developed), and 10 to 15 percent per year performance-related attrition (those who self-selected out or were forced out) after the initial purge of 10 to 30 percent of reps who weren't hitting the new minimum standards.

In our call center, once we increased the sales skills of some of our reps (who eventually were making upward of $25 per hour including commissions), we began losing a few to outside sales positions in other companies where they were making $80,000 to $100,000 or more annually. Initially, we thought, "Well, good for them." We took the high road and said we were all about making other people successful. That was our mission. If for the cause of peak performance we lost some reps to better lives, then so be it. We overlooked the fact that we had field sales positions within our company that could pay similar levels of compensation and provide similar satisfaction levels. Previously, we had never made the internal opportunities available to our reps because they never qualified before. The lesson? It is only bad to lose someone to an outside job that is significantly better when a similar job is available in your own company.

Additionally, we rethought the incentive program and removed the artificial cap. We realized the cap was simply limiting the company's revenue potential by limiting our reps' potential. Many high-performing companies do not place caps on incentive programs. Companies like Mary Kay Cosmetics and Enterprise Car Rental use their incentive programs as a catalytic mechanism for recruiting and sales profitability. Peak performers in these companies can literally earn hundreds of thousands each year, which the company is happy to pay since it reaps the profit benefits.

Bad attrition, on the other hand, includes huge turnover rates (more than 30 percent) due to the inability to meet minimum performance levels in the most important KPI, following the initial purge, or because of poor supervision or environmental issues. It also includes employees who quit because of poor managerial practices (e.g., poor training, coaching and reward systems). All of these factors are controllable and reside within the scope of the performance management process. If someone says they need to earn more money, we need to show them how they can do that in the redesigned sales job, and help them to gain the skills to realize the increased earning potential.

I once worked at a company where many of the managers, directors and VPs were reluctant to get rid of poor performers, employees with poor attendance records or those who could not work the shifts we needed. Their contention was that, in a tight labor market where the type of skilled position we needed was in high demand, they could not afford to lose anyone—not even the poor performers. Someone showing up and occupying a seat was better than having nobody in that seat. Unbelievable!

And yet, it's a management philosophy that is common at many companies when unemployment is low. What these managers fail to recognize is that employees will continue to turn in poor performance if there is no meaningful consequence to their actions. By not acting, management is basically telling employees that their performance is not really that critical.

Warning: Treat Your Top Performers Differently, or Risk Losing Them

When embarking upon the quest for peak performance in our call centers, the management team initially hypothesized that, if we could just duplicate everything our top-tier performers were doing, we'd be home free. In fact, we believed that we could even improve on the top performers' current results because they were not all adhering to the basics that we thought were tenets for peak sales, and they were not all doing the same things.

So we collected all of our top performers' best individual practices and set about scripting them to use the right key words, to use the best closing tools and to utilize a set grid for solving customers' problems in the form of a best practices diagram. We believed that, by training reps and monitoring for compliance to these newly found tools and practices, we would drive even better performance. We were excited; our reps were less so. But we used our best change management techniques to show them how they could both service and sell the customer even better *and* earn more money in terms of incentives because *they* were selling better.

It backfired. All of the additional training, scripting, new tools, best practices and coaching that worked so well in improving the performance of the medium-tier group didn't work at all on our top performers. Their talk time went up, their revenue per hour went down. Many of them simply quit, including some long-term employees who really knew what they were doing. Quite frankly, we mucked it up.

It was a revealing experience, and a hard lesson to learn. In the final analysis, we underestimated the value of our top performers' charismatic phone personalities and innate presentation skills. We had equally weighted their charisma with all of the other attributes, including product knowledge, tools, techniques and the script adherence. In reality, charisma sometimes compensated for the lack of script outline adherence (which had not been validated anyway at that point). Our top performers could use their phone charisma and personalized presentation techniques to get to "yes" much faster and without as many steps as our medium-tier performers. Also, we had assumed there was one "best way" to sell or describe a product. We were wrong. To say we were chagrined is an understatement.

As a result, we made immediate changes to the monitoring and QA program. Those top-tier reps who were consistently in the top third of the rankings for that department's KPI were immediately exempted from hitting the key script points required of those below the threshold. Of course, we continued to monitor them to find best practices for the other tiers, and to ensure that the customer got the minimum information required from a true

SALES REP RECRUITING BEST-PRACTICES

The following recruiting best practices were introduced in a sales center that I managed. They resulted from predictive hiring tactics and incentive research.

• Top producers were issued business cards to give out whenever they observed stellar service or sales performed—whether they were out shopping, taking care of personal business or if they knew of someone (e.g., a former coworker) with skills similar to their own. On the back of the business cards was an "advertisement" for the sales or service positions available in the call center. The program, called "Star Search," included recognition contests and luncheons for this select recruiting group of sales reps. The center recognized that, although the top-performing sales reps were ideal recruiters for the phone sales organization, they should not be the selectors. An assessment system was developed for that purpose. The Star Search reps served on a voluntary basis—there were no cash incentives paid for recommending the company. It was not necessary; great companies don't need to pay employees to recommend them.

• Recruiting bonuses to the rest of the organization were discontinued. Why pay low performers to bring in their friends? "Likes" tend to attract "likes" when performance and work ethics are concerned.

• New ads using a lot more graphics were created and placed in different media. The ads were listed under various headings. Instead of advertising: "$12/hour plus commissions and benefits for a sales associate," we advertised: "to $65K/year, plus benefits and advanced sales training for top internal sales representatives." I know of other companies that advertise "to $90K for inbound sales" for the phone channel, and one that offers "to $125K for full account management" for sales rep positions in their call centers.

quality point of view and that we were meeting all legal regulations—but, instead of force-feeding them, we decided to just let them do what they do best. Call it non-performance management from a prescriptive viewpoint!

WHAT SALES REPS REALLY WANT	
Poor Performers	**Top Performers**
• No or low performance standards	• High performance standards
• Higher hourly rate	• More risk/reward compensation
• No Incentives	• Cash incentives
• Safety	• Challenge

Eventually, our top-tier performers showed *us* the way they could improve. Instead of comparing each of their performance driver metrics to the team average, we either compared them to the top-tier reps' average on the team, or to the best rep for a particular performance driver, or to their personal best. Top performers like strong leadership, challenges, a little fear and a lot of money. We learned to provide enough of each to keep them.

Points to Remember

• Predictive hiring assessments ideally should include multi-hurdle tests, including job simulations from a company backed by qualified organizational psychologists.

• Customize the assessment process for each individual position.

• Set minimum standards for deselection.

• Find out who is leaving: Analyze your attrition rates by segmenting your rep population by new-hire, and then by performance quartile.

• Treat your top performers differently, or lose them.

• Do not tightly script any sales rep; use script outlines.

Chapter 8: Sales Training that Really Delivers Your Numbers

"I hear and I forget.
I see and I remember.
I do and I understand."
CONFUCIUS

One crucial element that is usually absent from call center training is instilling belief in the value of the product. Reps take an inordinate number of complaints compared with the service delivery reality. While not all orders come through the call center—a customer may be on an automatic order cycle or order through other service channels—the complaints come to the reps. They should not be made to feel as if the company cannot deliver on its personal commitment to the customer.

So how can you communicate a positive view of the company and its products? It's imperative to share your company's complaint-to-transaction statistics with your reps. Instead of percentages, deliver the results in terms of complaints per thousands or hundreds of thousands of transactions. This represents a relationship that all reps can understand. If reps don't believe in your company's products or ability to deliver, their lack of confidence will come across when dealing with customers. For instance, they'll typically use words and phrases that are tentative, like "probably will be delivered on..." or "should be delivered on..." rather than confident, such as "*will* be delivered on..." This lack of confidence in your company will cost you many orders and/or create repeat, non-productive calls.

If your reps don't have faith in your products, they will also tend to believe what customers tell them regarding a competitor's price or capabilities. Savvy customers who are trying to get a price reduction will frequently leave out information or mislead a rep about what the competitor has offered them. This gives rise to a self-fulfilling myth as to why the rep cannot sell at the current price point or with the current product features. The myth can be easily countered by having individual reps or the training class place calls to your competitors. That way, if a customer expresses "sticker shock" when discussing product prices, reps can confidently and knowledgeably respond because they have checked the competition's prices themselves.

In my call center, we used this approach every time we raised our prices. Each rep was required to make three calls a week to the competition and fill out a form for their supervisors that included competitive information and their observations on the competitor's selling techniques. Besides keeping up to date with our competitors, this activity produced a side benefit: Through evaluating our competitors' staff, our reps discovered that their own performance and skills were much better than the competition's. They were impressed and excited to relate their experiences with "the other guys." They loved monitoring and evaluating someone else. The exercise also reinforced the value and professionalism of the sales techniques they had been taught.

Another key influence on how your reps perceive the value of your products is their socioeconomic status. Most non-help desk reps earn $7 to $15 an hour, depending on the company, the technical difficulty of the position and the geographic region in which they're located. They're typically not within the same socioeconomic base as their customers, which often makes it difficult for them to understand that price may not be the biggest concern to a customer. In the car rental, airline and hotel industry, I've frequently witnessed customers being offered only the lowest-priced car, seat or room type because the rep couldn't envision paying the higher price to upgrade to a luxury car, fly first class or to stay in a suite. In many cases, reps will offer the price and product that they themselves would choose. Also, constant negotiating with customers over price tends to support their viewpoints.

To counter inhibitions caused by socioeconomic differences, it's helpful to compare the price of your products to those in other industries. For instance, a frequently used "rule of thumb" in the hotel industry is that the development cost of $200,000 for a hotel room (to build, furnish, etc.) requires a $200 room rate per night to cover debt service and a profit. Another example from the car rental industry would be: A car that costs $30,000 can be rented for $49 per day. To a rep who is making $12 per hour, a $200 per night room or a $49 per day car sounds like a lot, but then show them that a $300 lawnmower rents for $30 per day. Now those rates make the price of the hotel or car they are trying to sell sound like a really great value! Building a value equation for reps will help them to see the tremendous value of your products. I've shared this type of information with reps in the past, and they have found it to be very revealing. In fact, they came

---

TIPS FOR ENLIGHTENING YOUR SALES REPS ON YOUR COMPANY'S PRODUCT VALUE AND SERVICE TRACK RECORD:

- Have reps call the competition.
- Share complaint rates per thousand with reps.
- Have reps build their own value comparisons (price vs. retail cost of product) using examples outside of your industry.
- Have your marketing department share new product information and industry data with sales reps in periodic product refresher workshops.

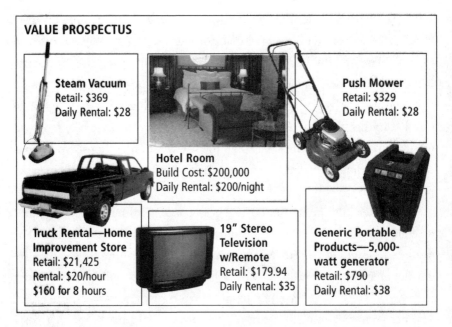

VALUE PROSPECTUS

Steam Vacuum
Retail: $369
Daily Rental: $28

Hotel Room
Build Cost: $200,000
Daily Rental: $200/night

Push Mower
Retail: $329
Daily Rental: $28

Truck Rental—Home Improvement Store
Retail: $21,425
Rental: $20/hour
$160 for 8 hours

19" Stereo Television w/Remote
Retail: $179.94
Daily Rental: $35

Generic Portable Products—5,000-watt generator
Retail: $790
Daily Rental: $38

up with several examples of their own that they posted on the call center's intranet, complete with pictures (see the Value Prospectus, above).

This approach is also used by Susan Searle, senior vice president of customer sales and marketing for Best Software, a provider of business management products and services for small and medium-sized businesses. She stresses that her sales reps' belief in the value of their product is crucial to driving sales. Searle personally visits new-hire training classes to drive this point home. She tells sales trainees: "Never apologize for the cost of our product, as it has tremendous value. Just think: a $500 software product is running and tracking the customer's entire business. Many of our current customers have given up much higher-priced products to use ours simply because ours works better. A one-time $300 software update costs very little, compared to what this business owner is spending per month on a water cooler or even window cleaning, neither of which is business-critical."

Sales Training for Phone Reps

When embarking on a new sales program, everyone in your call center needs to be speaking the same language, making decisions based on the same guiding principles and have a clear understanding of the new expectations. If formal sales training is not embedded in your new-hire training program, or if you're considering refreshing your current sales training, I recommend the following basic sales training program. The two-day core curriculum for inbound sales reps and subsequent four workshops can be easily tailored for outbound reps or service-focused sales reps. For the most part, all of these positions will need the same training. However, the role-plays, close tools and some approaches will differ; therefore, plan to conduct separate classes for reps depending on their job function. For instance, outbound reps will require additional courses for call planning and call follow-up. The training hours should be budgeted in the training project, in addition to any other technical or product refresher training. Remember to allocate funds for the trainer, training materials, reps' time off the phone and any small training "prizes."

TWO-DAY BASIC SALES SKILLS COURSE
(attended by sales reps and service-focused sales reps only)

Core Curriculum
Day 1 modules
Commitment: 8 hours
- Service-based selling philosophy
- Journey from order-taker to sales professional
- Product knowledge
- Using benefits, not features
- The product value equation
- Picking your sales style and dialogue
- Mandatory script points and rationale
- Listening for buying cues
- Asking for the sale
- Overcoming objections

- Reinforcing the sale through memorable call closes

Day 2 modules

Commitment: 8 hours

- Analyzing your own performance
- Understanding the sales KPI
- The role of the performance drivers
- Using the performance database
- How to read your performance graphs
- Connecting the dots: How you make a difference
- Call calibration
- Know your competition
- Calling the competition

ADVANCED SALES REP WORKSHOP

Commitment: 3 hours

- Building a relationship in less than 30 seconds
- Common presentation styles that derail sales
- Capitalizing on new close tools
- Computer shortcuts that increase sales productivity
- Knowing when to move on to the next call

SALES REP WORKSHOP: YOUR INCENTIVE PACKAGE

Commitment: 2 hours

- Creating a better lifestyle
- How the company wins when you win
- Incentive design principles
- The plan rollout
- Caveats on plan changes
- Minimum quality entry point
- Minimum standards
- Ideas on how to maximize the plan payout

SALES REP WORKSHOP: ADDING VALUE BY UPSELLING OR CROSS-SELLING

Commitment: 3-4 hours

- Listening for opportunities
- Using your computer to find opportunities
- Creating interesting segues to a great offer
- Cross-selling techniques
- Using second close tools
- When not to upsell
- Great questions that create customer interest
- Creating urgency
- Role-play
- Overcoming stalls, misunderstandings and resistance

While there are numerous excellent training programs for inbound sales and service-focused sales, most will need to be tailored for your industry and your company. This requires careful research by the training group. Make sure the partner you choose does not simply "tack on" a sales module to their existing customer service training program. Look for a training company that has a long history of sales training and that really understands the call center environment.

Outbound sales is its own beast. There are no recommended off-the-shelf programs, as each company, product and selling situation is truly unique. You should hire a sales consultant who has run call centers—preferably someone who actually has an outstanding track record (e.g., someone who has managed sales or training in outsourced outbound centers). Outsourced outbound call centers are better at sales because, frequently, they get paid only for actual sales produced, and must compete against other outsourcers for a portion of a company's call volume. Do not hire a consultant without a proven track record, excellent credentials and references that you can contact, or you risk seriously damaging your current performance.

Following are three workshop outlines with common themes that might be developed and customized according to your sales mission and product complexity. The time commitment will depend upon the actual content selected.

OUTBOUND SALES REP WORKSHOP: PLANNING THE CALL

- Time management
- Call scheduling for complex sales
- Dialer tips
- Analyzing your performance numbers
- Cold-calling techniques
- Calling existing customers
- Finding opportunities in analysis of customer history
- Using new presentation tools
- The second and third close tools
- Web-based product presentations

OUTBOUND SALES REP WORKSHOP: TERRITORY MANAGEMENT

- From suspects to prospects to customers
- National account rollouts
- Win-back call guidelines
- Account penetration techniques

OUTBOUND SALES REP WORKSHOP: FULL ACCOUNT MANAGEMENT

- Time management
- Presentations that sizzle
- Account follow-up
- Analyzing account revenue trends
- Growing an account from the inside
- Handling transitions from field sales

The diagram on the facing page illustrates a basic rep training approach used by RMH Teleservices:

RMH TRAINING APPROACH

New-Hire Training ⟩ Behavioral Training ⟩ Functional Training ⟩

Induction Program
- Organization overview
- Vision/mission
- Core values
- Operation philosophy
- Infrastructure
- Technology
- Quality awareness
- Team building

Sessions
- HR Policies and practices
- Compensation and career leadership
- Welcome address
- Industry and company overview

Voice and Accent Program
- Accent neutralization
- Cultural orientation
- Pronunciation and vocabulary
- Voice modulation
- Word stress and intonation

Soft Skills
- Skills sets for effective customer care/telemarketing
- Customer service skills
- Telephone etiquette
- Empathy and reflective listening
- Paraphrasing and call focus
- Collaborative negotiation
- Assertive communications
- Selling skills
- Role-plays and mock calls

Product Training
- Client specific

On-the-Job Training
- Closely monitored by coaches

Systems Training
- Quality Awareness
- Managing call quality

Source: RMH Teleservices, Inc. ©2003 All Rights Reserved; Training Approach used with permission of RMH Teleservices.

Proven Training Practices of Peak-Performing Sales Centers

Through past personal experience and interviews with numerous senior executives from top-performing sales centers, I've documented several training best practices that may prove valuable in your call center. They include:

- Have trainers become the reps' immediate supervisors for the term of the training, with evaluation and termination privileges.

- Make sure new reps meet their supervisors, manager and director on their first day of training.

- At the end of each day, managers should join training and review with reps what they have learned and explain how it fits into the company's overall goals.
- Maintain a trainer-to-rep ratio of 1:14 or fewer (1:10 is ideal for sales training).
- Insert "guiding principles" throughout training materials.
- Create a "nesting period" (one to three weeks) following classroom training, where reps can get individualized and immediate assistance from a supervisor or team leader. Ideally, the classroom trainer should serve as reps' temporary supervisor during the nesting period.
- Allow trainees to evaluate calls using the center's monitoring forms.
- Have sales reps, in teams, create their own value prospectus for the company's product(s).
- Incorporate role-plays and discussion into classroom training.
- Track sales rep scores and subsequent sales KPI by trainer for management follow-up.
- Ask trainees to evaluate each sales training class.

Sales Training for Supervisors

Your sales supervisor doesn't need to be the most accomplished seller, but he or she must know *how* to sell and how to coach that skill in one-on-one and group settings. Everyone who coaches sales should be required to experience the same training as the reps they coach. I recommend holding separate workshops to enable the sales supervisors and coaches to fully comprehend the sales theory behind the new sales processes, and to allow them to discuss issues that might arise during rep training. Sales supervisors will also need training on how to analyze performance trends and how to conduct root-cause analysis. They'll need to know how to set targets, deal with declining performance and manage top performers.

The following supervisor training program requires an initial commitment of about 10 days over the course of the first year. The training can be conducted during three- to four-hour workshops to minimize any adverse impact from taking supervisors off the call center floor. In fact, even the core curriculum days can be broken into half-day sessions. To maximize your call center's sales potential, frontload the training schedule as much as possible. In the years that follow, anticipate holding two to three hours of refresher classes every few months.

SALES TRAINING FOR SUPERVISORS

(same as for sales reps, but held separately)
- Sales rep training overview (2 days)
- Sales rep workshop overview (2 days)
- Outbound (as required)

SALES MANAGEMENT CORE CURRICULUM

(For sales supervisors only)

Commitment: 2 days
- Understanding the sales management process
- Sales monitoring assessments vs. policing tools
- KPI and performance driver analytics
- Performance trending
- Coaching for sales
- Coaching role plays
- Setting targets that move performance
- Creating innovative action plans
- Minimum standards and the deselection process

SALES MANAGEMENT WORKSHOPS

Commitment: 2-4 hours per workshop
- Finding opportunities using the performance database
- Creating performance visibility
- Creating and managing contests
- Leading sales meetings

SALES MANAGEMENT: HIRING SALES TALENT

Commitment: 2 days

- Predictive hiring
- Selecting the best
- Behavioral interviewing

Unfortunately, there are currently no strong off-the-shelf sales management training programs relevant to call centers that I would recommend, with the exception of predictive hiring and behavioral interviewing. Predictive hiring training is available from your assessment vendor. I suggest developing your own sales management training with the help of your direct sales management team (if they have the capacity and the time), hiring talent that has been through this process at a peak-performing sales center, or seeking out a proven sales consultant with experience in managing high-performing sales call centers.

If you go the consultant route, make sure they fully understand the analytics and are aware of the need to tailor their system to your company's culture. Ask them to explain correlation and regression analysis and its role in sales management. If they do not understand that it's used in predictive hiring and in setting script points and performance drivers, walk away. Ask them to explain how correlation and regression analysis is used in creating monetary incentive plans. Ask them what role standard deviation plays in setting incentive thresholds. If they "blank out," run and find someone else.

While there are several excellent leadership and general coaching programs available, they can improve only strong natural leaders or coaches; they cannot create leadership or coaching skills where the potential doesn't exist. The key is to hire strong leaders and coaches first, and then provide them with extra support in the form of specialized training.

Scheduling Refresher Training

There are several ways to schedule refresher training or "up-training." Core classes can be pre-scheduled and worked into traditionally low call volume valleys or days when you might normally solicit reps to leave early.

A Staff Retention Tool

Managing and retaining top-performing reps is one of the biggest challenges for call center professionals. Fortunately, today there are several tools that can help managers and supervisors in this endeavor. One of the better solutions is provided by a company called TalentKeepers. Its product—Retentionworks™—is a retention system with several components that help to reduce attrition among high-performing frontline talent. The product is being used by—and producing results in—several of the companies that I interviewed for this book. One of the primary product features is a strong leadership and coaching program consisting of 10 hours of online instruction and 18 hours of classroom training. Although it's not a substitute for hiring the right sales coaches or for specialized sales management training, it's an excellent model for advanced leadership training. You can reach TalentKeepers and see their demo at: www.talentkeepers.com.

The shorter product-refresher classes can be conducted during brown-bag lunch sessions, or scheduled on the fly when call volume unexpectedly dips. It's important to note that several e-learning vendors offer products that integrate with your ACD and workforce planning software on a real-time basis, "pushing" appropriate e-learning modules to the reps' desktop. A few of the leaders in this arena are Envision (www.envisioninc.com), Knowlagent (www.knowlagent.com.) and Ulysses (www.ulysses-systems.com).

Because of the need for flexibility in the call center environment, I recommend that the people who deliver the training report directly to the call center manager, not HR or the training department. You'll also need some flexibility to avoid increasing staff or using overtime to cover the training sessions. Other departments, like HR, typically are not accustomed to the maneuvering necessary to control costs in this manner.

However, I do recommend leaving the development of any training and computer-based training (CBT) to the professionals in the corporate training department. Adult learning is a specialty that requires years of education and alliances with professional organizations to stay current. Additionally, a corporate training department has the ability to see across the organization and can anticipate problems with procedures or material in your department—problems that could possibly create process disconnects along the service delivery chain.

Points to Remember

• If there is a socio-economic difference between your sales reps and your customers, have the reps build a product or service Value Prospectus.

• Sales reps should frequently call and evaluate the competition's sales presentations.

• Share complaint data to help the rep understand the strength of your company's service delivery process.

• Invest in a significant amount of new-hire and up-training on sales skills for both the rep and the sales coach/supervisor.

Chapter 9: Revitalizing Your Sales Coaching Programs

"Feedback is the breakfast of champions."
KENNETH BLANCHARD, MANAGEMENT WRITER AND LECTURER

Coaching consists of performance feedback, understanding an employee's thought processes, analyzing root causes, specific training for new skills, setting expectations and receiving commitment. It involves both positive reinforcement and constructive criticism.

If you don't think you have the time or inclination to perform a lot of monitoring, performance analysis and coaching, then save your company a lot of money and stop any continuous training efforts. Training is absolutely non-productive without immediate reinforcement. People retain very little of what they are taught, especially if they do not practice it immediately. Adults learn by doing. Coaching sets expectations that the new learning will be put into action. If the training content has been misinterpreted, as is often the case, especially in a classroom setting, then the coach has the opportunity to correct the misconception immediately before the rep develops bad habits on the job.

I have a friend, Joan Sims, the director of training for a large company, who laughingly comments: "Feedback is great, as long as it doesn't get all over you." This suggests that feedback is generally associated with negative criticism. But even when positive feedback is given, the individual is usually waiting for the other shoe to drop, as in: "You gave great customer service on that call… *but* you failed to mention our new promotion."

Supervisors generally have been trained to mitigate negative criticism, or to take the sting out of the negative by mentioning something positive first, usually in the same sentence. This approach only makes the positive unimportant or sound insincere, while the correctable behavior is not given sufficient emphasis.

Generally, feedback is so rarely given in the workplace, we don't do it very well. One of the biggest problems with feedback is that coaches usually know what is wrong—e.g., sales are too low; AHT is too high—but they don't fully understand how to analyze performance to pinpoint recommendations that might really work. The supervisors/coaches only know how *they* would improve their performance if *they* were in that job. The problem with this approach is there isn't just one "right way" to sell.

To transform your environment, coaches must be given a new toolbox—one containing four key tools:

1. Performance analysis using micro-gap analysis of performance drivers

2. Performance driver worksheets (planning for a performance conversation)

3. Error analysis

4. Exposure to a variety of "ways to sell" through role-play scenarios

Understanding an Individual's Performance Potential

One of the reasons for making the sales KPI the business outcome is that it will give you the opportunity to analyze the metrics that drive the end performance. To do this, first determine for each rep:

1. Individual KPI ranking.

2. Performance drivers that are below the team average.

3. Whether the low performance driver metrics are behavioral- or knowledge-based.

Let's look at each of these in a little more detail.

Individual KPI Ranking. It's not enough to merely separate service and sales performance metrics. You'll need to determine where each rep stands in the quarterly KPI ranking against other reps who are working the same shift and handling the same call-types. If certain service groups handle short call-types, then compare reps to that group only. If a sales rep receives mostly frequent-booker type calls due to dialed number identification services (DNIS) or prompt-routing, don't compare him or her to a sales rep taking calls from the general public. It must be a comparison of "like" calls.

The objective is to evaluate and show reps their performance potential, with all things being relatively equal. It's helpful for reps to know that others are achieving better performance—and that they, too, might boost their performance by adopting successful habits used by the top performers.

Determine whether individual reps rank in the bottom, middle or top third of all performers. I initially use a quarterly view so that any anomalies in the reps' performance are taken care of with enough data and enough time. Additionally, since shift bids typically take place semi-annually or quarterly, this fits in nicely, as call types may radically change by day-of-week and time-of-day.

Below-average performance drivers. Identify where each rep falls relative to his or her team's scores for the last quarter in each of the KPI performance drivers. By analyzing these statistics, you can determine where the problems and opportunities lie, as well as the appropriate diagnosis and remedy. (See the micro-gap analysis example in the table on page 146.)

Low performance driver metrics that reveal knowledge or behavioral problems. It is important to determine whether the lack of performance in the below-average performer is a behavioral or knowledge problem. This is the old "can do" vs. "will do" analysis you most likely learned in situational leadership. For example, if a rep "can do" the task, then the issue is a behavioral "will do" one. If the rep can't do the task, then the issue is knowledge-based. Understanding whether the problem is a "can do" vs. a "will do" problem is critical to knowing how or if correction is possible. A strong training manager once told me that she determines the answer to the "can do" vs. "will do" question by asking herself, "Has the rep ever been successful at the task before?" If so, it is a behavioral issue. The rep knows how to do it because he or she has previously demonstrated the capability. If not, it's likely a knowledge issue. Has the rep attempted to consistently use the recommendations given to him or her during monitoring feedback sessions? If so, then it's a skill problem.

Finding a Sales Rep's Potential Using Micro-Gap Analysis

Generally, properly selected reps do not perform poorly (sub-average) in all key performance drivers, just in two or three. The following micro-gap analysis example shows how you can target up to two areas for an individual rep's improvement.

In the box below, sales rep Rich Banks' sales performance data are com-

---

HOTEL RESERVATION CENTER: A MICRO-GAP ANALYSIS EXAMPLE

Representative: Rich Banks   **Room Type %**

AHT	CR%	XL%	NS%	Rm Nts	#Rms	A	B	C	NRPH	Incentive
180	33	8	5	2.1	1.1	44	26	30	$550	$100/week

Team Average (same skill-set/shift)   **Room Type %**

AHT	CR%	XL%	NS%	Rm Nts	#Rms	A	B	C	NRPH	Incentive
165	37	9	5	2.2	1.1	41	28	31	$680	$225/week

Rich's priorities for the next two weeks should be: Close Ratio Target: 35
                                                      AHT

Legend:
AHT—Avg. Handle Time   *#Rms—Number of rooms sold*
CR—Close Ratio (gross transaction/calls)   *A—Standard room*
XL—Cancellation Rate   *B—View room*
NS%—No Show Percentage   *C—Suite*
RmNts—Avg. number of room nights sold   *NRPH—Net Revenue per Phone Hour*

Note: Typically, this form also includes the amount of time the rep is scheduled to be on the phone, implying that the incentive can only be earned if he or she is there that many hours.

pared to his peers' average (for the same shift, same skill, same time period). Over a month's time, all of these individual reps experienced exactly the same conditions within the organization (e.g., products unavailable or percent non-bookable calls). The number

> TIP: It is helpful to have similar call-types going to the same center so that large enough groups of call-types and shifts can be compared with each other

of hours they've worked have been accounted for in the KPI, and therefore, all workers are at a similar parity.

Typically, no rep will be as good as the team average in every individual performance driver. However, should you be lucky enough to have such a rep on staff, simply compare and contrast his or her performance in each component driver with the team's best, instead of the average, or the best of another team under the same working conditions. This will show your high-performing rep that an even higher level of performance is still possible, which will give him or her a new target.

Have each rep concentrate on improving one driver over a two-week period—that will enable each to master the skill before moving on to the next performance driver. Trying to improve more than one key performance driver not only de-emphasizes the effort on that driver, it creates confusion. When one driver moves, another driver that was within an average range may go "out of whack." The rep needs to learn how to move the mark on one driver without detrimentally affecting another.

An example of this is attempting to increase first-call resolution rates (finding and solving the problem on the first call, or resolving the call without generating research and a callback). If a service rep's handle time was originally within a satisfactory or average range, you can be sure that the talk time will initially move outside the range. Throwing another driver for improvement on top of this one would not make sense.

In the hotel reservations center example, Rich, our sales rep, is not bad at everything. He is going to make substantially less incentive this week primarily because his average handle time is higher than the group average, while his close ratio is lower. He has a seasoned sales manager, Heather, who knows that a high handle time and a lower close ratio generally means that Rich does not know his products well enough and, therefore, is spending time searching his computer for the information. It could also indicate that he lacks confidence in his presentation, which causes customers to ask a lot of questions and eventually say they were "just shopping." While Heather realizes it also could be a lot of other things, the combination of these two performance drivers, and the fact that Rich is slightly underselling the higher priced rooms (B and C) leads her to believe that the problem lies with Rich's product knowledge. Like most of the sales reps, Rich has no confidence problem and is good at call control. In a coaching session, Heather

PERFORMANCE DRIVER DIAGNOSTIC WORKSHEET	
Performance driver: AHT	
Possible problem	**Development recommended**
Call control	Call-control refresher training.
Knowledge of products	Review product feature and benefits online.
Knowledge of policy	Pinpoint unclear policies and procedures for review with coach or trainer.
Keyboard skills shortcuts	Sit with a low-AHT/high-quality performer for review of computer shortcuts.
"Talk and type"	Do not use hold. Practice this skill. Monitor.

PERFORMANCE DRIVER DIAGNOSTIC WORKSHEET	
Performance Driver: Close Ratio	
Possible Problem	**Development Recommended**
Listening skills	Role play with rep to get him to pick up cues.
Problem-solving skills	Create scenarios for rep to solve by offering different products, discounts or solutions.
Image management	Recommend different presentation styles.
Dead-air syndrome	Ask for the sale.
No second close tools (e.g., discounts)	Actively monitor for use of second close attempt.

suggests that Rich spend some time—either in between calls or on his own—reviewing the computer tools available to him. This will allow him to quickly access the right information for his customers, and appear more polished in his presentation. Together, they develop an action plan and Heather schedules the training.

Creating Performance Driver Diagnostic Worksheets

In the previous example, Heather is an experienced sales supervisor. However, if she wasn't, she could have used a monitoring supplement to help her plan a development session with Rich. The table on the previous page is an example of a prescriptive checklist of performance "root causes" and recommended interventions for each performance driver and element of the monitoring form. This checklist is only representative, and certainly is not exhaustive of AHT and close-ratio performance drivers—generally, it would contain 10 to 20 possible problems and solutions. Be sure to identify and rank the top three to five "culprits" on each list as the most likely to solve the problem. You'll want to have your sales management, trainers and sales people participate when creating your checklist.

ERROR ANALYSIS TOOLS

Often, I see call centers committing to a minimum amount of training per rep, per year. They then construct elaborate and lengthy refresher courses that all reps are required to attend. This is fine for budgeting, but it's a waste of money since all of your reps certainly will not need refresher courses. Your better-performing reps will need advanced skills development, which is a better way to spend discretionary dollars.

There are six tools—which are easy to obtain or develop—that can serve as indicators of a skill deficiency or a simple misunderstanding that signals the need for refresher training or one-on-one coaching:

1. Periodic quizzes
2. Error reports
3. Complaint RCA (root-cause analysis)

4. Quantification of escalation call-types

5. QA department's overview and feedback of monitoring sessions and common problems

6. Role-play selling presentation scenarios

These six common indicators can help you to tailor informal courses or supervisor meetings to address the substandard performance issues with only those individuals who demonstrate substandard performance. If the problem is unique to an individual or two, then individual coaching is recommended.

Periodic quizzes. Quizzes that are administered to reps periodically (e.g., once a month) help to pinpoint training opportunities as well as create brief classes to address the concerns you may have with a select group of reps. Quizzes should never be used as a final performance evaluator for rating or termination purposes, or as a contest—they should serve only as an indicator for retraining. However, an exception would be during the new-hire process. I do recommend the use of quizzes and tests during the probationary period to determine whether to continue training or to terminate, as well as whether or not a new-hire is ready to get on the phones and have the privilege of speaking with your customers.

Quizzes can target anything you deem critical or areas in which you are experiencing problems. For instance, if you receive feedback from marketing or operations that promotional codes are being used improperly or that some reps are unaware of a policy, then develop a quick quiz to test reps' knowledge of proper promotional code use. You can then share the results with the other department and, if necessary, take corrective remedial training action.

Note: Make sure that whoever creates your quizzes has a strong training and development background. Quizzes that are poorly worded or that contain confusing answer choices can be counterproductive.

Error reports. Most companies lack extremely tight "edit rules" throughout their systems, and for good reason: Although business rules written into the system can reduce error rates, they can also cause considerable customer anguish when exceptions must be made to the rule. Systems with tight edit rules frequently do not have override capabilities—consequently, many centers have turned off a number of "system edits," thereby allowing a greater human error rate.

Some call centers have automated error detection, great statistics and error follow-up procedures. Others use an audit process or the monitoring process to determine procedural error rates. Regardless of which method you use, system error rates can be an excellent indicator for refresher training and can pinpoint the right individuals who need to attend. For example, an error report might highlight the percent of discount product by promotional code. If a rep has almost all of his or her sales discounted or is only using one code, refresher training is certainly in order.

Complaint RCA. Most companies have created their own customer complaint-handling systems, or rely on a customer relationship management (CRM) module for analyzing complaint data. Common root causes include policy problems, process problems or individual error problems. Using data from these systems to identify both the training topic and the individuals making the errors can reduce the latter problem. For example, a complaint report may show a statistically significant number of returned products for a particular sales rep, with an attached complaint code noting sizing problems on shirts from a catalogue with a new vendor. The supervisor would then individually coach the sales rep on a previous training bulletin stating that the shirt sizes from this vendor run very small. If other reps are having similar issues, the supervisor could call a short, 10-minute meeting for all identified reps. Eliminating returned sales will increase the NRPH KPI.

Quantification of escalation call-types. The quantification of call escalations by type and by individual, as well as your QA's analysis of performance problems, are excellent ways to identify training and coaching opportunities.

Companies handle escalations in many different ways. Some require immediate supervisors to handle the escalated call. In such cases, the supervisor often asks the rep to silently listen in to learn how the call should be handled. Other call centers put the supervisors in their own call queue to evenly distribute calls. Some have leads in an escalation desk or queue. Others allow more seasoned reps to take "supervisor" calls and identify themselves as a supervisor—particularly during the third shift when a supervisor may not be on duty.

Each approach has pros and cons, but it really doesn't matter which you do, as long as three things happen. First, you need to make sure the percentage of escalation calls to total calls is very low, since customers object to being transferred and having to repeat their concerns. Second, the customer should not be made to wait for longer than one minute without being offered a callback. Third, the call must be classified based on the nature of the problem and by the name of the individual who had to transfer the call. An automated report of all escalations should be generated for performance trending. This report provides an excellent means of identifying questions for your quizzes and training topics, as well as for reps who require additional training.

QA department's overview and feedback of monitoring sessions/common problems. Because supervisors/coaches only monitor a fraction of the calls to reps, it's difficult for them to assess whether a group training class on one or more topics is warranted. For this reason, the independent QA department represents a valuable source of topics for a short refresher training class.

Role-play scenarios. Your leads and the training department should create 15 to 30 role-playing scenarios representing a variety of selling situations for supervisors to use in their coaching sessions. Each role-playing scenario should provide the supervisor with several different selling approaches to play out. This will give your supervisor numerous suggestion alternatives when role-playing with sales reps.

The Importance of Positive Reinforcement

As a manager, and even as an executive, I rarely received personal feed-

THE SERVICE-SALES LINK

Although this book is primarily devoted to sales, I must take a moment to emphasize service. Your center must be running smoothly before you embark upon the journey to peak sales performance. The service levels must be consistently good, your complaint ratios low and your customer execution processes solid. But service is more than that. All staff, especially your customer interface staff, must exude a strong service orientation. Having a sales orientation is not enough—reps must understand that it starts with service. If reps try to sell something that the customer doesn't need or want, they might be successful once, but it's the lifetime revenue you're seeking.

Dennis Honan, chief operating officer of Lands' End, describes the direct merchant's very different approach to sales in his centers: "We don't have scripts, incentives or AHT goals due to our strong belief in service as the prime factor in driving customer satisfaction and revenue." Honan believes that, if they hire reps with the right "DNA" to take care of the customer, they will act as a customer advocate, understanding what the customer might want to purchase next. At Lands' End, cross-selling takes the form of "customers contacting an old friend with whom they like to go shopping, and the friend advising them about a great hat that would go perfectly with the coat they're buying."

Honan asks his reps to use their best judgment about when to offer additional products. For instance, if a rep is speaking with a busy mother with five kids yelling for her attention in the background and who can barely get her credit card number out, Honan trusts the rep's judgment not to suggest another "great go-together" product. On the other hand, he expects reps to take the "old friend" consultative approach to additional sales with someone who seems conducive to spending some time discussing the products.

Rarely can an executive share stories from his or her frontline staff about sales or the effect they've had on customers. Honan can—he hears them firsthand every week. He tells the following stories that clearly illustrate the service-sales link.

(continued next page)

One of his CSRs had a customer who was attending a black-tie event with her husband and needed cuff links that matched her husband's tuxedo. The customer lived in a rural area and had not been able to find any nearby. She remembered that Lands' End carried the product and called to place an order. Unfortunately, Lands' End no longer carried the item, but this particular CSR happened to have a pair that she had bought for her husband. The CSR mailed the cuff links to the customer to use for the big event. Needless to say, the customer was amazed and a lifetime relationship with Lands' End was cemented.

Another time, a customer who was getting married the next day called the company. She was staying in a small hotel that didn't have a wake-up service. She was worried that, in spite of the alarm clock provided, she and her sister would not wake up in time for her early morning wedding. She called a friend who she knew was reliable and had always been there for her—Lands' End. They called her the next morning, and she was married on time. These are bonds that no marketing dollars can buy. They are forged by happy people.

back, positive or negative, until it was time for my annual review. I told myself that I didn't need positive reinforcement—I was competent, self-reliant and self-motivated. I didn't need to see that my work pleased others. On the other hand, my husband observed that I always seemed inordinately pleased whenever I received praise or positive feedback, as I would come home and tell him about it. Do you think your employees are any different?

If a rep is doing something spectacular or performing at a high level—*for him*—then he deserves specific and immediate feedback, either on a one-on-one basis, in a group (peer recognition is always appreciated), or both. At the very least, send a brief appreciative email and copy the rep's supervisor.

While most managers understand the importance of positive feedback and reinforcement, many do not give nearly enough of it. Why? Because they don't see *spectacular* performance happening very often. They don't realize the implicit and positive impact that frequent praise has on employee morale and on maintaining peak performance over long periods.

I often hear managers lament, "Why should I thank someone just for doing their job?" Think about it: With senior management's high expectations for profit and productivity, any employee performing well in an environment of tough standards should be thanked and recognized frequently. If you don't do it, your reps will seek a company that does.

One of the easiest and most successful positive feedback mechanisms is to acknowledge and reinforce individual performance improvements. Low-, medium- and high-tier performers all periodically perform at new "personal best" levels. So while a medium-level performer may not be at the top of a forced ranking, he or she will occasionally move up in the ranking and, as a result, deserves prompt personal acknowledgement from the supervisor or manager.

Any manager or executive who walks through the call center will see just how many opportunities there are for employee recognition and praise (if they're paying attention to what's going on). You can hear reps using a caring and courteous tone of voice, or attempting a tremendous upsell. Giving a quick "thumbs-up" to these employees will make them beam and inspire them to continue to strive for peak performance.

Rules for Setting Sales Rep Targets

Remember, we're not trying to transform low performers into top performers overnight; we're trying to get them to sell at a significantly higher rate, which may very well be their personal best. They may have to improve their performance by 20 percent or more to get there.

While, certainly, we would be happy to move medium performers to top performers, the top performers are also moving and the medium performers may never catch up. That's OK as long as the KPI is moving in the right direction faster than can be otherwise accounted for (e.g., due to an increase in industry pricing). Following are three rules for setting targets for sales reps:

Rule 1: Set only two priority performance drivers in ranked order for each rep, based on how much they will affect *their* KPI, not on how far they are from the team average on that performance driver. The database worksheet will inherently be weighted to account for this.

Rule 2: Set a reasonable target for the top priority performance driver. This is the performance driver that will affect the KPI the most, and should be achievable in two weeks. *Note:* The target does not necessarily have to be the team average if the rep is very far from it.

Rule 3: Identify no more than three changes the rep should make to achieve the KPI goal. Usually, these suggestions will be selected from the performance-driver diagnostic worksheet developed for each of your performance drivers (see page 148). The form is created so you won't have to reinvent the wheel each time; however, there may be some new techniques the rep could use that are not listed on the form. Feel free to improvise.

The Target-Setting Process

The target-setting process is cyclical. The supervisor and/or coach and sales rep should schedule a performance planning and development session every two to four weeks. During that time period, they should follow the seven steps in the target-setting cycle.

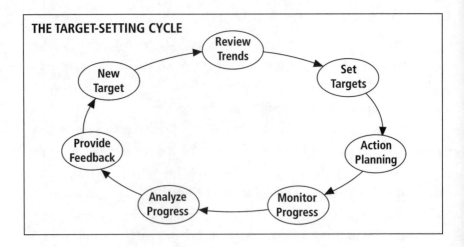

THE TARGET-SETTING CYCLE

Review Trends → Set Targets → Action Planning → Monitor Progress → Analyze Progress → Provide Feedback → New Target → (Review Trends)

Feedback Systems that Really Work

As previously mentioned, feedback is critical to correct behaviors, improve performance and inspire reps to achieve targets. There are seven traditional and new feedback systems that, when properly applied, can make a big difference in changing behaviors and increasing quality sales:

1. Monitoring feedback
2. Direct customer feedback
3. Real-time KPI feedback
4. Third-party feedback
5. Feedback on you
6. Performance-ranking feedback
7. Systemic feedback

Monitoring feedback. OK, monitoring isn't exactly new and cool, but I rarely see strong adherence in executing this basic process. The following are the best practices that I recommend, ranked in order of importance:

1. Ensure that *at least* 10 monitoring sessions per rep are completed each month, with face-to-face feedback provided within 24 hours. Record all calls to help the rep see the opportunities and successes. (Make sure you have written acknowledgement from the rep on file, as well as a message on your IVR system informing customers that calls may be recorded. If you do not have a QA system that records or allows you to follow the screens as you silent-monitor, then conduct a few side-by-side monitors every other month to ensure that reps know how to use all their tools.)

2. Have two different parties conduct the monitoring sessions (e.g., a QA evaluator and the supervisor). Some organizations use only supervisors or developmental coaches to do all of the monitoring. The problem with this approach is that supervisors are not always consistent in their objectivity. I've also seen monitoring being conducted only by QA staff, with supervisors feeding back someone else's impression of what happened and what the customer perceived during the call. With this approach, not only does the rep receive second- or third-hand information, the supervisor frequent-

ly doesn't deliver the feedback with any sense of ownership or, in some
cases, even agreement. The ideal method is for the supervisor (depending
on team size) to conduct about half the monitoring sessions (calls) per
month for each rep (more, if the supervisor or rep believe it is necessary).
The other half of the sessions should be conducted by someone with no
skin in the incentive game—in other words, a QA person or qualified supervisor who reports to another center or manager.

   3. Calibrate calls frequently between:

• Managers and executives, including Operations and Marketing
• Supervisors in the same center
• Supervisors in different centers
• Reps
• Supervisors and trainers
• Supervisors and QA

   4. Minimize administrative tasks by creating diagnostic monitor forms
and prescriptive feedback mechanisms (performance driver diagnostic
worksheets).

   5. Have managers sit in on at least one performance feedback session per
supervisor per month to evaluate the caliber of the coaching.

A FEW THOUGHTS ON MONITORING

   A number of years ago, I worked with an organization that provided
mediocre service and achieved sub-par sales. In my first week working with
this consumer inbound business, I brought together marketing, customer
sales supervisors, managers, directors and executives. I gave them the monitoring form and had them listen to and evaluate recorded calls.

   The results were fascinating. Calls that marketing and I rated as atrocious
from a service and sales standpoint were rated as "good to perfect" by most
of the customer service and sales management staff, including call center
executives. They made their checks on the forms and heard all the monitoring points hit by the rep. They were thrilled; they were in the spotlight and
their people had performed brilliantly. The only problem was that the calls

were terrible. The desired business outcome—a sale and a satisfied customer—was nowhere to be seen.

What was wrong? In the past, when faced with the news that the customer interaction was not acceptable, the first thing the service and sales management said was: "Change the form! The format, weighting or criteria must be wrong!" The monitoring form, like that in most contact centers, had been changed 20 times in the previous 10 years. Of course, some of the criteria still needed to be changed, and there needed to be new training regarding what "acceptable" meant, but the real problem was that management didn't understand what the business outcome of calls ought to be.

Many industry experts share this concern regarding current monitoring practices and the need to offer consistent feedback and coaching in addition to monitoring. "There is a tendency for many call centers to use a detailed set of checklist items to measure their people against," says Denise Cooper, a partner with call center consulting firm The Wasatch Solutions Group. "In this case, monitoring becomes more of a mechanical, policy process. The company may have a robust point system and hold regular calibration sessions during which supervisors try to 'get the points scored right,' but they tend to lose focus on the customer."

Mike Kennedy, also a partner with The Wasatch Solutions Group, stresses that, "Companies should concentrate on measuring things that are important to the business they are in and to the final customer experience." Too frequently, he adds, call centers focus on internal measurements with arbitrary targets that are not derived from their customers but from old benchmarking across multiple industries (e.g., ASA, number of rings to get a rep, etc.). When Kennedy asks supervisors and managers why they monitor, the most common responses are: "for quality purposes," "for compliance" or "to get it right." They rarely make the final connection to the company's goals, he says, which is to improve the company's profitability.

The Wasatch Solutions Group recommends monitoring 20 calls per rep per month. You can meet that objective without increasing your supervisory staff by including self-assessments and QA. Kennedy also suggests that a center might shoot for 20 calls as a center average, doing more observations for low to medium performers, and fewer for higher performers.

PLANNING FOR A PERFORMANCE CONVERSATION

There are a number of activities that should be completed before initiating a feedback performance conversation, such as gathering facts and observations through data collection, monitoring, micro-gap analysis and Performance Driver Worksheets (see page 148). Supervisors should assess the rep's mood to ensure that he or she is receptive to feedback. If it is clear that someone is having a bad day, for whatever reason, reschedule the feedback; the rep wouldn't hear you anyway. Deliver the feedback in a location that is private, comfortable and free from distractions. Although this sounds obvious, I've often seen feedback given on the open floor.

A FEW THOUGHTS ON MYSTERY SHOPPERS

A disturbing trend in some organizations is the use of mystery shopping to replace a certain amount of inhouse monitoring. I caution against this practice. Mystery shopping and quality monitoring are not the same.

Mystery shopping should be used when a company wants a view of the consistency of the customer experience from the time that the number is dialed to the end of the phone call. Typically, mystery shoppers are part of a virtual call center, usually working from home. Generally, the shopper's purpose is to validate whether or not something is being done—for example, whether a script is being followed, if the recording is correct, or if an attempt to overcome an objection is made. However, shoppers usually do not know your company and are rarely skilled enough to properly evaluate a call. When mystery shoppers are used as a substitute for monitoring, reps who receive the feedback often see the skill deficiency of the evaluators, argue the judgment on the interpretation, and invalidate all of their findings.

That's not to say there is no place for mystery shoppers. It's a good way to confirm that all your phone numbers are being routed correctly, that customers are receiving the right experience from a recorded message standpoint, or that previously identified "black-and-white" problem areas have been corrected. However, anything that requires judgment should be left to a supervisor or an internal QA evaluator.

Direct customer feedback. I recently saw a great system for providing direct customer feedback. Hilton Reservations utilizes a back-end IVR to reconfirm the reservation details and give callers a confirmation number. Clearly this reduces rep talk-time and, therefore, labor costs, but it also gives the call center the opportunity to solicit immediate customer feedback on their experience with the call center.

Nearly 30 percent of their customers who confirm reservations provide feedback. This has enabled Hilton to drive changes in rep behavior and, consequently, increase customer satisfaction and loyalty. The customer score for each individual rep is tabulated, given back to the rep weekly, and is included as part of their monthly evaluation. Customer comments are transcribed verbatim and passed along to reps.

Just think, *actual customers* giving feedback to reps at a rate of approximately 240 customers per rep, per month. Amazing. Given the high scores the average rep receives, this is great positive reinforcement.

Real-time KPI feedback. Leave it to those folks at Hilton, they also have an outstanding process for providing real-time KPI feedback. At the reservations center, the KPI for individual sales reps is "close ratio" (number of reservations divided by calls handled). Managers provide real-time performance feedback to their reps through an active scoreboard on each reps' desktop. The scoreboard contains only three metrics for each rep: 1) calls handled that day, 2) number of reservations made that day, and 3) the close ratio. Each group (of similar skill-set and call-types) has a monthly "close ratio" target, so they know what they are shooting for.

Hilton Reservation's system works because it's focused on the most important metrics for its reps, and lets them know how they're doing in real-time. When something is critical, it must get attention. Your customers are critical. Your revenue is critical. Your employees deserve the most timely feedback you can give them.

Third-party feedback. Formalizing a process for tabulating and feeding back *internal complaints,* which sometimes include third-party customer complaints, is another best practice that I've used with success. It's cathartic for operations, marketing or customer service staff to be able to get their complaints about training issues off their chest, and they're always most impressed when their complaints are tracked and addressed. Some organizations refer to this as the ATTM ("As Told To Me") process. Here is how it works: Anyone in the organization, including reps, can fill out an ATTM form online. The supervisor addresses the feedback with the individual and determines whether there is a coaching opportunity. Keep in mind that this type of feedback should never be used for evaluation purposes since it is third-party information; however it can focus the entire organization on highlighting the need for individual feedback. Additionally, and most importantly, it will eventually reduce complaints as the coaching and retraining processes kick in to address the problems raised.

Getting feedback on you. One of the best ways to help an individual or team perform at a higher level is to understand how *you* can help. Sometimes that takes the form of formal 360-degree feedback (an anonymous written survey), which, if you have the trust of your direct reports, can advise you of something you could do to help your reps or something you might need to change.

You can also use a technique to gather informal 360-degree feedback. Every time you give someone feedback, especially if it is not positive, ask them two things: 1) What can I do to help you?, and 2) What can I do to improve my performance? I learned this technique from a great boss for whom I was privileged to work. She often asked me those two questions, and I was regularly able to provide her with assistance that helped her to grow or enabled her to help me be more effective.

The first time you use this technique with your direct reports, they might think the latter is a trick question. They probably won't believe you really mean it. But don't let that deter you. When I used this technique on my assistant, I received no feedback. So I suggested that she should give it some consideration, and I would get back to her again with the questions. I asked her a few more times over the next few weeks, but she could think of nothing. Then one time I forgot to ask. She asked me if I still wanted some feedback. She said that it would be helpful if I could call in twice a day when I was traveling, instead of once, so she could expedite some matters for me that had come her way. Easily done. She helped me to help her.

Performance-ranking feedback. The Wasatch Solutions Group's Denise Cooper mentioned that, in a recent informal poll of her performance workshop management attendees, only two of 20 centers indicated that they posted ranked or stacked performance results of any kind. When asked why, most responded: "It might have something to do with privacy issues."

We must increase the business acumen of our management. The use of ranked performance measurements, especially with respect to sales, is a demonstrated best practice for call centers. It's a technique that has been used in direct sales and general management for years—driving recognition and competition, and helping everyone to understand who the performance role models are. It drives poor performers to either improve or self-select out so that you will not have to do it.

There are no privacy issues with respect to quantifiable performance measurement (e.g., close ratio, revenue or sales per hour, etc.). However, don't overdo the rankings; limit them to the major KPI and several critical performance drivers.

Page 164 shows an example of a simple performance board. In this case, it describes and recognizes the performance standings of all team members in a supervisor's group. To be fair, for comparison purposes, all reps on the board should be of the same skill set and on the same shift. Performance boards can be posted online, in a report or on a bulletin board.

Systemic feedback. As discussed in earlier chapters, systemic factors include rules, conditions, policies, procedures, processes and practices that

EXAMPLE OF A PERFORMANCE BOARD

Rick's Team—Sales Performance Rankings

Friday Top Performers Team Average $850/hour	MTD Rankings Top Performers Team Average $841/hour
1. Susie............................$1,101	1. Mark................................$998
2. Mark...............................$984	2. Susie................................$989
3. Amy................................$948	3. Marcia.............................$952
Complete Team Rank	**MTD Team Rank**
4. Maria..............................$947	4. Amy................................$943
5. Denise.............................$840	5. Derek..............................$941
6. Ashanti............................$838	6. Andrew...........................$870
7. John................................$820	7. Denise.............................$849
8. Derek..............................$817	8. Ashanti............................$841
9. Andrew...........................$812	9. Marc................................$822
10. Marc..............................$801	10. John...............................$817
↓	↓
18. Lucy..............................$602	18. Charles...........................$620
Sales Tip of the Day Offer the 2-for-1 packages to all new customers.	**MTD Most Improved From Last Month** 1. Amy..............................+$103 2. Jack...............................+$58 3. Heather.........................+$47

frame *how you do work* in your call center. Systemic feedback, therefore, involves whether or not what is occurring within these areas is what you had created and intended to have happen to the customer. There are several proven practices for systemic feedback:

1. While monitoring calls, have QA and supervisors call-type and time calls by handle time, time of day, and day of week.

2. Perform a "mystery shopping" call yourself at least once a month. Call your organization and go through the myriad prompts, including the IVR. Listen to the on-hold recordings. Doing so will give you completely different information and feedback than monitoring, but remember, it is not a substitute for monitoring.

3. Have someone call each phone number for your organization—sometimes from a cell phone, sometimes from a different part of the country—at

different times of the day to see if they can access each number.

4. Call 411 and 00 directory assistance from a land-line phone and from a cell phone to see if they can find listings for your organization's local and/or 800 numbers. Look up your organization in all of the online yellow pages, as well as in major printed directories from throughout the country. Make sure you are listed and competitively placed. While your company may already have another department or individual who is responsible for this activity, you'd be surprised how often it's not done properly. At the end of the day, if you are really responsible for your center's revenue, then you'll want to make sure that the phone is ringing.

Scripting Vs. Script Outlines

Once your reps have mastered the general call flow, it's important that the words used when speaking with customers not be rigidly scripted. You want to let their personality and confidence—their phone charisma—flow through. This is how to increase sales.

To be sure, the major points need to be outlined, and in some cases, key words and/or phrases must be used to ensure that regulatory compliance requirements are met. Nevertheless, all reps who are past the training probationary period should be allowed to find their own way to sell. They will invariably borrow lines, vocabulary and presentation styles from their colleagues—the things that feel natural and work for them.

Without a doubt, *every* customer knows when a rep is reading from a script. When customers sense this, they think the company lacks confidence in its employees. Call centers install IVR systems to cut costs and free reps to handle calls that require human intelligence and sensitivity. Taking away your reps' freedom to think and express themselves dehumanizes the call center—and alienates customers.

Best Software's Senior VP of Customer Sales and Marketing Susan Searle asks her management to create a script outline, which is used for rep training. The reps then tailor the script using *their own* language. Monitoring ensures that customers are grasping all the key points.

But even with general script outlines, reps may get frustrated. In a recent focus group with reps, Searle heard the following complaint about a required script outline: "I don't understand. If I have *already* sold them the tax services, why do I have to say something about the rest of their system?" Another rep agreed, saying, "I'm in tech support. Why do I have to comment on our great software that they have *already* purchased?" Supervisors, attempting to cut call handle time, basically concurred with their reps, commenting, "The customer already knows what kind of software they have. Why are we going over it again?"

Searle first helped the supervisors resolve their AHT problem by suggesting that most of the buying reinforcement can be done during the silent time or dead air time that occurs during the transaction. This shows the customer that the rep knows them, and which products they've previously purchased and installed.

Searle then explained to the reps and supervisors the rationale for telling the customer on every call that they have the best software in marketplace, or that it is the most current version, or that a new version is on the horizon. To illustrate, she used a car maintenance simile of "checking under the hood."

Here's her explanation: "Let's say you brought your car into a repair shop because your brakes required servicing. You picked it up after the repair was completed and then ran out of oil or water in one mile. How would you feel? You want someone to 'look under your hood.' You want them to say 'I checked your oil and water, and you are in good shape to drive.' Or you want them to fix it. Your customers are buying our tax software to run their businesses, as well as to do their taxes. You want to let them know that you have 'looked under their hood' and they are in good shape from a software point of view. You are their expert. You want to take every opportunity to reinforce the customer's buying decision, to be credible and caring, and to have them hang up feeling confident that their system is in shape. It will make the next buying decision much easier."

While Searle does not rigidly script her staff, she does create general outlines that must be delivered in their own words. She stresses the need to reinforce to everyone the *why* behind the outlines. "You need to connect the dots for your reps. When you do, you'll find that rep compliance goes much easier," she says.

We can become myopic by merely looking within the call center industry for innovation. I have often found it helpful to share analogies from other industries with my sales management staff—both to find new sales techniques, and to reinforce a tactical sales direction that we put in place. Like Susan Searle, I, too, was sometimes faced with sales management questioning the wisdom of reinforcing the value of a purchasing decision that was obviously already made. Sharing the following experience seems to help them to understand: I'm a clothes shopper, and I love a good bargain. Consequently, I sometimes shop at Loehmann's, a discount designer store. Although Loehmann's is a discount store and does not have a typical sales staff, I realized that all of my buying decisions were being subtly reinforced at the checkout counter. The checkout clerks always comment on one or two articles that I'm purchasing, seemingly in awe over my superior taste, selection and discount-sniffing capabilities. I leave feeling great—thinking that I rooted out great values. After shopping at this store at least 90 times over a 15-year period, I finally figured it out. I asked if the staff was required to compliment customers on their shopping choices. Yes, I was told, it is

DILBERT by Scott Adams; reprinted by permission of United Feature Syndicate, Inc.

mandatory to reinforce the buying decision on each transaction, but management leaves what to say up to the individual clerks. They never overdo it. It is subtle. It certainly can't be scripted since everyone in line can overhear the dialogue. Imagine, I was being "sold" on the Loehmann's brand all along and never knew it was happening. I just came back 90 times!

Be a Manager, not a Messiah

Many years ago, I read an article in the *Wall Street Journal* that changed my performance management strategies. The article, which was titled "Benefits of Working with the Best Workers,"[i] postulated that there are far too many "messianic" managers in business today (i.e., relating to a "messiah or savior"). They try to "save" each employee. The author's point was that many supervisors and managers—and leaders in general—really take their role as coach to heart. Many do this to such an extent they become employee counselors, losing sight of the ROI on their time.

The author also stated that most managers devote 80 percent of their time to the bottom-third performers, and the remaining 20 percent to everyone else. He believed this to be upside-down. Although you can turn around a consistently poor performer once in a while, it's rarely worth the manager's time when you consider the investment made. Instead, the author contended that managers should give almost all of their time to the top performers, who will soar to even greater heights as a result. His view was that the medium-tier performers should be ignored essentially because, when they noticed that the top performers were getting all of the attention, they, too, would want more attention and would strive harder to produce. He also believed that managers should do everything possible to eliminate the bottom performers who failed to respond to retraining efforts.

I agree with many of his ideas. To be sure, motivation, at least sustainable motivation, comes entirely from within. It requires long-term discipline and an interest in the subject-matter, which, in this case, is sales. The best you can do is recruit and select the right people for the job, using validated predictive hiring assessments and behavioral interviews, provide the environment and training to do the job at a consistently superior level, and inspire them through coaching to be their best.

However, I disagree with the author's suggestion to virtually ignore the medium tier. In my experience, this group has the most upside potential from a retraining and coaching perspective. Ignoring them will not motivate them to do better. With properly selected sales staff, the motivation should be there. In many cases, medium performers have the "right stuff," they merely lack the advanced skills. They need to be inspired and coached, which you can do by giving them new material and techniques to hit higher performance levels. Show them how the top performers are accomplishing their amazing feats.

> **"When people tell me they don't have time for coaching, I say, 'Spend ALL of your time on coaching—the rest will come easy.'"**
> *—Herb Kelleher, Chairman, Southwest Airlines*

The extent to which your supervisors should delve into personal issues that affect a person's work performance is, indeed, an issue. When top performers begin to fail, supervisors often feel it's their duty to take on a counseling role. This is never a good idea—it's a role for which the majority of managers and supervisors are not trained. Supervisors can act as a "broker of counselors" and assist employees in getting the resources to help them resolve their situation. However, we do the employee a disservice if we attempt to play amateur psychologist or crisis counselor. The next section will help you to further define supervisors' roles in coaching and training.

Role Clarity: Who Should Do What?

It is critical for everyone to understand their role when it comes to coaching and training. Frequently, well-intentioned supervisory and/or training staff misunderstand their roles—they do what they like to do, or are most skilled at, or what is most visible, instead of what must be done. Without role-clarity documents, critical performance support tasks like training, monitoring and coaching frequently fail.

I worked with a company once where coaching, monitoring and feedback rarely took place. Supervisors said that they didn't have enough time. The results of a one-week time study of the supervisors' detailed calendars revealed that, indeed, they were busy doing a lot of very important customer tasks, but they were failing to complete the tasks for which they were hired. In their perception, which was somewhat based in reality, the people who got promoted in the company were those who demonstrated strong project management skills. Therefore, when a customer called or a project had to be implemented, supervisors would take on those tasks at the expense of managing and developing their reps.

What these supervisors failed to realize was that there were already people in the company who were responsible for new customer implementation and projects—people who were paid and trained to do these jobs. Sometimes a supervisor's immediate manager would inappropriately delegate projects or administrative work that they didn't want to do, or an implementation manager would fail to deliver the project, so supervisors would volunteer or be volunteered.

All of this happened because of poor role clarity. Identifying and documenting the tasks or activities that are formally out of the call center supervisor's job-scope allows them to "push back" on inappropriate manager delegation and refocus on the most critical task and role—being a developmental coach to their reps.

The aggressive career-minded supervisor who's bucking for a promotion will surely counter, "How do I get promoted to manager if I can't get any project management experience?" The answer lies in the fact that experienced supervisors frequently accomplish their core tasks in less time, and can then be formally assigned limited project management duties—assuming that their staff does not pay the price.

In addition to the formal, results-oriented job descriptions that most organizations have in place, it's essential to develop role-clarity documents that contain the following descriptive information for each position:

Core tasks. Tasks—such as monitoring, evaluations and feedback sessions—that *must* be accomplished within prescribed timeframes.

Core task time allotment. Percentage and average number of hours typically required per day, week or month to accomplish each task.

Required and mandatory ongoing meetings. Includes daily "game plan" meetings, calibration meetings, management staff meetings and rep communication meetings.

Discretionary tasks. Includes all activities that are not assigned to anyone as part of their essential job. Examples might include contest creation, holiday party planning, process revamping, etc.

Tasks outside the scope of a position. Clarifies what the person in a certain position should *not* be doing, especially if it requires further training, is someone else's job, or is done at the expense of a core task.

A formal role-clarity document should be constructed for every position in the call center, including QA evaluator, supervisor, trainer, manager, project manager, scheduler, etc. A hypothetical example of a role-clarity document for supervisory position in a mid-size call center follows on page 172. Your categories and allocations will vary with the size and complexity of your center. Another form that can assist supervisors in allocating more time to the role of developmental coach can be found on page 173.

Have your staff estimate the time they spend in each of the 14 to 20 roles noted in both columns in the role-clarity document. They can use the supervisor role-prioritization form to figure out an action plan to offload all the other tasks they have been assigned or have sought out.

In *ICMI's Call Center Monitoring Study II Final Report,* 62 percent of supervisor respondents said they have enough time to provide effective

ROLE-CLARITY DOCUMENT FOR SUPERVISOR POSITION		
Supervisors control 60 percent of the costs of a call center and manage 80 percent of the sales. Your job as supervisor (development coach or team leader) is critical. You make a difference every day.		
Percentage of Time	**Your Role**	**Not Your Role**
50%	**Coaching and development** (Off-peak hours) • Monitoring • Performance analysis • Performance appraisals • Recognition • Feedback	• Handling incoming calls
20%	**Monitoring and managing service levels** • Service level monitoring • Managing schedule adherence	• Customer relationship management of large accounts
15%	**Leading and managing** • Miscellaneous administration • Contest planning • Management training • Product rollout planning	• Account implementation • Technical services • Facility management
8%	**Product pre-receipt customer escalations**	• Product post-receipt customer escalations
5%	**Communication** • Team meetings • Monthly one-on-one performance meetings with reps	• Data gathering • Report generation
1%	**Consulting with Training**	• Training
1%	**Hiring**	• Special projects (Mastery of job will allow project time for top leaders)

monitoring/feedback. While dismal, that number has improved substantially since the previous study was conducted in 1999, when just over 50 percent of respondents believed that to be true.[ii] If you want to significantly improve sales, service or quality in your center, you must find a way to make effective monitoring and feedback the No. 1 priority for your supervisors and managers.

SUPERVISOR ROLE-PRIORITIZATION FORM			
Supervisor Role	Critical Role (Must Do)	Maintenance Role (Should Do)	Time Wasters (Stop Doing)
Monitoring, coaching and development			
Managing service levels			
Managing change			
Pre-product receipt escalations			
Communication			
Training/consulting			
Hiring			

Points to Remember

• Use micro-gap analysis to highlight individual rep potential and to drive improvement.

• Focus on one performance driver at a time, building action plans and setting reasonable targets.

• Develop performance diagnostic worksheets (one for each performance driver metric) to expedite coaching and highlight the way to higher revenue.

• Use error-analysis tools to build a refresher training program—just for those who need it.

• Do not underestimate the power of positive reinforcement at all levels in the call center.

• Sustaining peak sales performance begins with a real service orientation.

• Try traditional and new feedback systems that, when properly applied, make a big difference in changing behaviors and increasing quality sales.

• Have managers sit in on supervisor feedback sessions once a month for each supervisor.

Chapter 10: Using Employee Feedback to Remove Barriers

"Those workers want to know how much you care before they care how much you know."
A MANUFACTURER OF FARM EQUIPMENT IN IOWA

Wouldn't it be appalling to spend a lot of effort, not to mention money, overhauling and constructing the perfect selection, training and coaching processes, only to find that something hidden in the environment is counteracting all your best efforts? It would be like a car manufacturer building a superbly designed high-performance car, creating a great marketing plan and offering a ground-breaking 10-year warranty—but failing to realize that they neglected to mention in the operating literature that the car requires 93 percent octane fuel. Otherwise, it would not perform very well, would it? Sometimes, it is the little things that can sabotage our best efforts. We need to know what they are.

What elements must be in place to create a workplace environment where peak performance happens? There are several key areas of focus that will help you and your sales reps to build the workplace of their dreams. In this chapter, we'll look at common problems in call centers and how you can remove real or imagined job impediments and irritants through the use of an environmental assessment. We will also examine the manager's role in enabling reps to achieve higher performance.

The Call Center as a Community

I can walk through a call center, any call center, for a half-hour, not speaking with anyone, and know if there are problems that distract reps and supervisors from achieving peak performance. How? Take a little tour of your organization with me, and I'll show you. First, we'll walk into your lobby and see if we can tell what business you're in. If one cannot tell from the lobby, then there is a focus problem. Also, there must be visible evidence of pride and excitement about your products or services. If there isn't, then an opportunity is lost to make a positive impression on all of the visitors, potential customers, and prospective and current employees who pass through your lobby.

Then, we'll walk through the call center seeking graphs and scorecards that are posted that show team and individual performance rankings. Are they found only at the one or two team managers' stations who believe in performance boards, or are they everywhere?

When sitting in the break room or walking down the hall by the water cooler, what are employees discussing? Is the tone negative and angry, or are they discussing how to change a process for the betterment of the customer or the company? Are they discussing their incentives positively? Are they discussing how to achieve higher metrics?

When we walk by reps speaking on the phone with customers, what words are we constantly hearing? Words like: "I can't," "It's our policy, sir," or *"They* didn't tell us about this new program"? Do we hear a loud, high-pitched voice across the room indicating that a call is going wrong? If within minutes we can hear more than one of these symptoms, you can bet that your reps are hearing negative comments about your product and your company's ability to deliver on its implied promises (in its mission or company tag line) hundreds of times a day. Not good. These are dangerous signs, and they reveal a need for an environmental assessment.

Conducting an Environmental Assessment

An environmental assessment is not an evaluation of the asbestos in your walls, nor the quality of your water. This assessment is similar to an employee opinion survey, but it is much more focused on your call center and its performance potential. While there are outside firms that excel at this process, outsourcing the assessment is not absolutely critical because the survey is internal, very brief and for your use only.

A word of warning: Embarking upon your own employee survey, albeit informal, will scare the heebie-jeebies out of your HR folks, who think they own employee opinion. They will give you all the reasons why their employee opinion survey is the only valid and official survey that should be done. But what are they really worried about? They're concerned that you may be having a short-term burst of focus on employee "care and feeding," which will dissipate when you read your next management book. Their concerns are valid—they've seen it before. A survey is conducted, expectations are raised that things are really going to change, and then nothing happens. Actually, something *does* happen. The bees in the hive get angry, really angry, and they direct their complaints to HR. This "buzz" is not a productive one.

An environmental assessment should be conducted at least every six months, but only if you take action and have reliable communication and feedback mechanisms in place. If you don't have the time, inclination or the resources to act upon what the reps tell you, then don't do it. It's better to let sleeping dogs lie.

The environmental assessment is very different from the annual employee opinion survey. It has several purposes. It focuses on tangible areas that are affecting performance—areas that you can change. For instance, the assessment often focuses on the quality of the relationship between front-line coaches and their reps. Research on employee attrition has shown that people quit their bosses, not their companies. The quality of the sales reps' relationship with their immediate coach is the No. 1 reason they will stay with a company.

The assessment may extract elements of a 360-degree feedback tool and the employee opinion survey to get to root causes of company-caused performance issues. ScientificSelection.com, FurstPerson and TalentKeepers all have assessment tools that can be tailored to suit this purpose. Generally, they are more accurate than tools that are internally developed because they have been put through correlation analysis.

Environmental assessments differ from employee opinion surveys, in that they are:

• Much more performance-focused.

• More actionable because the questions can be much more narrowly focused on your department (e.g., sales).

• Shorter. They can be conducted more frequently and progress can be readily tracked.

A typical environmental assessment questionnaire does the following:

• Explores retention issues, such as, what would make an employee stay? What would make an employee leave?

• Asks whether reps feel respected by their supervisor, and by the organization.

• Explores the trust, communication and flexibility demonstrated by their supervisor.

• Asks whether reps are clear about their goals, targets, incentives and how their performance is measured. Do they think the process is fair? Are there conflicting measurements or messages?

• Explores feedback issues, such as does their coach or supervisor offer suggestions or insights that actually help them improve their performance?

• Identifies job irritants, such as what gets in the way of performing at a higher sales level (e.g., policies, procedures, colleagues, training, systems or service conditions)?

TIPS FOR CONDUCTING A SUCCESSFUL ENVIRONMENTAL ASSESSMENT

• Do not imply promises in the phrasing of questions.

• Require that everyone fill out the assessment, including supervisors.

• Hold rep focus groups within one week of administration to clarify unclear data.

• Carefully evaluate the feedback.

• Start making immediate changes based on the feedback.

• Have a logo or stamp designed: "Courtesy of the EA" and use it on every new policy, procedure or practice that was changed as a result of the assessment.

ELIMINATING COMMON JOB IRRITANTS

A properly executed environmental assessment—and subsequent sales rep focus groups—should provide a list of employee "irritants." If left unresolved, these irritants will create poor sales performance, attrition among high producers and problems with customer satisfaction. Following are just a few common irritants that can be found in most call centers, along with some suggested solutions.

Marketing/advertising surprises. Many centers still face the chronic problem of first hearing about a marketing program or a new advertisement via their *customers*. There is nothing more upsetting to reps than to be caught off-guard or uninformed during a customer transaction. It makes them appear unprofessional and incompetent, and can have a devastating impact on their confidence level and ability to gain customer trust.

If this is a regular occurrence in your center, I'll bet your attrition rates are high. This situation must be corrected immediately by gaining commitment from the appropriate senior marketing, advertising or Internet executives to fix the problem. Show them the frequency of the problem, using specific data and examples, and explain the consequences. With their assistance, assemble a crossfunctional team to map the current process, identify the "process disconnects" and map out a new process. The new process should, at a minimum, require physical sign-off from the call center management group and the data-entry group (for codes). It should include a review and formal sign-off of the advertisement or media, the promotion policies and the dates. The timing should be such that, if the call center or the data group has a significant issue, the media or plan can still be revised. Whenever possible, the actual print ad should be available on the center's Intranet for review with the rep and the customer. In addition, it's a good idea for the call center and data managers to receive proposed quarterly and annual media plans and revisions.

Poor communication. When it comes to spreading the word on changes, it's amazing how call center rumor mills are so effective, and training and memos are not.

Let's face it, we and our staff suffer from information overload. Learning specialists say today's adults have to hear something at least seven times to retain it, especially if it requires a behavioral adjustment on our part. Moreover, we all absorb information in different ways. Some people are visual, others respond to oral instruction and some learn only by doing or repeating it over and over. To "get the message out" on something very important, it's best to use a variety of methods, including the following:

- Team meetings
- "Daily game plan" messages that flash on the reps' screen upon sign-in
- Quizzes
- "Drive-bys"*
- Info-boards
- Statistics and reports

*A "drive-by" is a phrase coined by reps in a call center that I managed. It occurs when management walks through the call center on the way to a meeting and takes a few moments to stop and ask a rep or two how a new promotion is going, or if the new computer shortcut they implemented last week is working, or what they think of a new policy. If the rep knows nothing about it, then the manager must look further into the communication process.

Bad information tickets. In every call center, a process should be established that allows anyone, especially reps, to report what they believe to be inaccurate information. This allows reps to report problems or errors pointed out to them by customers during calls (e.g., mistakes or misleading information on the Web site), as well as any problems the reps themselves discover (e.g., a code that doesn't work).

These types of problems, if not corrected, will generate costly rework, customer ill-will and employee frustration. Often the cause of bad system information is the proliferation of many new channels and services, and the lack of a company database that feeds all the systems. Information easily becomes out of date. Clearly the best, and often costly, solution is to develop a central database or use an enterprise resource planning application, but even then, that database can be wrong. Peak-performing organizations find a way to quickly eliminate bad information by allowing reps, or anyone who identifies incorrect information, to notify the data department by filling out an online form detailing their discovery.

The critical component to make this work is feedback to the rep on the resolution within 24 hours, whether it be that the bad information has been corrected, or a company error (e.g., a store closed earlier than it should have) was followed up on, or a training issue was fixed. If reps don't see that management is acting on their feedback regarding errors/bad information, they will stop documenting the problems.

The Manager as Muse

The role of upper-level management in an organization is to create the conditions and the environment in which employees with clear goals and proper support can accomplish great things. The role of the immediate manager or supervisor is similar to that of a muse. A muse provides inspiration, not motivation. Motivation always comes from within. The old proverb, "You can lead a horse to water, but you can't make it drink," is derived from a basic truth that is valid in the workplace today. An individual must take responsibility for his own motivation to do a good job, for he cannot obtain it from anyone else.

The manager is there to diagnose performance problems, redirect energies, build trust and to provide emotional support when self-confidence wanes. A supervisor can help a sales rep with self-esteem problems by inspiring him and teaching him new techniques to try to reach new targets. If an employee cannot motivate himself, then most likely, he's in the wrong position, wrong company or both. Let's face it—we don't like to give up on anyone, but there are, in fact, some people who just don't have the perseverance, work ethic or resiliency required to be successful at sales. When confronted with such individuals, be clear and unwavering about the level of performance required, and in holding these individuals to high-performance standards. Don't waste time attempting to work with those who aren't suited for the job. They will drain vital energy from their coworkers, from the call center and from you, depleting the energy required to inspire those who crave inspiration.

I have a good friend, Rosemary Wilkie, a highly successful sales vice president at AT&T, who advocates *"performance non-management."* She contends that her job is easy. She hires highly intelligent, motivated people who have a strong drive to win, and she gets out of their way. She believes in servant leadership, wherein managers are there merely to "block and tackle" for their employees. She creates an exciting environment in which her sales executives can flourish, make mistakes, take some risks and grow. I have simplified her philosophy, of course, but it's not really that far from the one espoused in this book. Although she doesn't run a call center with a lot of non-exempt employees, her point is this: Hire the right people and half your job is done. Give them the right support and take the obstacles out of their way as they occur. Not only will they be more successful, they will want to be more successful *for you.* The manager as muse instead of overseer or motivator provides a refreshingly new viewpoint; it invites a redirection of your talents and energy.

It is important to redefine your job; if you don't, you'll always be the same type of manager. You must ask yourself: Am I the best I can be? If not, it might be useful to reframe your job. Reframing is a classic problem-solving technique. When you're stuck on a problem that you've been working on for a long time without progress, it's helpful to consider the issue from various different perspectives. Reframing your job works the same way. A number of years ago, I made a major change as a manager of people. I reframed my managerial mission: "To make other people incredibly successful." After I adopted that as my personal mantra, many things changed, in fact, they turned upside-down, including my energy level, how I gave feedback and how I viewed the goal of my job as a muse, not a manager or controller of people. I encompassed in this mantra a different way to think about my customer's business, and how I could make them more successful. I thought a lot more about my boss, and how to make her more successful. I gave myself permission to give my boss and colleagues feedback in a manner that let them know I cared about their success. Suffice it to say, after reframing my job, I became more successful, and so did my staff and the people I cared about.

Remember, rarely are *we* performing at peak levels in *all* the areas within in our scope. Like all change in business, it starts at the top. When we, as managers, and the organization begin performing at our peak, then our reps have a chance. Get enough reps, managers and support staff performing at *their* peak, and you will have a peak-performing center.

Points to Remember

- Employees quit bosses, not companies.
- Take a physical "walk-about" your center for a fresh eye on environmental concerns.
- Conduct periodic environmental assessments to find new problems to fix.
- Eliminate common job irritants and impediments by fixing processes, and eliminating bad data and unwelcome surprises.

Chapter 11: Sharing the Wealth: Incentives that Matter

"Money is better than poverty, if only for financial reasons."
WOODY ALLEN, DIRECTOR, SCREEN WRITER, ACTOR AND COMEDIAN

The last chapter touched on the point that the relationship between frontline employees and their supervisors is critical to their decision to stay with a company. While that's true for companies across the board, in my own research on call centers and in rep focus groups, good compensation and schedule flexibility rank almost even.

So money *does* matter. If you manage one of the few call centers in the world that pays its staff what they are worth—i.e., a decent living wage—then you can skip this section. But if your center is like most in the call center world, where compensation structure is poor to dismal, then you will want to pay attention.

Many HR and senior executives like to cite job satisfaction surveys in which employees, when asked what they value, rank money below factors like recognition for contributions and the relationship with their boss. But a word of caution here: averages skew the numbers. Those results might be true for the average worker who makes $30,000 to $50,000 per year—but while job satisfaction and recognition are very important, they don't feed the children or keep the lights on. We all know our demographics. For the most part, our centers are staffed with 25- to 40-year-olds, and many single women with children. When you consider that many are supporting a family, these reps are earning at or just above the poverty level. So, yes, money matters—particularly at the rep level where money means having heat in the house, not which model BMW to buy.

Management Can Make a Difference

It is up to management to find a way to increase productivity or revenue enough so that we can pay our employees a decent living wage. Not one that is mandated by the state or federal government, but because we have given the right people the right skills to create enough value for the company to pay them well. I'm suggesting self-funding compensation levels by including incentive pay at a level that can actually change your sales reps' living standards.

Incentive plans that are properly constructed and executed usually carry a high return on investment. According to a study by the American Compensation Association, an incentive plan that pays an average of 3 percent provides a 134 percent net return, while higher paying plans provided even higher company returns. The top quartile firms in this study reported a net return of 378 percent.[i]

When you find a way to add $1,500 per month to a top rep's paycheck by showing him how to add $10,000 per month in profitability to the company, then you are really making a difference—not just by boosting corporate profits, but in actually changing someone's life for the better. I've had experience with making this vision a reality in several companies. It's quite a rush to know that someone could take a vacation for the first time in her life or could afford to go to school, live in a better apartment or purchase a reliable car.

Raising the minimum performance standards, developing new training and performance management tools, and new recruiting techniques to find better-qualified candidates are all prerequisites to being able to afford higher incentive levels. The investment requires, in part, faith by management. You must find ways to provide a fail-safe so that you don't end up paying more for the same performance. In this chapter, we'll explore a few ways that companies accomplished this goal using probability theory. You'll also want to ensure that your finance department is included in your undertaking so that when they see the incentive costs increasing, they can relate that to increased sales. Also, it's important to be proactive and advise finance that you are to be held personally accountable for the effect on the bottom line.

Proven Practices for Constructing Rep Incentive Plans

There are 12 essential elements of a successful incentive plan. These elements are the result of years of trial-and-error, and blood, sweat and tears by some of the best call center managers in the industry.

---

12 PROVEN PRACTICES FOR CONSTRUCTING REP INCENTIVE PLANS

1. Use minimum quality thresholds, not a weighted quality/sales index, to qualify a sales rep for participation in the plan.

2. For reps, pay out the plan at least monthly and more frequently, if possible. For supervisors and managers, pay out the plan quarterly.

3. Keep the plan simple, pay out on the sales KPI only.

4. Don't use weighting or a point system.

5. Audit, audit, audit.

6. Immediately, and somewhat loudly, terminate staff for any falsifications.

7. Pay on net, not gross revenue or gross sales.

8. Create a plan that pays out to 80 to 85 percent of the population. Ramp-up to this payout level may take up to six months.

9. Create a safeguard that lets you revamp the plan if it does not payback in the first six months.

(continued next page)

---

10. Leverage incentive pay on top performers. Pay the top 10 to 20 percent of performers substantially more than other reps (pay them more, even as a percentage of revenue).

11. Constantly communicate new performance levels and the return on the incentive plan to Finance, HR and your boss.

12. Don't cap the incentive program, unless you want to cap your revenues.

Examples of the influences and effects of the right incentives appear throughout the book. So, to avoid repetition, I will not separately address all 12 practices here.

The role of quality in incentive structures. In a sales skill incentive plan, make sure you have a quality-level prerequisite, not a quality component, prior to paying any incentive. It's wrong to include quality as some sort of index to calculate an incentive payout. It's very easy and too tempting for reps to shortchange the customer on quality in order to get the money. Such a tradeoff cannot be tolerated; the customer always comes first. Many employees view quality or service as a sliding scale to be balanced against the end revenue or productivity outcome for themselves and the company. They frequently cannot see the big picture—the cost of rework and the cost of customer loyalty. For these reasons, I highly recommend instituting a fairly high-quality threshold, below which reps are not able to participate in the monthly incentives. It only takes one month of missing out on $200 to $1,500 in incentives to remember the only duty is to the customer.

Pay out monthly. If you want to sustain peak performance and institutionalize it, you need to ensure that reps do not view their incentives as a windfall or something that happens by accident. Help them to recognize how hard they worked that month by reviewing their monthly statistics, and forecast a monthly payout so they can begin to plan, budget and anticipate a lifestyle change. If a rep's new performance level has allowed her to afford a car, then you'll want to ensure that she continues to perform well enough to earn the extra money to meet her monthly car payment. Reps should be able to estimate their payout during the month, and whether they will hit their sales numbers and quality threshold. No one likes surprises—not your boss and not your reps. Knowing how they're doing will also help to keep reps motivated and sustain high performance.

Rewards at this level cannot be paid out quarterly or annually—they must be as immediate as possible. A monthly payout is the bare minimum schedule; bi-weekly is better. Later in this chapter, you'll read about a call center incentive program that pays out daily. I realize that this can be an administrative nightmare, but ideally, reps should receive their rewards as close to the performance event as possible. I've spoken with several companies that issue each of their reps a real bank account with a debit card into which the incentive is paid. This allows the center to pay out more frequently, and the rep to tap those resources daily.

Always keep it simple. Trust me on this one: You must establish just one KPI on which to base an incentive. If you elect to adjust for anything, weight the employees' multiple performance drivers or use a point system, you'll create an administrative nightmare from which you'll never awaken. Your employees will be confused, their supervisors will not be able to explain it, and you'll end up discontinuing the program within the first two months. Your performance database should be automated enough to generate the incentive projection reports, the final incentive reports and the backup to payroll.

Audit and terminate abusers. It's important to audit your incentive system to ensure that you're not paying someone for performance they didn't achieve, and also to discourage those who might try to defeat the system. Auditing will also allow you to continue to afford rewards for those who do their very best. You probably already know where to look for "funny business" in your operational statistics, but listen to your reps, as well. They'll know who might be playing with the numbers and how, and they're usually really irritated when no one sees it. Many companies have instituted a

"Fraud Hotline" where employees can report any company abuse. Use one that your company has already in place, or set up your own. Abuse will happen, so when it does make sure that everyone knows it will not be tolerated. Blatant cases, not misunderstandings, should result in swift termination.

Payout distribution should favor top performers. It is important that most, but not all, of your sales reps be seen as winners. Quality thresholds, sales performance minimum standards and attendance patterns will typically limit the payout distribution rather naturally to about 85 percent of the sales staff. Most of the companies that I've spoken with that have incentive systems in peak-performing sales centers pay their top sales reps a much higher percentage payout or commission on revenue or units sold. Not only do reps receive more money because they sell more, the rate of payout is higher, as well. For example, a top performer might receive the same percentage commission for the first 700 sales he makes in a month (where 625 represents the average units sold by reps), but is paid at 150 percent for the next 100 units sold above 700 that month, and is incented at 200 percent for any units sold above 800 in the month. In a number of call centers, sales executives said their top performers could double their base pay. In a few centers, the very top performers were making $80,000 to $90,000 per year; and at Hibernia Bank, top sales reps make $130,000 (including a $15,000 base salary). You must ensure that if you increase their payout, you do so for a higher performance level than they had previously attained. You don't want to pay more for the same amount of work. An example later in this chapter perfectly illustrates this point with a real incentive plan for "personal best" performance.

Make sure you see a payback. Some call centers create incentive programs that simply provide more money to incent improved performance without putting in any fail-safes. Sometimes this works, sometimes it doesn't. Everything discussed thus far requires a great leap of faith: If you execute well all of the changes—instituting predictive hiring assessments for reps and coaches, creating minimum performance standards, developing new performance management tools and new training programs—you'll see a major improvement in performance. I believe it. I've seen it work. But I'm not in your business. What if significant performance improvement doesn't happen in three to six months? Do not initiate incentive plans that don't require sales performance improvements as part of the program. Make sure that you communicate to your staff upfront that the sales rep incentive plan will be a six-month test, and that you reserve the right to withdraw the plan at any time if it doesn't deliver an acceptable profit after wealth sharing. They will appreciate your honesty and your efforts to benefit them, and they'll want to be an instrumental part of the plan's success. They will help to make it work—for themselves and the company. Later, you'll read about one company's incentive system that ensured an improvement in revenue for every dollar spent.

Communicate to keep your resources. After leaving a company, I have often learned of perceived "secret techniques" that my staff believed I knew and had not formally shared with them. Invariably, one question was: "How did you get the resources to pull off what you did?" Actually, this is not the right question. Getting the resources is relatively simple. In most organizations, whoever has the most credibility (i.e., has delivered the goods in the past) and the best business case wins. This is especially true if the initiative is immediately self-funding, such as a performance-based incentive program. It's much more difficult to *keep* the resources, especially when times get tough or when another great idea that must be funded comes along. So how do you keep your resources and your incentive package? Involve HR, the finance department and your boss intimately in your business case, and deliver sales progress reports to them. Constant communication of your successes, at least on a monthly basis, and perhaps even the need for program modifications, will go a long way toward ensuring that your resources are not withdrawn.

WANT A DIFFERENT CANDIDATE POOL?

If you want to attract a different and better candidate pool, advertise your new compensation package and environment. After we had implemented a much more lucrative package, our recruiters continued to advertise: "Call Center Sales Associates wanted. $12 per hour plus incentives, plus benefits." In the minds of our potential candidates nothing had changed, even though we had changed everything. However, we soon altered the way we recruited, as well as how and where we advertised. In one company with whom I worked, we rewrote the job advertisement this way: "Inside Sales Reps to $65,000 per year, plus benefits and extensive sales training programs." We promoted it as a professional job with risk-rewards. At least 15 percent of the staff attained that compensation level. We also focused on training, because peak-performing sales reps really value training and coaching.

The "Personal Best" Incentive Program

Dr. Mark Haug of the University of Kansas School of Business designed a highly effective incentive plan for a privately held collection company with a single contact center. The incentive plan was based on the concept of "personal best."

The company's president had budgeted $1 million annually for contact center incentives. Haug recommended creating an incentive program that rewarded each individual rep $20 for each day he or she performed "statistically significantly" better than his or her running average (statistically significant is two standard deviation points). In addition, if reps "collected" better than their straight average for five consecutive days, they received another $20 kicker. Collections is much like sales, but it's the recovery of revenue (the customer must again agree to pay for the product or service).

Here's how the plan worked: For the sake of simplicity, let's say that one rep, Joe, as illustrated in the table on the facing page, is collecting at an average of $1,000 per hour. On the first day of the incentive plan, Joe collected $1,011 per hour; on the second day, he collected $1,434 per hour; $1,123 on the third; $1,080 on the fourth; $1,141 on the fifth; and $1,557 on the sixth day. On the seventh day, his performance dropped back to $1,300 per hour. Joe is rewarded with $20 for Day 2 and Day 6, since his performance on those days is statistically significantly above his average. He is rewarded another $20 for Days 5 and 6 since he beat his overall monthly average of $1,000 per hour for at least five consecutive days. On Day 7, Joe did not hit the threshold set by the two standard deviations, which would discount normal fluctuations, but he is given $20 for sustaining performance over five days and exceeding last month's average. On Day 8, Joe wasn't focused, and therefore, didn't perform as well as last month's average. He received neither the payout nor the sustained performance kicker for this day.

PERSONAL BEST INCENTIVE PLAN			
Joe's Last Month Avg. $1,000/hour			
Day	$/Hour Avg.	Payout	Kicker
1	$1,011		
2	$1434	$20	
3	$1,123		
4	$1,080		
5	$1,141		$20
6	$1,557	$20	$20
7	$1,300	$20	
8	$997		

Haug also recommended that, since a best practice is to reward employees as immediately as possible, they should actually receive the money the very day they earned it. Reps viewed it as almost like having a contest with themselves each day. The program was wildly successful for both the employees and the company. Reps came to work every day with smiles on their faces, because every day had the possibility of reward.

If this all sounds a bit "Pavlovian" to you, then you understand the process. Incentives are all about modifying behavior. Although this particular example was for revenue generated through collections, it is an excellent example of an incentive plan's ability to boost productivity. As a direct result of the incentive plan, revenue productivity increased by 11 percent. The personal best incentive plan can work equally well with sales. Other organizations that implemented this incentive plan, including those with sales, reported a 12 percent increase in revenue productivity.

Statistical Tools Help Set Performance Targets

In the collections center example, we can determine how high Joe will have to jump each day to beat his average. By inputting the data from Joe's last month performance ($1,000/hour average) in Excel using the STDEV formula, we find the standard deviation for this data to be 120. Multiplying 120x2 (standard deviations), tells us that he must collect $1,240 in revenue per hour {1,000 avg.+ (120x2)} to get a payout on the program. As you can probably deduce, as he does better each day, his personal average begins to rise and the new target will eventually be higher than the $1,240 per hour. It will continue to change throughout the course of the incentive program.

Building these types of incentive plans generally requires help from a strong internal compensation analyst or a sales incentive consultant. To get a good ROI for your plan, use probability theory to set each rep's daily targets, understand how many consecutive days a rep should exceed his average to earn the second payout, and to determine the appropriate payout level ($20).

You need to ensure that an increase in productivity is not a fluke of circumstance, but a true positive performance trend. How? By selecting the right number of standard deviations. The standard deviation threshold ensures that the variance was not a result of normal fluctuations, such as seasonal fluctuations, price consciousness of the customer or a day-of-week phenomenon. In the collections center example, two points of standard deviation mean that there is only a 2.3 percent chance that the results were caused by random variation. Therefore, the only plausible explanation is that Joe improved his performance. If one standard deviation point was used, there would be a 15.9 percent chance that the results were caused by normal variation.

The two-point standard deviation is a statistical process control tool and level used for service processes. It represents a threshold of plus or minus X percent from the baseline mean number. In addition to assisting you in creating incentive plans like the "personal best" plan, the two-point standard deviation is often used to build process scorecards; measuring the processes that are out of control, or to help understand if your intervention in the out-of-control process had positive measurable results. In the call center world, one might build a scorecard on any of a variety of process measures, such as "first point of contact close" or "reopened complaints."

Determining if two standard deviations is the right number for *your* incentive formula will depend on several variables, including the total amount of money budgeted for the incentive plan, number of reps in the plan and the daily plan payout amount. Perhaps the right standard deviation for your set of conditions may be 1.6 or 3.0, or the payout $10 or $25. All of these variables require the analysis of an expert. I highly recommend

---

STANDARD DEVIATION SIMPLIFIED

Standard deviation is a measure of how erratic or volatile your data is, and how widely the values are dispersed from the average value (mean). The calculation is imbedded in Excel as a tool. You can use formula (STDEV), below, in Excel, and apply it to data such as the collections center incentive example.

$$\sqrt{\frac{n\sum x^2 - \left(\sum x\right)^2}{n\,(n\text{-}1)}}$$

A Standard Deviation Process Example
1. Compute the standard deviation and the mean for your population.
2. Determine the number of standard deviations that is reasonable for your plan. We chose two standard deviations on the advice of our incentive expert.
3. Let's say the net revenue/hour for a rep over the last month averaged $600, the data is normally distributed and the standard deviation is calculated to be $50/hour using the first Excel formula.
4. If the sales rep now achieves $700/hour, then that is two standard deviations from the mean ($50x2).
5. This means there is only a 2.3 percent chance that the $700/hour average achieved was caused by normal variation. The sales rep should definitely get a reward!

investing in some advice. The business results can be exceptional if the program is properly designed, but you can really lose your shirt if the targets and incentives are the result of guesswork.

Where to Find Inspiration for Effective Incentive Systems

I have often advised call centers to look outside the industry for innovation and inspiration on subjects in which we are not as sophisticated as we might be. Incentive systems is one of those areas. So when interacting with other companies, if you should observe a noticeable turnaround in employee behavior in a company, investigate whether they have just implemented a new incentive program, either for the frontline staff or the managers. Get the details of how it works from the frontline staff, and ask them about the pro's and cons of their system.

Whenever I see good sales performance, I like to speculate on the performance measurements and incentive programs that must be in place. Likewise, if the sales performance is sub-par, I wonder about the program I might put in place if I were in charge. It doesn't matter whether I'm calling a call center or in a retail store making a purchase. For instance, I live near a CompUSA retail store. During past visits to this store, it was obvious to me that, if there was an incentive system for the line staff in place, it was not working. No one ever seemed to be around, and no one ever asked me if I needed help (when I really did need help!).

I've often fantasized about improvements I would make if I managed their store sales. I would have an automatic counter installed in every "entrance only" doorframe in the chain. This would provide a tally of how many people entered, which then could be compared to the number of transactions. In effect, it would be the store's "close ratio." I would also measure revenue dollars per employee on the floor and implement a sales incentive system.

About two years ago, I observed a change in the CompUSA environment. Suddenly, there were people everywhere who wanted to help me. They were knowledgeable and went out of their way to assist me, sometimes going to extraordinary lengths. My average sales per visit increased, but I didn't care. Whenever I decided to purchase something, the sales rep would put a sticker with a number on the item "so that the cashier would ring me through quicker." But I knew what they were doing—the number on the sticker identified the sales rep. They finally had an incentive plan in place (or at least, one that worked). Now they could afford more floor staff, or the ones who were already there finally came out of the woodwork. Incentives really do change behavior.

Incentives that Change Lifestyles

In the years that I spent researching best demonstrated practices for this book, I interviewed many managers and executives, most of whom were still trying to determine how to create an incentive package for their sales or service reps. They wanted a plan that would be clear to the reps, pass the compensation department's fairness and equity tests, and actually drive the right behavior at a significant enough level that would matter to the company and to the rep.

Confidentially, the executives in several of the best companies—those most adept at driving sales—said they had their own "litmus tests" for whether or not their incentive programs were working. Some would privately note the percentage of individuals who could afford to own their own homes based on their individual paychecks. If no one could afford to buy a house or condo, then the executives didn't think they had solved the career, attrition or performance potential issues in their centers. For a person in a call center rep's socio-economic level, many of whom have no savings account and can never foresee retiring, building equity in something they can borrow against and can call their own is important. Even if only a few in your organization can afford to buy a home, it gives hope to all.

Tim Cook, VP of North American Reservations at Hilton, believes incentive and recognition programs, designed correctly, can really inspire top performers. Hilton's basic program for sales reps consists of incentives that average 6 percent of their pay, with the top performers earning 12 percent. Eighty-five percent of their staff qualifies for incentive payments. While an incentive of $200 to $300 a month to a top performer doesn't seem like a lot, it helps them to afford a new car or a nicer apartment. In other words, when reps have a real opportunity to earn incentives every month, it can change their standard of living.

RMH Teleservices Inc., a large customer care and sales outsourcer, pays a market-competitive base wage. Their average incentive payout runs approximately 15 percent of a rep's base pay, or approximately $250 per month. A top producer there can enjoy as much as $1,600 a month in incentives, almost doubling their base pay. These are also incentives that certainly change lifestyles.

Incentives mean different things to different people. The key is to know your constituency and build general incentives that address their needs, hopes and desires. Incentives can take the form of recognition and compensation, as at Hilton Reservations, or in flexible scheduling and time-off policies at Lands' End, or in aggressive monetary incentives as at RMH and Cox Communications (in a later case study). It is the wise manager who doesn't treat everyone alike and who takes the time to ensure that their "rainmakers"—their peak performance sales individuals—are very happy. Some top performers will not necessarily conform to the "one-size-fits-all" incentive and/or reward systems that work for most reps. We must look further to satisfy their particular needs; they really are special people!

Best Software's Susan Searle tells a great story about one of her top performers. This individual transferred into sales from technical support, and was in the second year of his contact center sales job. Thus far, he had sold $1.6 million in software a year. Considering the average sale for this company is about $325, you can see how truly remarkable a salesman he had become. One day he approached Searle in a hallway and asked her how the 401K benefits actually worked. This top salesman, and many others in the workplace, were afraid to participate because they thought it was all tied into the stock market, and they knew that the market had been down for the last three years. He also thought a 401K plan was just for retirement and couldn't imagine putting money away for retirement when he was saving to purchase his first home. Although the company conducted benefit sessions to explain how a 401K works, he commented that he and his colleague didn't attend because "it's like inviting someone who is deathly afraid of water to take swimming lessons."

Searle invited him into her office, and took the time to explain the benefits of a 401K program, especially given the company's matching percentage. She also explained how he could use it to fund a home. All he needed was one-on-one time with someone he knew and respected. He wanted to be treated as an individual, and he was afraid to ask what he thought were dumb questions in a large group.

Searle spends a lot of one-on-one time with her high performers. She realizes that high performers can go anywhere and get paid a lot. And when they get really good, they realize they can sell direct and make significantly more money. Although Searle acknowledges that there is a fine line between education and advice, she believes that one-on-one time with the top performers is extremely valuable in creating a loyalty connection with the company. In an era when most of us have kissed the thought of a loyal and caring company good-bye, there are those executives who will not give up on the "big connection." Thanks for reminding us, Susan.

Let me tell you about another executive who created a customer service bonus program that dramatically changed the lifestyles of many of her front-line staff. Georgia Eddleman, who has held executive call center positions in many industries, recalls a rebudgeting process she initiated at a former company to fund a service incentive program.

Initially, her budget for rewards consisted of allocating each supervisor $10 per month per employee to use as they saw fit in incenting the service staff. Some of the supervisors were creative and performance-oriented in their use of the money; others simply arranged a pizza party at the end of the month for their team. In addition, management gave away merchandise in contests and awarded plaques for achievements on a monthly basis. All of this consumed a lot of time and money, and attrition was still high at 30 percent (I know, some of you think this would be a good problem to have!). During exit interviews, typical comments surfaced, such as: "I am not going to stay with you just because I have a star on my desk."

At this point, Eddleman killed all the reward, contest and incentive programs. She challenged her management team to build a new incentive program from scratch. They developed new job descriptions, redefining and rerating the positions, and built an incentive system based upon the five performance indicators that they believed reps could control: accuracy, courtesy, schedule adherence, after-call work time and attendance. The management team believed that the key to their program's success would be aggressive goals, clarity, ownership and simplicity.

The team set up four bonus pay tier levels based on corresponding performance targets, with the following group percentages (allocated for the budgeting process only):

Level	What they receive	Target % Reps
Tier 1	Reps must improve in 90 days to keep their job	5%
Tier 2	5% of salary paid monthly	50%
Tier 3	10% of salary paid monthly	25%
Tier 4	20% of salary paid monthly	20%

The top tier had never been reached by anyone at any time in the history of the company. This would seem to fly in the face of one of our earlier tenets regarding goals: That the goal must be reasonable, and that one of the ways you can tell whether it is reasonable is if someone somewhere has already reached it. Although that performance goal-setting rationale is basically sound, Eddleman and her team exercised good judgment and overrode this principle based on their current base level of performance. Remember, every situation is different. They believed that significantly better performance was definitely reasonable, even though no one had actually accomplished the new top tier level.

When the management team rolled out the program, naturally, there was significant push back on the top tier level from the reps. The reps said it was impossible because it had never been done before. However, the first month's results proved them wrong—4 percent of the rep population achieved the performance targets and rewards of the top tier. Within six months, 20 percent of the rep population had stabilized in the top tier. In addition, attrition decreased from 30 percent per year to 12 percent. The attrition calculation counted all exits from the department and the company, voluntary and involuntary, unless it was an internal promotion.

After listening to their reps following the initial attrition reduction, the management team realized that many of the reps didn't have the capacity or the desire to be promoted through the management ranks, but they did want a career with the company. The company subsequently developed a senior CSR position. There were three criteria for the position: 1) a minimum tenure of two years, 2) achieving a top tier level for 12 consecutive months, and 3) passing a number of tests. Once reps fulfilled the criteria and became Senior CSRs, they received a 15 percent differential pay rate over and above their hourly rate and a 20 percent bonus. The management team was now truly controlling the attrition at the *very* top tier of performance.

Like the other incentive plans described in this section, this one truly changed the lifestyles of some of the reps at Eddleman's company. A 35 percent increase (20 percent bonus, plus 15 percent pay differential) in compensation, as well as attaining such high performance levels can give an individual a real shot of self-esteem. To illustrate the impact on employees' lives, Eddleman tells the story of Marcia. Marcia thought she was stuck in a dead-end job with no prospects for a better one elsewhere. She was a single parent with a young daughter, lived in an old trailer and drove a car that barely limped along. Her clothes were held together with safety pins, and she had low self-esteem. Marcia worked to improve her performance, and fulfilled the criteria for a higher-level position. Two years later, she was a senior CSR wearing a business suit and pulling into the parking lot in a new economy car. She lived in a nice apartment and took night classes in order to obtain her degree. Clearly it was not just a 35 percent increase in pay that created this transformation. It was also the pride in her position, her success at attaining the "unattainable performance" targets, and an inkling of hope for her future and that of her daughter. Incentive plans *can* change lifestyles and lives.

For those of you who have, unfortunately, found employees living out of their cars, or actually living *in* your centers and taking showers in the gym locker rooms, you know that your job is bigger than the bottom line. It is making a difference in people's lives.

Do Your Reps Really Understand How They Are Compensated?

So you have decided to make some major changes this year. You're beefing up your training and making major inroads in recruiting top talent from new and proven sources. You've made some major improvements in your incentive plan that will focus your staff on cross-selling a few high-margin ancillary products. You're ready to sit back and watch the sales pour in… or are you?

Although you may *think* you have all the right ingredients for success and have tweaked all the right components of your performance model, you have to make sure that you've really made a change that will work. An important sign that you're on the right road is whether your reps really understand how they will be compensated under the new plan.

Best Software's Susan Searle confides that her No. 1 indicator that she has *really* made a positive change in the compensation plan is to listen to hallway and break-room conversations—when reps are really being honest with each other. She offers the following comments from a rep, which she overheard in the break room: "I'm really nervous—I don't know if I'll make my 'add-on quota' for the new sales program. If I make three more of these sales, I'll hold my close ratio and make $100 more in my paycheck this month, which I'm going to use to buy my daughter's cheerleading uniform."

Searle noted that it was *only* at that point she could confirm that a change in behavior was going to take place in her center—because the rep had confirmed that she knew what she had to do differently in the short term, and that it would make some difference in her life. This is a great story because it illustrates that we must take the time to validate that our programs have been rolled out effectively. A program that is not understood or that is not perceived as different or that creates no change in behavior will not succeed.

Searle believes that a successful incentive program must meet three criteria: 1) It must be simple; 2) it must be consistent with other programs and policies; and 3) it must be repeatable. The first two are self-explanatory. The third implies that the incentive program can be explained accurately by one rep to another or by a rep to his or her spouse. If any program does not meet these three criteria, it will fail in execution and should not be approved.

To determine whether or not a new program has been accepted into the culture at large, Searle recommends that management staff put on a headset and do side-by-side monitoring. If done frequently enough, reps become accustomed to your presence, which will allow you to hear some honest discussion that would never have materialized from mere focus groups.

Incentives that Go Wrong

Just as a well-conceived and executed compensation plan can boost profits and morale, a poorly constructed plan can actually drive profits down. Georgia Eddleman recalls such an experience with a former company where she was a customer service executive. When she first joined the company, a shopping network, she met with all of the customer service reps in focus groups. From management reports and the focus groups, she found that customers frequently complained of call "hang-ups" in the inbound sales organization. The data indicated that first-time callers to the shopping network generated all of the complaints.

The order-entry leadership, who didn't realize that they were really in the sales business, had recently implemented an incentive in this group for calls handled per hour. First-time callers required a comparatively long interaction due to all of the customer information that had to be input into the computer. This critical first call generally lasted about 15 minutes, compared with the calls from existing customers which took 30 seconds. You can probably guess what was happening. Several of the reps were doing exactly what the plan incented them to do. They hung up on first-time customers. Through a few simple calculations (estimated number of customers lost x lifetime value of a customer), Eddleman was quickly able to demonstrate that this incentive program would cost the company a significant amount of revenue per year. Although Eddleman was running a service organization, she was able to dramatically affect company sales by listening to the customer through her reps and her data. Eddleman comments: "At a certain level in an organization, everyone is in sales."

The Three Biggest Mistakes in Building an Incentive Plan

According to Susan Searle, the three most common mistakes in designing compensation and incentive plans are: 1) indexing too many factors, 2) engineering a plan around the "sneaky dogs," and 3) failing to prepare HR. Many successful sales executives with whom I have spoken echo her views.

As discussed in Chapter 4, indexing and weighting many different factors never works. Searle also believes it defocuses and confuses reps. Before the rollout of any new program, Searle asks her staff to answer the three questions that make up the criteria for a successful program, which were mentioned earlier: Is it simple? Is it consistent? Can the rep correctly repeat it to a peer, friend or spouse?

Often, companies try to develop compensation and incentive plans that will eliminate cheating by the "sneaky dogs," or those who will always be out there trying to find holes in your plan. In trying to cover all the bases, companies end up with overly complicated and administratively burdensome plans, which break the rule of simplicity. I'm not saying that, where possible, you shouldn't establish incentives for the right ultimate outcome—e.g., net revenue production instead of gross revenue production—just don't go overboard trying to catch every possible way to abuse the program. A better way to foil the offenders is to conduct periodic audits. Former reps are the best at conducting these audits since they know most of the system holes and overly creative revenue techniques. Plus, the word will get out that unethical behavior will not be tolerated.

> **The three most common mistakes in designing compensation and incentive plans are: 1) indexing too many factors, 2) engineering a plan around the "sneaky dogs," and 3) failing to prepare HR.**

The third, most common mistake call centers can make in designing compensation and incentive plans is not getting sufficient buy-in from HR. Doing so will help you to teach the organization to be more emotionally resilient around the subject of compensation plans, according to Searle. Most organizations are reluctant to change their traditional plans. Why? It would require exceptional change management skills and considerable time, as well as the understanding that the competitive marketplace is very dynamic and new plans may be required more frequently to ensure that your company's market is being properly serviced. Additionally, the organization should be made to understand that if a plan is not working, it needs to be tweaked or replaced. Setting the expectations of your reps and the organization that the plan will remain in place only if it achieves the desired results will ensure that all parties will be better prepared to deal with any future changes that might be required.

"In the old days," Searle explains, "we would roll out a new incentive plan. A week later, I'd be contacted by HR, who were hearing from reps who were nervous about the new incentive plan. HR was obviously concerned that the employees were concerned.

"Today, we use a new technique. A week before the rollout, we walk HR through the actual incentive presentation, and ask for their input in crafting the language that we use. We also give them the top 10 questions we antic-ipate being asked, and the recommended responses. Not only does this approach ensure HR's buy-in to the process and outcomes, we get great input for the presentation and help in fielding the natural employee con-cerns that are inherent in any compensation change."

Recognition Is Always in Vogue

Earlier we discussed how the relationship bond that a rep has with his or her supervisor can positively or negatively affect employee retention and performance. One of the best ways a supervisor can positively influence that bond is through sincere recog-nition.

> "The greatest gift you can give another is the purity of your attention."
> —Richard Moss, M.D.

In fact, personalized and immediate recognition from an immediate supervisor is the most powerful performance motivator, according to Dr. Gerald H. Graham, professor of management at Wichita State University. In a study of more than 1,500 employees in a variety of work settings, Graham found that the type of recognition that employees wanted most—personal thanks for performance—was the type that they received the least.[ii] Another study conducted by Graham found that employees perceived that company-

TOP RECOGNITION INCENTIVES REPORTED BY EMPLOYEES	
Top motivating techniques by rank	% of Employees Receiving
1. Personal thanks	42%
2. Written Thanks	24%
3. Promotion for performance	22%
4. Public praise	19%
5. Morale-building meetings	8%
Source: Dr. Gerald Graham, Wichita State University, "The 1993 National Study of the Changing Workforce"	

sponsored recognition for "presence"—that is, for being present with the organization, such as length of service, attendance, etc.—was much more prevalent than supervisor- or manager-initiated rewards.

It's interesting that the least costly, most desired and most productive types of recognition are the ones least used in most companies. Recognition and incentives experts agree that the best way to praise an employee for performance is to follow five key steps: Do it quickly, sincerely, specifically, personally and positively. Share these steps and research with your management staff, and see what actions ensue.

Adopt Great Recognition Ideas from Other Companies

I once worked with a travel company that really believed in recognition. At that time, when the travel business and the airlines were relatively healthy, the company had the opportunity to reward their top travel advisors in a unique way: The top 10 percent of their sales staff and their spouses or significant others got to spend a week in Hawaii with the senior staff and president of the division. While this may be "over the top" and beyond the budgets for most of us, what the staff appreciated most was the recognition in front of their peers and, more importantly, in front of the person they held dearest—their spouse. Additionally, the company recognized the spouses for their support in making a great travel advisor great, such as putting up with late work nights, handling the stress when the work environment infiltrated the home, and providing backup and other support so advisors could be there every day for their customers. Besides being able to recognize and appreciate sales staff and their spouses, the informal setting

---

HILTON'S PERFORMANCE RECOGNITION PROGRAM

In addition to its monetary incentive program (see page 197), Hilton's management team has devised a very rich formal recognition program for top performers using many of the recognition components advocated by experts. Although, initially, the center's "Commitment to Excellence" program may sound like one that you have previously put in place, read carefully—there are big differences that really matter.

The winners of this quarterly award typically represent the top 10 to 12 percent of the rep population. Reps must place in the top 30 percent of productivity and meet high minimum standards in four categories: close ratio, attendance, adherence and availability. Those who achieve all these measures receive the following:

- A day off with pay
- $250 (grossed up to cover taxes)
- A "Commitment to Excellence" T-shirt
- First pick at the next quarterly shift bid
- Balloon notification on the floor of their selection
- Invitation to a quarterly, upscale awards dinner with their spouse

Hilton's Tim Cook notes that the winners are seen as a very exclusive and competitive group, and once in, no one wants to slip out. In fact, one individual has won 16 quarters in a row. Reps who win all four quarters in a year receive $400 grossed-up cash in addition to the quarterly award.

Trophies are also awarded to individuals who attain the top results (for the top producer and most improved) in each of the five categories. A rotating trophy goes to the top team for the quarter. In addition, two large crystal cups (based on the Stanley Cup) also rotate among the offices—one is awarded for the highest close ratio over the goal; the other for quality.

allowed senior management to spend quality one-on-one time with the advisors to solicit and hear valuable suggestions from the "best of the best." Rarely does anyone in senior management get to spend enough quality time with their best staff. This company found its own way.

It is always interesting to look beyond one's own environment to find interesting solutions. Several years ago, I was at a Chef's Catalogue warehouse sale. Chef's Catalogue is a place that sells upscale cooking equipment to chef "wannabes" like myself, and is owned by Neiman Marcus (although recently purchased by Pikes Peak Direct Marketing Inc.). Their warehouses stood side by side in a Dallas warehouse district. I was standing in a very long line on this particular morning, waiting to get into the sale, when I observed the magic of service recognition at work. Several items on Neiman Marcus' warehouse walls caught my attention—in fact, they caught my eye because they were so large. There were blown-up, poster-sized customer compliment letters hanging on the walls. They were in their original form, some handwritten, some on corporate letterhead stationary, some even contained misspellings. These were real people who wanted to thank a Neiman Marcus employee for going the extra mile. Thousands of other people saw those letters that day, but more importantly, the employees who received the letters were memorialized on their informal "wall of fame."

I love great ideas wherever they come from, and I wasn't the least bit ashamed to steal this one. I had some of our customer letters blown up and hung on our center's walls. It cost $50 to do this at a local print shop, but I can't begin to describe the pride expressed by our employees, their management and their departments to see these letters framed and hanging on the walls.

I noticed in the lobby of another company I visited, large poster-sized black-and-white pictures of their top performers who recently had been awarded "Employee of the Quarter." I liked their idea, and decided to improve upon it for my center. We hired a professional photographer (someone who was working nights in our call center) to produce similar photos of our top 10 percent performers. We encouraged them to go with the photographer anywhere they chose, within 10 minutes of the center. The photographer took a picture of each top sales rep with a prop, or doing something that represented who they were individually. We recognized that our staff had another life outside of the call center. They were husbands, wives, mothers, sisters, artists, photographers and athletes first, and employees second. Oftentimes, it's who they are outside of the call center that helps to make them successful at work. We displayed the poster-sized photos of reps with their children, a racing bike, a collection of 300 Beanie Babies, on a Harley, holding a Tiffany's shopping bag, painting... anything they chose that represented who they were as individuals.

Within several weeks, there were 100 framed photos hanging all over the building. We received more positive comments on that recognition program from employees, spouses, new-hire candidates and other departments than all of our of other programs combined. The cost for that project was $8,000—it was definitely worth every cent.

Create Contests that Drive Focus

Although contests play an important role in improving call center performance, they're not a long-term solution. They are not a substitute for truly meaningful, long-term incentives. Contests can make life in the call center more fun; they can highlight and create temporary focus to reach a goal; they can help to launch a new product or move distressed inventory; or they can help to find solutions to problems. Contests should be thought of as a traditional "sales blitz."

I previously worked for a cable television company whose suppliers—HBO, Showtime, Disney and the other channel providers—were most generous in supplying valuable prizes to our reps for selling their products. They offered items with logos, trips to Australia, large Disney dolls and sometimes cash. Another company with whom I worked offered a car or truck as a quarterly prize for sales. Still others are well-known in the industry for offering a plethora of contest prizes, including "lunch with the president," paid time off or even roulette games with theme-based prizes. At most companies, senior leaders and marketing managers usually guess that the expensive trips and prizes are the most effective at driving top performance in a sales blitz.

I disagree. In my experience, the most effective contests have been the ones with high visibility and less expensive prizes. They featured prizes like balloons, lottery tickets, management dunking pools, management car washes, company logo items and food. Never underestimate the pride that call center employees, and really, all employees, have in their company's local, national or global brand. I've seen reps go to incredible lengths to win a jacket with a logo or something deemed "rare" in the company's culture. Use your brand proudly.

It takes a lot of work to create an effective low-cost contest that actually drives the right numbers without endangering other metrics—but this is the fun part of call center management! I worked with a company once that had numerous large call centers. Instead of always standardizing and rolling out contests from corporate, we allowed the local sites the autonomy of creating, designing and implementing their own contests. We also continued to roll out a few corporate-inspired contests to create some competition among centers, and which also inspired a lot of geographic pride.

We gave the centers contest *guidelines* developed from ideas culled from the best call center managers with peak-performing sales centers (see the box on page 212). We asked the centers to work within those boundaries and a set budget. Later, we solicited the best contest ideas to create a toolbox for each center. We called this tool, which was based on a recipe box, "Recognition in a Box." Each box was filled with all of the recipe ideas for recognition, rewards and contests that we could think of, and included plenty of blank "recipe cards" for new ideas. We included in the recipe kit a commercially produced book with 1,001 ideas for creating a fun environment. It was a huge hit.

A Few Words of Caution about Contests

Contests can have a powerful influence and, therefore, should only be used to drive performance and the KPI. Some call centers have used contests to try to improve their attendance levels. I don't recommend it. Although attendance entails costs that must be managed, it is not a KPI. Instead, use minimum standards as a way to keep attendance on track. Having said that, there's no harm in, say, announcing the results of a KPI contest on a Tuesday following a three-day holiday, and requiring that the winner be present to collect his or her prize. I used this strategy to get

---

15 GUIDING PRINCIPLES FOR CONTESTS

1. Build contests that end on a logical reporting period.

2. Use contests only to drive a KPI or performance driver.

3. Develop contests in which people other than top producers can win (e.g., include a "most improved" category).

4. Do not use attendance as a contest goal for which one receives a prize.

5. Creativity and fun should win out over costly prizes. Instead, put the money into incentives that change lifestyles.

6. Audit, audit and audit.

7. Do not build long-term contests (longer than one quarter).

8. Do not create contests that feature "frequent-flyer" points.

9. Frequently change the contests, the goals and how you win.

10. Take some time off between contests, even if for only a week.

11. The more visual, the better.

12. Involve your senior management, president or chairman.

13. Create a contest calendar. Plan out the year, delegating contest construction to strong supervisors (those who complete their coaching).

14. Ensure that your accounting office makes provisions for payroll taxes for anything of high value. Check with your accounting office for their official guidelines.

15. Check with HR to ensure that "imaginative" prizes do not create legal liabilities.

everyone to show up on a day that was our busiest and when we traditionally had poor attendance, and it worked. In general, attendance problems are minimized when you have a peak-performing call center. Your reps understand how important every individual is to the center, and how hard their coworkers must work in their absence. Sometimes you just need to "connect the dots" for some individuals and let them know how their attendance affects everyone else.

Generally, it's best to minimize the amount of administration involved in running a contest. This is why I advise against developing contests or incentives based on frequent-flyer points. The frequent-flyer type award scheme was first introduced by an airline company to reward its most loyal customers with free flights by utilizing unused seat inventory. The competition thought this was a good idea and matched them. Then the innovating airline upped the ante and began offering trip packages and merchandise. Soon a department and an entire administrative industry was developed to support a program originally designed to inexpensively reward loyalty. I spoke with one director whose call centers have a manager and two coordinators just to administer their sales employee points program.

Many companies like the idea of customized programs that offer merchandise that their employees can select from a catalogue. Theoretically, they are allowing their employees to choose how they want to be recognized and rewarded. In addition to being administratively burdensome and costly, these programs presume that the employee wants or needs "things," when they may need to make a car payment or to buy food.

Lengthy, complicated contests consume a lot of management time, and reps just lose interest. The longer the contest, the more those winners who always win will pull out ahead. Instead, I recommend short, frequent contests. Use creative statistics or drawings in which anyone who improves substantially or hits a new higher standard either wins or gets put into the drawing to win.

Providing Incentives for Management

In addition to frontline contests and incentives, provide your sales managers and supervisors with a sales incentive that is paid quarterly or on the shift bid cycle. Since high and low performers may change teams or even desks on a shift bid cycle, the incentive period for management should be closed out at that time. Tie management goals to targets set against the KPI performance levels of their reps. For example, let's say a supervisor or manager has a team with an average NRPH of $550, the center average for that skill set on that shift is $650, and there is not a significant difference in the number of new employees. He or she might set an incentive payout of 5 percent of quarterly salary if the team reaches an average of $600 per hour, 10 percent of their quarterly salary if the team hits $650 or the current center average, and 20 percent of their quarterly salary if the team exceeds a $750 stretch goal. This is only one of many ways the payout might work. An alternative might be to pay out on a small percentage of actual revenue improvement. The amount to pay out depends, among many other factors, upon the profit potential of an individual sale, as well as the span of control of the supervisor or manager. It's best to consult an incentive specialist when determining the amount of payout and the ranges for your supervisors and managers.

Essentially, management's ante to get into the incentive game should be the QA team's quality rating of their sales reps. If the group's overall quality fails to meet the minimum quality standards, the manager should not receive a payout. If one out of 20 reps fails to meet the minimum quality levels, it is not a problem; if five out of 20 reps fail, it's another matter.

Since your goal is much higher performance than in the past, your management should share in the increased profits. This helps to create a self-sustaining peak performance environment.

Points to Remember

- Recognition is critically important, but it is not a trade-off for proper compensation for a sales rep's excellent contributions.

- Recognize improved performers as well as top performers.
- Supervisors should praise their reps personally and often.
- Incent with money, not points-based reward systems or just contests.
- Money incentives let reps choose a different long-term lifestyle.
- Use contests for sales blitzes or to create focus. Establish minimum quality levels as the ante to get into the incentive game.
- Make sure your incentives are big enough to matter.
- Pay out to only the top 80 to 85 percent of performers.
- Leverage the payout dollars on the top 20 percent of performers.
- Keep the incentive program simple: Can reps explain it accurately to their friends or spouses?
- Hire incentive consultants who can build a program using standard deviation process control tools to ensure that you only pay on improvements or sustainable high performance.

Chapter 12: New Processes, Tools and Technologies

"Make the complex simple. Make the simple work."
I.M. PEI, INTERNATIONAL ARCHITECT

There's a well-known management adage that says, "What gets measured, gets done." So most call center organizations measure everything they can because it's fairly easy to do. Unfortunately, when it comes to sales, we don't always measure the right things. Chapter 4 discussed the importance of correlation analysis to address this problem.

Once your organization selects its sales KPI and the most important supporting performance drivers, the most critical tool to be developed is a performance database. One problem for many of us is that none of our databases talk to each other. There's a lot of data strewn about, but not much actionable information.

Our new sales KPI—net revenue per phone hour—is typically a derivative of data resident in the databases of several systems. Generally, the performance drivers for the sales KPI can be found within a second set of databases. This makes getting the right data in the right formats time-consuming for supervisors, who must spend much of their time pulling reports and extracting the key information to determine how reps perform against their skill and shift group. Many centers do this work manually. This is definitely not a good use of management's time, which is better spent putting real-time performance information into action via coaching.

At one call center where I worked, my management team and a contractor, on a very limited budget, constructed a performance management database comprised of relevant data extracts from the following systems: administration, HR, payroll, quality assurance and workforce management. It resided in an Oracle database on a server with Crystal reports that we converted into HTML files. We used what we had. It worked, but the reps didn't have direct access to the reports without going through a supervisor. The total cost of the database came to approximately $75,000. If we had had extra money that year, we would have bought the licenses to bring the data to the reps' desktops.

An Integrated Performance Data Mart Is Critical

An integrated performance management database, or a data mart, is a critical analytic tool that doesn't exist in most call centers. Whether you build your database from scratch, patch one together as we initially did, or buy, integrate and customize a new off-the-shelf package will depend on your financial situation and your company's buy vs. build philosophy. What's important is that you acquire a performance database quickly.

The cost to build or buy is not inconsequential. If you build it from scratch, it will cost approximately $150,000 for a contract programmer or an in-house developer. Add another $100,000 if you want a GUI (graphical user interface) front end, and slightly more if you want to give your reps access to reports from their desktops.

You'll also need to budget approximately $25,000 per year for software support, plus additional funds for the upgrades and improvements that you'll inevitably want. In addition, be sure to budget for one or two servers and the cost of their support. Also, ensure that you have a system to back up the data on a daily basis. Remember, you'll be paying incentives from this database—it would be a disaster if the data got lost.

The biggest cost will be management labor, as you determine the necessary reports, formats and roll-ups. Retention, print, backup, security and access issues must also be addressed.

Typically, the current standalone databases that should be integrated into your data mart are:

- Payroll
- ACD
- Workforce management
- Host computer system(s), POS or CRM system
- HR and/or administrative system
- Quality database

All of these must be integrated into one database, or the data should be able to be extracted to a reporting tool (e.g., Crystal reports) in order to automate the incentive payout and quickly access online performance reports. If your HR or administrative systems do not include the following information, it will need to be manually keyed: team or desk standards, team or desk call-types, hire date and source information, training information and leave-of-absence information.

Formal user requirements must be documented and screen/report formats identified for discussion with the programmer. Following are a few considerations for developing your user requirements:

- Reps must be able to access their individual performance statistics from prior days and compare them with the average for reps on similar shifts. They should be able to view their standing by quartile at any point in time, and have access to these statistics from their desktops or a designated desktop in the center.

- Decide whether or not reps should be able to view other reps' individual statistics. However, supervisors and management should have access to those statistics.

- Supervisors and managers should be able to export all statistics to another program (e.g., Excel or Access). This allows the supervisors and reps to conduct "what-if" analysis by moving performance drivers and incentive outcomes.
- Report-tracking statistics should be available upon request, allowing supervisors/managers to view the date and frequency with which online management reports are accessed and by whom.
- Historical tracking of all statistics should be provided, both on a team level (supervisory relationship) and a desk level (call-type relationship).
- Trend graphs for all statistics at all roll-up levels should be available on demand.
- Fraud detection alarms should be provided to highlight suspicious data.
- The estimated incentive payout should be projected daily based on quality assumptions and current trending of the performance drivers.
- You should be able to create analytic reports that allow drill-down analysis from the KPI and the performance drivers.

Hiring a programmer analyst with prior experience in creating a performance management database in call centers will speed up the process and help to reduce costs. There are a number of programmers and analysts on the market who create general performance databases, but as we all know, the call center is a unique beast. Someone experienced in call center statistics will recognize, for example, the importance of retaining both team- and desk-level statistics from an historical perspective, insofar as shift bids create confusion in data performance statistics.

Nearly all of the best-of-breed sales centers with whom I spoke had an integrated performance database, most of which were developed using the companies' own resources or contractors. Perhaps the reason for this was that they were developed before 1998, when commercial products became available, or that the company wanted more control, or that there were cost issues involved.

Tools in Today's Marketplace

The cost estimates mentioned on page 218 are for the performance database and reporting system only. Off-the-shelf programs provide additional performance management functionality. You will have to evaluate whether this added functionality is worth the extra cost for your operation.

The best-known, off-the-shelf call center performance management software packages—usually sold as part of a "performance optimization" suite of products—come from Blue Pumpkin, Envision, etalk, Nice, Performix and Witness, among others.

I prefer Performix's award-winning *Emvolve Performance Manager* tool because of its logical hierarchy design, data integration, performance analytics, performance development tools and user-friendly GUI interfaces. (Performix was originally developed by an outsourcing company located in Ireland to address their own performance management processes.) Emvolve integrates the data from the call center systems previously outlined, then breaks down business objectives into KPIs, and then into individual performance targets for reps. Aligning high-level business objectives with individual targets "connects the dots" and shows reps how their performance contributes to the overall company goals and health. It paints a numeric picture.

The product has six core software modules:

1. Performance Review
2. Appraisal Manager
3. Personal Development Plans
4. Reward and Recognition
5. Reports Manager
6. Key Performance Manager

Emvolve is targeted toward mid-sized to large call centers. Its Reports Manager module has reporting roll-ups that provide a centralized view of individuals, supervisory teams, multiple teams, skills, departments and centers—and it's scalable to 10,000 reps. The vendor touts a payback of less than six months for its product, and resource requirements of six man-weeks for implementation. These numbers are reasonable, if all of the performance management correlation analysis and sound KPI decisions have been made prior to the system implementation. (For more product information, visit Performix's Web site at www.performixtechnologies.com.)

Off-the-shelf packages generally cost significantly more than an internally developed performance analysis and reporting package only, although most providers have published business cases which "prove" that buying the software is less expensive than developing it internally. That may be true if you desire all the "bells and whistles" of their systems. Many companies will never build a system or develop one themselves if something is available from a third party—it's simply part of their management practice. You'll have to do the research and the financial analysis to determine the best solution for you.

The benefits of purchasing an off-the-shelf package are, of course, time and convenience. The previously mentioned vendors have all gone through the painful creation of requirements, software development and testing. They have addressed hierarchy, format and access issues. Having said that, you'll want to review the product's features and business rules to determine if the decisions the vendors have made for their products are right for your organization. If they're not, consider customized alternatives—but keep in mind, you'll still have to do all of the analytic work, such as choosing the right KPI, doing the regression analysis to set the supporting performance drivers, as well as creating new incentive, recruiting, coaching and training programs.

One important concern regarding off-the-shelf performance analysis software is that the companies offering these solutions have focused on driving performance optimization from a cost and quality standpoint; none of them appear very experienced in driving sales or understanding sales performance drivers and improvement analysis. While their systems could probably be designed to manage sales performance, they currently don't exhibit a wealth of sales performance management experience.

HILTON'S ROBUST PERFORMANCE MANAGEMENT SYSTEM EMPOWERS STAFF

Hilton Reservations recently built and copyrighted its own performance management system. All 1,300 reps, as well as 100 management and support-type personnel, can access the system directly from their desktops. This is critical, as power comes from knowledge.

In the first three months, 249,000 online performance reports were run, mostly by reps, who felt empowered and in control of their performance. There were no surprises at their monthly performance review sessions. They knew exactly where they stood at all times.

Hilton has also designed a performance database that is integrated into an employee information system, which they call Connect. All reps can access Connect from their desktops and can review their performance on a daily basis. They can view all of their phone and reservations performance statistics, the amount of sick leave taken, paid time off available, and all of their employee information. A projection of each rep's incentive, based on his or her current pacing, is also provided. All data is updated nightly and is available in numerical format as well as in bar or line graph format so that reps and their leaders can easily spot trends in their performance.

Once all the tools and feedback mechanisms are in place, administration of this amount of feedback becomes manageable. While gathering the individual and team statistics used to take each Hilton supervisor three hours a day, with the performance database it now takes only minutes. In addition, feedback checklists by performance driver make monitoring feedback a snap. An automated feedback form creates monthly, quarterly or annual evaluations in minutes—no more working on evaluations at home all night for Hilton supervisors.

Using CRM to Drive Sales Performance

Although this is not a book on customer relationship management (CRM), we must discuss its potential for driving a call center's sales performance. CRM can be a formidable tool when properly implemented. Defining it is always a challenge, so I'll borrow a passage from *ICMI's Call Center Management Dictionary:*

"CRM is the process of holistically developing the customer's relationship with the organization. It takes into account their history as a customer, the depth and breadth of their business with the organization, as well as other factors. CRM generally uses sophisticated applications and database systems that include elements of data mining, contact management and enterprise resource planning—enabling agents (reps) and analysts to know and anticipate customer behavior."

Commonly misunderstood as a database and a large suite of software applications, CRM can be more correctly thought of as the sum of all customer strategy in its detailed, executable form, including processes, information, business rules of all parties, and an understanding of which customer segments will be serviced and the manner and level of personalization they require.

Since CRM came into vogue over the last 10 years, the technology associated with it has received somewhat of a black eye. There have been too many poorly sponsored or overly ambitious CRM software implementations. Many of us have heard the horror stories about some Fortune 500 companies' forays into CRM—installations costing twice the projected cost, taking twice as long to implement and executive sponsors not lasting through the rollout. However, there have been some notable successes, as well, primarily in the pharmaceutical, telecom, high-tech and banking industries.

Even if you have not implemented a CRM suite of applications and a common customer database, your organization probably has elements of CRM applications, such as a proprietary customer interaction system and customer transaction history. If you are in a large business-to-consumer enterprise, your business would be too large and complex to manage without some form of CRM, although it may not be one of the current popular application suites.

The question is, "What else do you need to successfully drive sales in your contact center?" Almost all of the best-of-breed sales call centers that I've interviewed have a CRM strategy and have installed a number of additional modules of systems with CRM functionality. These systems are either of a proprietary, home-grown variety, or an ERP version that ties in with Oracle, SAP or Peoplesoft (Vantive), or a CRM-focused suite like Siebel, or something from one of the CRM niche players like Epiphany.

J. Bruce Daley is founder and executive editor of *The Siebel Observer*, a magazine dedicated to CRM practice and focused on the market leader Siebel System (although the magazine is independent of the software firm). Having led or participated in 13 different CRM implementations, Daley believes that the greatest ROI from CRM projects come from those anchored by call centers.

But as great as the potential is for driving ROI, so is the complexity of a CRM system. For instance, Siebel has 120 different software application modules. Not all are important to your business, and not every call center module is important in driving sales in the call center. How do you know what you need? To drive sales in a contact center, Daley suggests focusing on the following six areas of functionality:

- Customer contact management
- Scheduling of follow-up and call-backs
- Interface with the phone switch to manage personalized phone routing
- Customer history tracking
- Marketing analytics for campaign management
- Upsell and cross-sell applications

Note: Most application suites touted as CRM have these six areas built in.

If CRM is something you think you might need to drive sales, by all means explore it, but know that it should be at the bottom of your project priority list if you're looking for an immediate payback. According to Daley, it isn't unusual for a large CRM implementation to take over a year or two to complete, with the real benefits not appearing until after five years. And if you've ever lived through a major system change or implementation, you know that it's also difficult to focus on anything else. However, Daley adds, "Once implemented, contact center agents can't imagine how they lived without it."

There are exceptions, of course, to the dismal view on the timing of CRM benefits. Daley indicates that it is misleading to look to a finite ROI benchmark for any one CRM application module. He cites an example of a well-known global consumer product manufacturer with each individual inbound phone rep selling $1 million in product per day to wholesalers. "When you're selling that amount, the ROI for the right CRM applications can be amazing."

That is, *if* it is implemented properly, which is not often the case, according to Daley. He points to the following three biggest mistakes companies make when implementing CRM:

- Poor executive sponsorship
- CRM decisions not aligned with company goals
- Too much customization

In Daley's opinion, the company's processes need to change to match the CRM workflow, as they often represent the industry best practice. Also, too much customization of the software creates ongoing cost problems when the vendor issues new releases. This is especially true now that there is a strong trend in CRM toward creating industry vertical applications.

As you're making your list of which sales performance management strategies to focus on over the next two years, you may need to make a choice. You cannot embark upon a CRM project at the same time as implementing a variety of other initiatives, such as creating a performance database, revamping coaching processes, searching for and implementing a predictive hiring assessment tool, and creating new incentive plans. My suggestion to most call center professionals is that the low-hanging fruit of the latter initiatives should easily win out over CRM. However, if you are further along in your journey to peak sales performance, then some applications of CRM should be on your radar screen.

LANDS' END GETS CLOSE TO ITS CUSTOMERS

Lands' End uses a home-grown CRM system with cross-sell recommendations developed by its vendors, as well as the merchants, who know best how to accessorize their products to add more value for the customer. According to COO and Co-President Dennis Honan, customer information and extensive affinity analysis in the CRM system allows CSRs to see the customer's purchase history. It screen-pops recommendations to go with current and previous purchases, making the CSR sound very knowledgeable. Like a friend, they know what is in their customer's closet.

Quick-Wins on the Path to Peak Sales

Speaking of low-hanging fruit, there are a number of quick-wins that you'll find on your journey to peak performance. The following technologies and processes can enhance your department's credibility and support your proposal for the additional resources required for peak performance:

Skills-based routing. An easy way to immediately improve your revenue and sales ratios is to put your best sales people in a sales queue. It's surprising how many organizations still lump sales and service together. While many organizations separate call-types through prompting, some do so only to reduce the complexity and the error rate; they still fail to put their best sales people in a sales queue to drive more revenue. Sometimes it's because they don't really know who their best sales people are, they don't have the right sales KPI, or because they want everyone to have a chance at lucrative incentives.

Supervisors always present this classic dilemma to management: "How can the service reps get better at sales if we don't give them sales calls?" It's easy. In all prompting situations, there are a significant number of customers who dislike the prompting systems or who simply don't listen. In my experience, no matter how you reword the prompts for clarity, at least 20 percent of customers will select the wrong prompts. Don't worry, the service reps will still get these sales calls. However, the calls with the most sales potential need to go to the sales reps with the competencies and personality traits most conducive to sales. The airlines came to this conclusion years ago, and those that were the first to adopt skills-based routing showed incredible growth in reservations sales.

If you run a very small center, and separating sales and service causes a service level problem, create a slightly smaller service queue and overflow calls to the sales skill, instead of the other way around. Someone with the correct sales mindset (doing what is right for the customer) must first be good at service. The reverse does not work.

Regrets reporting. One technique that I used in a hotel reservations center to increase revenue and reduce service-related calls was to have reports automated from the host systems to report the number of times (percentages) that individual room type or product type requests were turned down due to lack of availability. General managers, revenue managers and product managers could then view the unfulfilled demand and readjust pricing, or get more product. These reports were automatically generated based on computer queries on products to sales (non-close ratios) that were trended over time.

New revenue-focused positions. In peak-performing organizations, we usually find one or two project managers with a title like "Call Center Revenue Manager" who is dedicated to rooting out sales performance issues within the department and between other departments. These managers perform root-cause analysis and manage the resulting projects to remedy the problem. When coaches and/or supervisors attempt to fill this role, their focus on the sales reps and on the revenue projects is usually lost. In addition, the skill sets required for each position are very different.

Test kitchens. This is a part of your call center where you can try a lot of new ideas, one at a time. Each test should be separately constructed, utilizing a control group within the same center and call-type group for 30 consecutive days. Assign a test kitchen to an analytic sales manager. Test kitchens are not pilots that are constructed prior to a large program rollout; they are attempts to validate prevalent hypotheses on performance improvement opportunities. Examples might include dialogue changes, new close tools, and new policies and procedures that might increase sales.

Pay by sign-on. One way to immediately increase productivity—and to create self-managed reps—is to create a policy whereby reps are paid based on ACD sign-on. You can automate this all the way through your workforce management system into the payroll system.

Typical productivity gains can be as high as 5 percent. If reasonable, eliminate after-call work or alternate "unavailable" ACD states so that reps cannot "hide" in these work states. Require reps to completely sign-off whenever they are not at their positions taking calls. If they need an extra smoke break or restroom break, or if they are slightly late, don't make a big deal about it, but don't pay them for this time off.

Instituting such a policy can require a great deal of leadership initially—some supervisors and HR people may even think it's illegal. When I've opened new centers with this policy, the reps are rarely concerned with the policy; it's simply seen as a standard operating procedure. In existing call centers, implementing it as a new policy is more difficult, but strong leadership skills can overcome the change-management obstacles. After

> **Tip:** Implementing a pay by sign-on policy at the same time as increasing an incentive program or implementing another positive change makes the new policy more palatable.

I "borrowed" (unashamedly stole) this innovation from a colleague, I shared this secret over the years with many other centers, all of which have implemented it with success.

Create products and promotions for customer "sweet spots." Partner with marketing to create products and promotions that are conducive to the frequent selling opportunities that your reps encounter on service calls. There are natural "sweet spots" that occur when a certain call-type (e.g., change of address or name) aligns with a certain customer-type (e.g., basic service customer with good credit). These are service calls that reps don't have to work hard to sell when they are armed with the right product and promotion.

Informal call-typing is not a natural thought process for many reps, so they must be trained to think about a call as a combination of customer-type and call-type. Once they get used to thinking this way, they begin to recognize "sweet spots" or "golden combinations." For example, a newly married woman who has just gained three teenage stepsons calls her cable television provider to change her name and/or address (call-type). She has no premium cable TV packages (a customer-type). It's a golden combination—there is a higher probability she will purchase a sports channel package. The rep should recognize the call- and customer-type, and know the best product to offer after servicing the account.

While some call-types and customer-types are conducive to sales, others are not. For instance, one call-type that a rep should not try to upsell would be a billing inquiry that turns out to be a complaint about a rate increase. A customer whose account is severely past due is an example of a customer-type one would not want to upsell or cross-sell. Creating a "call-type matrix,"

CREATE PROMOTIONS AND TRAIN OFFERS FOR THE "SWEET SPOTS"
Customer-Types

Call-Types	Product Sweet Spot		
		Product Sweet Spot	

like the one on page 230, can help reps to successfully identify and sell to customers who have service issues.

Points to Remember

• Develop an integrated performance database available to all reps and supervisors at their desktop.

• Prioritize CRM initiatives appropriately based on ROI and organizational readiness.

• Implement technologies and processes to ensure some "quick-wins" on your journey. It will enhance your department's credibility, and support your proposal for additional resources.

Section 4: Staying on the Path

Chapter 13: Execution: Organizing and Tracking Projects

"A great many people think they are thinking when they are merely rearranging their prejudices."
WILLIAM JAMES, AMERICAN PSYCHOLOGIST AND PHILOSOPHER

Project management is a process—and a unique set of skills—that allows you to manage the development and implementation of your initiative. The methodology addresses cost control, schedule and scope management, and ensures the best chance of delivering the business results projected in the business case.

How complex or comprehensive you want to make project management is entirely up to you. If your company doesn't use a project management approach to non-technical initiatives, you can use the processes outlined in any introductory project management book. For additional assistance, basic forms are included in the appendix of this book that you can tailor to fit your call center.

Keeping project management simple for those not formally trained in this discipline is critical to the team's buy-in. It's imperative that you have a plan, a budget and a way to track the implementation and success metrics. Your commitment is to deliver on your promise to your staff, to your company and to yourself.

Project management will give you the best chance at success when making changes in an organization that already has a lot of moving parts, but you also need to make sure you can back out of a change that isn't working, or regroup, if necessary.

Organize the Peak Performance Program into Projects

Organizing the changes necessary to achieve peak performance is more manageable if it's structured as a series of sequenced projects, utilizing project management methodologies. The sum of all authorized projects constitute the Peak Sales Performance Program. Each project should have team members and a project manager who reports to a program manager, as well as an executive sponsor. The program manager and the executive sponsor may be the same individual, if you work in a small to medium-size organization. Your project management team will define the common project management tools, templates and communication timetables and distribution lists that the project team will use.

It's easy for a detailed and organized person to go overboard on project management methodology and forms. For the sake of your team, do not make this common mistake. Your staff could easily be overwhelmed with what they consider to be bureaucracy. You want the depth of project management rigor to match the level of complexity, risk and benefits that are at stake.

All project managers should store their data on a common server. Project agreements, project plans and risk assessments are some of the tools that will be used. Beginning on page 273 (in the appendix), you will find numerous project forms (see the list on the facing page) that have been simplified for non-technical process projects, such as those that you'll be managing. A project plan document is not included—it's a form that resides in Microsoft Project, Microsoft Schedule or any other good project software.

Additionally, there is no work breakdown structure form *per se*, since it is a critical process best learned in a project management class using a real example from an upcoming project. Suffice it to say that work breakdown is similar to using a fishbone diagram in root-cause analysis—it will assist you in defining all of the tasks necessary to create the deliverables that define the project. A work breakdown structure (WBS) example is also provided in the appendix of this book.

Minimum project management tools for sales performance program management include:

- Common server
- Project binder
- Common project plan software (e.g., MS Project, MS Schedule)
- Project agreement form*
- Project plan
- Risk assessment and mitigation plan form*
- Project updates or status report form*
- Project communication plan form*
- Project organization chart and team roster
- Project issue log*
- Project change requests form*
- Project work breakdown structure*

Forms included in appendix

The Project Management Organization

You'll need to assign project managers who will be responsible for the process transformations. Do not assign supervisors to this role—their primary focus should be inspiring, monitoring and coaching reps. Nothing should distract them from this task; however, they can sit in on a team or two as subject-matter experts, provided that it takes little time (less than two hours a week). Some project managers or team members will come from outside your department or functional area; for instance, a marketing project manager for dialogue changes, and an HR manager for the recruiting and selection process. Other departments from which you may need to draw project participants include operations, revenue management and finance.

A director or vice president of the major functional area should be the program sponsor. Each of the project managers will report to the program sponsor for the length of their projects. Understandably, this matrix management may create some political problems, but most problems can easily be anticipated and avoided if the sponsor first meets with relevant department heads, walks them through the program overview and the ROI, and receives permission to use their employees in a matrix environment. Although many companies frequently use this methodology, if it's new to you, you might want to ask your boss or HR expert for advice on how to navigate through the politics. Eventually, an organizational chart for the program and related projects should be created.

Keep in mind that not all project participants—particularly those outside of the call center—will be fully trained in project management, nor will they all understand the impact that their actions will have on the call center. Make sure that, as the executive or manager in charge of the call center, you have final approval on all decisions that will change anything in your organization.

Teach project participants from outside the call center the impact that key metrics will have on the center. For instance, one second of centerwide AHT is worth $220,000 per annum (or whatever your number is) in terms of variable costs (telecom + rep and supervisor salaries + cost per facility seat); that the direct cost of one rep lost to attrition is between $5,000 and $7,000; that the average low-performing rep can cost $240,000/year in lost profit; and that one point of real close ratio improvement is worth $10 million to the bottom line, and so on.

A note on getting other departments involved in your program and projects: Be prepared for a clash of cultures when you integrate teams that have not spent a lot of time together. While each company has its own unique culture, individual departments often have their own versions of that culture. It's like a group of people speaking English in various regional dialects or accents. Sometimes we don't understand each other despite sharing a common language. This is especially true of the call center's relationship to other departments within the enterprise since many centers are geographically dispersed from their "mother ships" (the corporate offices).

There may be rocky roads, but the project team members will also develop lasting friendships and the participants will gain new respect for each others' jobs.

"I don't know how it started, either. All I know is that it's part of our corporate culture."

New Management Skills Will Be Required

Trust me when I tell you that changes of this magnitude will require new skills for your staff and perhaps for yourself. I recommend that the following management training be done on a group basis, with the entire project management team in attendance:

- Meeting management and facilitation
- Process redesign

> **TIP: This training should not be conducted individually nor via the Internet. Use real-life examples of the changes you are going to implement to provide the greatest insight and learning experience.**

- Change management
- Project management
- Influence management

Unless you have a strong analyst at your side, one person will also need to brush up on correlation and regression analysis. There are a number of online training sites that can help you with analysis training.

PROJECT MANAGEMENT BREAKS PROJECTS INTO DELIVERABLES

The following example illustrates a list of possible deliverables for the multiple projects you'll be launching. I've organized the deliverables into six major projects that might be associated with a program to improve sales rep performance. Separate projects are launched in a similar fashion for structural or systemic sales improvements. This list of projects and deliverables is not intended to be exhaustive.

Project: Results-Oriented Metrics
- Define one sales KPI and the validated performance drivers
- Validated new monitor form
- Validated new script outline
- Performance management database
- Online evaluation and development modules (optional)

Project: The Right Sales People
- Recruitment strategy and tactics
- Predictive hiring assessment system for sales reps and supervisors
- New call center revenue positions
- Minimum standards (reps, supervisors and managers)
- Deselection process
- New evaluation process and frequency tied to KPI
- Skills-based routing design

Project: Training for Higher Performance
- Rep and management sales training plan
- Rep and management sales training materials

- New sales training delivered to all sales reps and supervisors
- Change management training
- Project management training

Project: Compensation, Incentives and Recognition Programs that Matter
- New compensation and incentive programs
- New contest guidelines
- New recognition programs
- QA program and link to incentive program
- Environmental assessment survey
- Retention programs
- Environmental assessment technology
- Elimination of employee irritant plan

Project: Coaching for Peak Sales Performance
- Role-clarity documents for supervisors
- New coaching tools
- Coaching standards and processes

Project: Structural and Systemic Changes
- Policy, procedure and product changes
- System changes
- New close tools
- Selling on calls previously handled by the IVR
- Synergies with another division or possible acquisition

Project Prioritization

To prioritize all of the various projects, first divide them into two categories: 1) individual rep performance, and 2) all other projects (systemic and structural). They need to be divided in this manner because if you choose to improve rep performance, you must do all the projects outlined in the box. You cannot simply put in hiring assessments without changing the training, coaching and environment. On the other hand, you could easily launch several of the projects that are structural or systemic in nature without creating simultaneous projects that all of the systemic and structural opportunities identified. So if you are embarking upon a project to improve sales rep performance, you'll want to choose only a couple of the systemic or structural projects. You can use a Prioritization Quadrant, like the one below, to plot all of your projects, and decide which (if any) you'll take on in addition to improving sales rep performance.

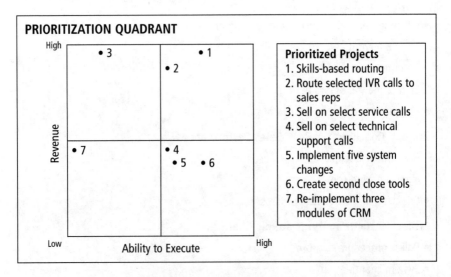

Usually you'll have so many revenue opportunities that you'll want to plot them using numbers, with a corresponding legend of named projects. At this stage, I typically look at the impact on revenue instead of ROI since it would take considerable research and time to produce even an approximation. Eventually, in the formal project agreement, you'll have a high-level ROI, but you can use simple revenue here as a proxy for initial prioritization. Choose from those projects that fall in the upper right-hand quadrant first for quick wins. Selecting projects with large revenue potential and low difficulty will also allow your team to test their project management competencies.

Obviously, your organization can do more than one thing at once. Nevertheless, no single manager should focus on more than one project at a time, in addition to his or her people responsibilities. If a project clearly has a major ROI, or the bottomline impact is huge, assign a dedicated project manager who has no other people responsibilities.

When to Use Consultants, Contractors or Executive Coaches

I don't advocate hiring a consultant to help you with every change. You and your organization must own and lead the peak sales performance program, and all of the changes that go with it. The changes will not stick if an outside consultant leads it.

However, all of these projects can be more difficult than they appear, and you generally have only one shot at implementation. Outside resources can be helpful when any of the following conditions are in play:

- You need to move faster.
- There are not enough permanent resources.
- Other departments' priorities are such that you cannot access their resources.
- Specialized skills do not exist internally (e.g., predictive hiring, incentive design, performance analytics, technology integration, etc.).
- No revenue opportunities appear obvious.
- Your organization values the opinion of external experts.
- You have never managed a change of this magnitude—you need a coach to help you organize and plan the change.

Points to Remember

- Utilize a simplified project management approach to define the project and track progress.
- Ensure that the project management requirements are not overly bureaucratic and onerous.
- Train your new matrixed team on all the relevant skills required for these changes.
- Use the prioritization quadrant tool to prioritize all projects.
- Selectively use outside resources to organize and supplement—not lead—change.

Chapter 14: Leadership When Times Get Tough

"There go the people. I must follow them, for I am their leader."
MOHANDAS GANDHI, INDIAN SPIRITUAL AND POLITICAL LEADER

Over the two to three years it will take to institutionalize the amount of change required to become a peak-performing sales center, you can bet there will be numerous obstacles that you did not anticipate. Here are a few that my management teams have dealt with in the past:

- Initial "lip service" from supervisors who do not believe that you are serious.
- HR resistance.
- Not all new tools initially work perfectly.
- Response time issues from databases.
- Manual processes are too labor-intensive.
- Leaders not sticking to training schedules after the initial rollout.
- Loss of focus because of outside influences and demands.

Generally, the hardest obstacle to deal with is the last one. As you can imagine, there will be unexpected new projects or changes that the organization will thrust on you or your staff, over and above all of your work on peak performance management. Knowing when to accept new work, when to say no to "bad business," and when to reallocate resources is the job of the senior leader. You'll make your staff crazy if you keep accepting new projects without new managerial resources. It is your job to either say "no" or to renegotiate your project deliverables. Make sure that any new work comes through you first, and keep a log of total workload by management individual.

When the going gets tough, and it will, the following tips will help you to get through it.

TIPS FOR "TEAR YOUR HAIR OUT" TIMES

• Fortitude, resilience, discipline and endurance are underrated qualities. Buck up. In most cases, those who win are simply more perseverant. This stuff takes time.

• Give people a part to play in the changes.

• Communication is a two-way street... make sure you're listening.

• Hire new managerial talent with a strong performance management track record.

• Ask for help when you need it. Seek an executive coach for you and your team. Perhaps look to an internal trusted advisor—someone with a successful performance management track record.

• Remember, 1 percent improvement a day, compounded daily, is more than 80 percent improvement in two months.

• Find the humor—it's there somewhere.

• The project plan is only a guide—change it if it isn't working. Refocus the project if necessary, but make sure that your boss signs a change control form acknowledging the change in approach, scope, timing or costs.

• Terminate resources (e.g., consultants, systems, team leaders, matrixed managers) that do not prove effective.

• Recap the learnings of the project teams often in meetings and on electronic bulletin boards.

Communication: Up, Down and Sideways

Before you kick-off a new program with balloons, meetings and a lot of hoopla, think about the last five times someone did that in your organization. There was probably a lot of skepticism, hallway talk about the "management du jour" program, and then little action for a while. Words like "initiatives" or "programs" can be rather frightening to a rep or a supervisor. Their experience with these terms has not always been good.

I recommend not conducting any large program rollout that is visible to the reps or the organization. Sometimes the belief that *"everything* is about to change," even if it's positively announced, can be frightening and intimidating for employees. To the reps, the "look and feel" of the transformation to a peak-performing sales call center should be exactly what it is: a series of "just-in-time" communication—over the course of four to six months—regarding incremental improvements, opportunities and investments in the call center that are well-executed with input and feedback from all levels in the organization.

So think twice before giving the program a catchy title or a fancy kickoff. Save your money and energy to celebrate the successes that will soon arrive.

Identify the Moles

Every organization has them—"upwardly mobile moles" and "downwardly trusted moles." The former are the people below you on the organizational chart, or with an outsourcer or vendor, who can be counted on to share their personal opinions on everything that is going on in your center with your senior management, whether they happen to catch them in the cafeteria, out smoking on the patio or at the water cooler. They generally have a personal agenda.

The downwardly trusted mole does not necessarily have an agenda, and frequently does not have aggressive career ambitions. Often they are people who have a personal link with a member of senior management or some important constituency; e.g., they grew up with someone, is the son or daughter of an executive, was a peer of a senior manager, or was previously managed by someone in upper management. Sometimes the important contact is a peer, major customer, president, chairman or board member who informally calls up the trusted mole to ask, "How's it going?"

As discussed in earlier chapters, it's best to get only 20 to 30 percent of your information from asking your direct reports how it's going. You can be sure that those who made it to the top of the executive food chain have already learned that lesson. Therefore, it's very helpful to ensure that both types of moles are feeding off the right rumor mill, and that the "dots have been connected" for them. When you know what they think, you have the opportunity to re-educate them, if necessary. These individuals can also be very influential in the frontline organization, so make sure you have the right informal contacts with them.

> "Because a thing seems difficult for you, do not think it impossible for the team to accomplish."
>
> —*Marcus Aurelius*

Part of managing and communicating "upward" through the organization is understanding the informal communication channels and actively managing them. It always lends credibility when the information you present to your senior management on how it's going actually matches or resembles what they've learned from their informal communication network. Keep your knowledge of the informal network to yourself—don't share your knowledge of the trusted mole network with the moles or the important constituencies. Just use them appropriately and discreetly.

Celebrate Successes

Celebrating successes never happens enough. Yes, it's about recognition of the team's success, but at this stage, it's bigger than that. It's a confirmation that you're on the right road—you have the right roadmap and you know where the heck you're going.

Celebrate successes early and often. Cut out early one night with a project team, or if a big obstacle has been solved or a major deliverable accomplished, then cut out early with the entire program, management or supervisory team. It doesn't matter what the celebration is—just that you are all together reveling in the success. It doesn't involve a plaque or trophy, it involves camaraderie. It could be a luncheon or a wacky prize or whatever. The important thing is that you spend time together reminiscing about how hard it was and how good it feels to "win one."

Points to Remember

- Senior leaders must act as gatekeepers for new workload outside the projects.

- "Tear your hair out" times will happen. Make sure your team has coping mechanisms.

- Don't spend a lot of time and energy on big kick-offs for the frontline organization.

- Use the "trusted mole" network to help you carry your message to senior executives.

- Celebrate your successes informally and often.

Chapter 15: Sales Excellence: Winning Strategies and Success Stories

"Look over your shoulder now and then to be sure someone's following you."
HENRY GILMER, DEMOCRATIC ATTORNEY

In the course of interviewing dozens of companies and many more individuals whom I deemed candidates for peak-performing status, I found that many of the best-of-breed companies were not using the same processes or strategies to attain peak performance. They didn't all agree with each other. Just like our top-performing reps, each company found its own path to peak performance in their call centers, with different nuances and emphases that fit their corporate culture, missions and strategies. However, there were more commonalities than differences between these top-performing companies. The box on page 252 lists 20 strategies for stellar sales performance—they come from my own experience, as well as the experiences of these industry leaders.

The pages that follow include three fascinating accounts of well-known companies that have been pursuing peak sales performance for a number of years. I chose these examples because they incorporate many of the guiding

20 STRATEGIES FOR STELLAR SALES PERFORMANCE

1. Determine your center's minimum peak sales potential using macro-gap analysis.

2. Focus on fewer performance measures. Set one business outcome KPI per function.

3. Validate supporting KPI performance drivers using correlation and regression analysis.

4. Use micro-gap analysis to show individual sales reps the way to their "personal best."

5. Hire top-performing sales reps by using validated assessment tools.

6. Develop a detailed and rigorously followed sales training and coaching process.

7. Explore structural and systemic revenue opportunities, reducing the number of times the rep must say "no" to a sale.

8. Do not tightly script top sales performers.

9. Utilize skills-based routing to drive sales calls to the best sales reps.

10. Rethink channel profitability. Selectively move IVR calls back to sales reps.

11. Deselect the bottom performers through minimum sales standards and higher risk/reward compensation programs.

12. Reinforce the reps' faith in the company's product value and delivery systems.

13. Build a dynamic performance database.

14. Allow the reps access to as much customer information as possible.

15. Construct incentive systems that can change lifestyles.

16. Remove environmental irritants.

17. Design a CRM strategy and implement selective customer- and call-type tools that enhance sales reps' ability to cross- and upsell.

18. "Connect the dots" between reps' performance and the company's success.

19. Tighten the bond between the sales reps and supervisors using recognition and advanced leadership training.

20. Drive changes through a series of prioritized and well-orchestrated projects using project management methodology.

principles outlined in this book.

American Express' story is about its *customer-focused sales* philosophy that is strongly tied into its branding strategy. Their philosophy is that selling the customer the right products builds strong brand loyalty.

RMH Teleservices reinvents a number of tired, traditional call center tools and processes, and delivers outstanding sales results on some of the most difficult call types. Their commitment to *flawless execution of feedback* has made them an industry leader in the telecommunications retail sales space.

Another organization, Cox Communications, sold only cable products a few years ago. The company now sells a host of other complex services, as well, demanding a more professional approach and sophisticated sales staff than in years past. Their story is one of an *enlightened path to sales profession-alism.*

Read on for three prime examples of what can be accomplished.

Case Study: American Express Builds Brand Loyalty with Customer-Focused Sales Program

American Express is well-known for its service delivery, but what many don't know is that they became innovators in cross-selling in 1995, when they embarked upon a sophisticated program called "Customer-Focused Sales," or CFS.

American Express has thousands of customer service representatives in locations around the world. This initial buildout of a distributed service network was a prerequisite to the rollout of their CFS program. Judson Linville, executive vice president of the company's Service Delivery Network, describes American Express's philosophy, noting, "The American Express inbound service network has a massive opportunity to shape the brand. It is shaped by each customer experience. We use the momentum of the inbound service call to deepen both the relationship with our customers and their loyalty."

Linville credits four major strategies as key to driving sales in his organization: 1) structured call routing, 2) predictive hiring assessments, 3) a focus on fewer metrics, and 4) leveraged variable pay.

STRUCTURED CALL ROUTING

At American Express, approximately one-third of all service calls have an opportunity for cross-sell or upsell. Linville explains that the process to determine whether a customer will be made an offer is extremely structured:

- All customer service reps understand that their first and only real priority is to service the customer.

- Call-types that are eligible for cross-sell are identified in the routing system; then the card members who are eligible to receive the offer are identified.

- If both the call-type and caller could be handled through an IVR, but American Express has not spoken with the customer to make an offer in a designated period of time, the routing system directs the caller to the Customer-Focused Sales Unit (CFS).

- If American Express has made a recent offer, their eligibility criterion suppresses these calls from being routed to a sales rep, and either keeps them in IVR or routes them to a service-only rep.

- On certain types of calls that require specialized knowledge, a call may be dial-transferred to a more knowledgeable rep after the service the customer requested has been provided, and after the customer has agreed to a transfer to hear about a product. American Express research shows that customer satisfaction actually increases when a customer is transferred to the best rep to handle the call—but only if *one* transfer is required.

- After the service issue is resolved, the system "screen pops" the most appropriate offer for the rep to sell.

Here's a specific example of the process in action: The American Express suite of routing and CRM systems identifies an inbound customer who is not enrolled in the Membership Rewards program, but who spends a lot each month in eligible reward point categories. If the customer's call-type is eligible—meaning the customer is in good standing and has not had the offer made to him recently—instead of routing him to an IVR, the system routes the caller to the Customer-Focused Sales Unit to be serviced first, and then offered the Membership Rewards program. The sale is important of course, but even more so is the opportunity for American Express to reinforce its branding and create a depth of loyalty through educating its customers on the value of its products.

FOCUS ON FEWER METRICS

American Express, like a few other forerunners in marketing and sales, has come full-circle regarding the use of automation in optimizing its call centers. The company has realized that the old metrics of cost-per-call or cost-per-unit-sold are no longer appropriate. The call centers now measure and assess a contact channel's desirability based on the prof-

> **No longer does the company drive a call to the lowest-cost channel. They selectively route the call to the most profitable channel based upon call and caller type, as well as customer interaction history—a real breakthough in the call center industry.**

it contribution, or net present value (NPV). No longer does the company drive a call to the lowest-cost channel. They selectively route the call to the most profitable channel based upon call and caller type, as well as customer interaction history—a real breakthough in the call center industry.

American Express is a metrics-driven organization that requires all of its employees to take personal responsibility for their goals. However, the company recently made a big change in how they view their metrics. They moved from an operational characteristic view of goals (e.g., heavy weighting on the typical 80/20 service levels) to transaction-based surveys on key processes and competencies.

When American Express began its CFS program in 1995, they utilized virtually every conceivable metric. According to Linville, "In their infancy, most companies take on too many process metrics that make it to the floor too quickly. Paradoxically, the more sophisticated our company has become regarding performance measurement, the fewer measures we actually have." He recommends that companies use fewer performance measures, and only those focused on business outcomes.

THE IMPACT OF MONITORING AND COACHING

Monitoring and coaching play critical roles in improving sales performance at American Express' call centers. They record 100 percent of calls, and monitoring is conducted by both team leaders (supervisors) and a centralized quality group. Although some critical components of the call are scripted, American Express realizes there are many ways to sell, and it should be a very personal experience. Accordingly, they allow for considerable deviation in the selling dialogue. The monitoring staff focuses on three areas: 1) compliance, 2) the customer experience, and 3) the rep's decision quality.

By analyzing the CFS unit by quintile, management is able to profile the performers in each group and tailor coaching experiences that are more likely to be successful. Linville shared one example of a rep who had been in customer service for some time, but who was still struggling with his performance. He was in the bottom 20th percentile overall. His team leader "buddied" him up with a top-producing peer so that he could see all of the key skills properly modeled. In a short period of time, this bottom performer rose to the top 1 percentile in all performance categories, and within the top 10 percentile in sales. Not surprisingly, Linville believes modeling and peer coaching to be a powerful way to influence and change behavior.

EFFECTIVE RECRUITING, TRAINING AND INCENTIVES

Another important strategy in driving sales for American Express is a strong competency for selecting the best sales people through the recruiting process. American Express' recruiting selection team is comprised of a number of members, including several Ph.D.s, who identify strong service ethics and sales abilities through the development of proprietary predictive assessment tests.

All reps begin training using a computer-based program that features a simulated sales environment. Since reps are under a 90-day probationary period, the selection process to determine whether they will be placed in a service or sales-skilled team is delayed until their skills have been proven.

American Express' compensation plan includes variable pay based on line-of-sight metrics—metrics that are very visible to the reps and that need little explanation. The organization firmly believes in paying out as closely as possible to the actual event. The pay is fairly leveraged, with top producers able to double their base pay. Bottom producers do not make variable pay and eventually self-select out of the call center. Like most best-in-class companies, American Express has not capped the incentive. They believe that capping incentives is like telling the rep not to sell anymore, that the company does not want more revenue.

In addition to base-pay incentive programs, American Express leverages short-term (three months at the longest) programs, with additional monetary awards or prizes that are visible on the call center floor (e.g., mountain bikes). They find this particularly effective in areas that are time-critical to the business, such as relaunches of products or programs.

American Express has all of the same performance management elements as other companies, but they execute each of these elements more rigorously, methodically and flawlessly than most. In addition, they have woven their branding strategy into a sales and service philosophy that is well-thought-out and continuously communicated throughout the organization.

Case Study: RMH Teleservices Cites Feedback Quality as a Key to Success

RMH Teleservices is one of the top players in customer care outsourcing, with 10,000 reps in 15 customer contact centers located in the United

States, Canada, the Philippines and Panama. Their clients are almost exclusively Fortune 500 companies, including telecommunications firms, technology companies, financial services providers, and travel and logistics businesses.

With the outsourcing business becoming increasingly competitive, third-party outsourcing agencies are taking more of a risk/reward position with their clients in order to acquire new business. This means delivering what you promise or not getting paid. Sometimes, it means getting paid only for actual sales produced, with additional business directed to your agency if you produce better than the other outsourcers. To survive and thrive in this environment requires strong operational excellence, the ability to execute new programs and to deliver measurable value.

Tom Morrisroe, a senior account manager for RMH, describes a spectacular performance turn-around in sales that his operations group achieved for a major telecommunications client. When RMH first acquired this account, they received the fewest number of calls of the seven outsourcers handling calls for the client. They had to prove themselves to receive a higher share of the calls.

THE MOST DIFFICULT TYPE OF SALES CALL

The type of call that RMH handles for the client is the most difficult sales scenario that I have ever reviewed. It is a very difficult service call from a non-customer. Let me explain: When a phone company handles an operator-assisted call or a collect call for customers who don't have an account with them, they provide the service requested and then bill the customers through the phone company (the one they don't have an account with). When customers receive charges on their bills from phone companies that are not theirs, they frequently will call the company in question to dispute the bill. This is where it gets interesting. RMH's reps answer these calls and agree to have the problem reviewed. The reps then suggest to customers that their company might have a better telecommunications product and pricing plan than the customers' existing phone company. They either sell customers on the conversion to the new phone company or not, and then transfer the call to the client's customer service rep so that the original problem can be resolved. The net conversion rate of these service calls to an implemented sale averages 18 percent. It is an amazing track record, and a tremendous improvement from just 10 months ago.

RMH's original call volume of 60,000 per month from this client has doubled to 119,000 per month, Morrisroe says, dramatically increasing their share of the client's business. He attributes their share increase directly to his contact center's ability to move the conversion ratio from 15 percent to 18 percent. (In this case, the close ratio is the same as the conversion ratio since they are attempting to convert all service calls to sales).

Then, when the phone company client redistributed calls to RMH from other outsourcers who were also servicing this account, it moved them from a last-place share position to first place. Morrisroe attributes the 20 percent increase in their sales close rate to a few major changes. The center hired a new general sales manager, who ensured that two key processes which RMH had designed were flawlessly followed. First, he made sure that they had the right team in place, with the right people in all the key positions. The right team meant people from a broad range of areas: from HR, to training, to floor management, to supervisors. It meant people with the right outlook, attitude, skill set and sales experience.

RECRUITING FOR A DIFFICULT JOB

RMH's recruiting process consists of a four-stage selection process: 1) an assessment of language skills, psychometric profiling (a predictive assessment tool), voice test and preliminary interview; 2) background check, reference check and document verification; 3) final interviews with HR and operations; and 4) an offer. The client's program and performance requirements are carefully outlined for each candidate during the interview process. Anyone who appears afraid or does not look at the job as a challenge that can be met is quickly eliminated from consideration. While many of RMH's reps have prior sales experience, the company also hires anyone who appears "sales-trainable"–those who are not afraid of high targets and standards, have high self-esteem, and have excellent listening and language skills.

ADVANCED COACHING

The second core process is an absolutely rigid adherence to the rep and sales supervisor development methodology. It consists of the usual monitoring and feedback cycle, but with several differences. Each supervisor has an average of 18 sales reps and each rep has two to three calls monitored each week by their sales supervisor. No exceptions. It always happens. There is no other priority considered more important in the sales supervisor's position.

> **Instead of listing the items that the sales supervisor heard go "right" and "wrong" during the monitoring session—which can sound tedious and nit-picky—the sales supervisor is trained to bring to the surface the *behaviors* they observed.**

The development-coaching process is very formalized. Considerable planning is conducted before the one-on-one development coaching with the rep occurs. The sales supervisor carefully considers his approach to the session, including an assessment of the right time to conduct a session. If the time is not right, the rep may not really be listening, and the development session is rendered ineffective. The feedback is always given in a quiet room specially designed for these conversations. It's outfitted with easy chairs and couches. Instead of listing the items that the sales supervisor heard go "right" and "wrong" during the monitoring session—which can sound tedious and nitpicky—the sales supervisor is trained to bring to the surface the *behaviors* they observed. They get the rep to discuss his thought process in using certain words or approaches with the customer. In doing so, they are able to get to the rep's root belief structure, which may be driving the observed behaviors. Only then are supervisors and reps in a position to effect change. One or two goals are focused on each week, and reps commit to make the agreed-upon changes. Supervisors follow up with reps in the next monitoring session to ensure that the changes occurred.

Sales supervisors also follow a development process. Each is initially given a one-hour training session by their sales manager on how to effectively deliver feedback and coaching. The sales manager is required to sit in on at least one development-coaching session with each of their seven to eight sales supervisors each month. New supervisors, or those with lower sales results, are visited more frequently. Much like the supervisors' development session with their reps, the sales manager conducts a feedback session with supervisors in a subsequent

> *"Coaching is not something you do to your employees— it is a gift you give them."*
>
> *—Tom Morrisroe, RMH Senior Account Manager*

meeting. They discuss the approach, techniques and behaviors the supervisor exhibited. According to Morrisroe, "This formal development process is our No. 1 competitive advantage."

MINIMUM SALES STANDARDS

Like many peak-performing sales centers, RMH has minimum sales metric standards that fully tenured reps are required to consistently reach to retain their position with the company. The client has minimum sales conversion ratios, which makes RMH eligible to receive a certain percentage of their call volume. Consequently, RMH shares this burden with their reps who, in turn, must deliver a minimum sales close ratio. This "consequence management" approach drives a 48 percent annual attrition rate, but the client's and RMH's standards are high. Each call that cannot be converted is a lost opportunity. The chance to have a phone contact with another com-

---

FISH! THE POWER OF PERSONAL CHOICE

The FISH! Video is a companion to the bestseller of the same name that came out several years ago, inspired by the workers at Seattle's Pike Place Fish Market. The FISH! Philosophy has four basic "life lessons":

- You choose your attitude each day.
- Make the customer's day.
- Play.
- Be present to the moment.

More information can be found at their Web site: www.charthouse.com.

---

pany's customer is rare and not likely to happen again. The company cannot afford to have anyone but the very best on the phone. When one considers the unique conditions—that these reps are dealing with the toughest sales call possible—this attrition rate is remarkably low. It is a tribute to RMH's selection, incentive and development processes.

ATTITUDES LEAD THE WAY

There is another factor Morrisroe mentions that is less tangible than the formal processes in place. It is attitude. Morrisroe and his team embrace the now famous "FISH!" philosophy, adapted from a Seattle-based seafood company (see the box above). They believe that employees have the choice to make work fun. They choose their attitudes every day. All teams in RMH's center go through the formal FISH! training program, and the philosophy is reflected in the center's décor—ocean waves and fish adorn the walls.

Case Study: SHARKS in the Cox Communications Call Center

Nelson Elmore, director of sales for Cox Communications in Southern California, has an outstanding team of 110 inbound sales reps who have increased their sales of Revenue Generating Units (RGU) by 68 percent over the last four years—with the same incentive budget and number of staff. For Cox, an RGU is any monthly unit of revenue, whether basic cable TV service, an HBO package, a local telephone service, or a high-speed Internet service. The sales group has labeled themselves the SHARKS—an acronym for "Sales Happen and Revenues Keep Soaring."

Instead of the traditional revenue per hour, close ratio or conversion ratio as the KPI metric for sales success, Cox measures RGU per person per month, with the lowest producers averaging 600 RGUs per month, the middle producers averaging 675 RGUs per month, and the top producers averaging 900 RGUs per month. The spread between Elmore's low and high producers is only about 30 percent, indicating that his team is doing a very good job of selection and deselection of sales reps. As mentioned previously, in most sales organizations that are not operating at peak performance, the spread is much higher, typically in the 100 to 300 percent range.

> **Employees at Cox joke that the best cars in the parking lot are owned by sales reps. Individuals in traditionally professional positions within the company, like trainers, now compete for jobs in phone sales.**

REPS ARE "PAID FOR PRODUCTION"

Elmore notes that his reps do not need minimum standards for sales production because their base rate of pay in this high cost-of-living area is acknowledged to be too low for an adequate lifestyle. In spite of that, most sales reps are well-paid because their sales compensation plan uses a *pay-for-production* strategy. (Remember, top sales performers typically prefer a higher "risk/reward" ratio.) If the sales rep cannot produce, then he or she doesn't make money and will eventually move on to another job. A low producer (bottom 5 percentile) will not make commission and typically grosses $21,000 to $30,000 per year. Average reps earn about $46,000 per year, and the top 5 percent command $80,000 to $90,000 per year.

Employees at Cox joke that the best cars in the parking lot are owned by sales reps. Individuals in traditionally professional positions within the company, like trainers, now compete for jobs in phone sales. It is no wonder that the Cox sales department enjoys single-digit rates of attrition.

FOUR SUCCESS FACTORS

It's not compensation alone, however, that drives low attrition and stellar sales at Cox. Elmore credits four major factors:

1. Implementing a new hiring process. A few years ago, Cox deployed a new selection methodology that, in addition to incorporating interviews and role-playing, utilizes psychometric testing to predict candidates' success on the job (Hogan's Personality Profile and Quiz Cognitive Program). For each candidate, the test produces a personality profile and a skills-based competency assessment that is compared to Cox's ideal rep profile. This enables Elmore to find people capable of competing with his best performers. He seeks individuals with a *high advantage score*–those who have enough "it's all about me" attitudes. Too high an *advantage score*, however, might result in the customer being improperly serviced. "It's a balance," says Elmore.

He adds that it's important to not "get too hung up on sales experience" when selecting new-hires. "Three of my best sales people had absolutely no previous sales experience. Our assessment and role-play interviewing program allowed me to feel comfortable hiring them. We can now predict that they will be successful."

Once this hiring program was implemented, attrition in Cox's phone sales group decreased from 25 to 30 percent to less than 10 percent, and sales production began rising.

2. Setting clear job expectations. This involves not only setting performance targets and goals, but also helping reps to understand *the part they play* in the company's goals and success. Whenever a new policy, procedure or process is rolled out, management ensures that they use a "double-message" technique–illustrating what's in it for the customer as well as what's in it for the rep.

3. Designing new training methods. Another key to Cox's sales success in its call center was the revamping of their training over the last few years. This included reducing new-hire training from six weeks to four weeks by extracting a few components that are better digested after the reps have been on the floor with customers for a few weeks.

Every session in new-hire training now includes role-playing sessions. Two of the sales training programs are held in the first week of training—instead of as an afterthought at the end of training. Elmore describes the training class as "rallied each day by the trainer first explaining the policy and procedure, followed by the sales manager joining in to explain the importance of the topic. The sales manager explains the downstream consequences for the rep and the customer if the process is not followed."

This is a prime example of Cox's "double-messaging" technique. Important messages are repeated from different points of view so that the sales reps will understand the interconnection of everything they learn. They then begin to really understand the part they play in the their own success and that of the company.

After Cox restructured its approach to training and behavior modification, Elmore noted that: "28 of our 30 new-hires are in the top 50 percentile of performers."

4. Creating a dynamic incentive program. The dynamic nature of the call center's incentive program has also helped to drive results. Elmore has a set zero-sum incentive budget. If the company requires another product line to be driven harder or introduces additional products to the mix, Elmore reserves the right to change the incentive plan to put a higher commission on one product and reduce it on another. His expectation is not that the product with the lower incentive will now generate less units, but that the new structure will focus the sales reps on finding new ways to better sell the product that needs additional focus. His reps are taught a "top-down" selling approach, with no one assuming that the entire package of products is unaffordable to a customer. Reps are trained to envision a full-package sale as a tremendous value and a trade-off decision that the customer can make against other forms of entertainment. If the sales rep believes that the Cox full package of entertainment and services is a much better value than other entertainment and services, then their customers might, too.

SKILLS-BASED ROUTING AND NO SCRIPTS

Nancy Peinado, director of broadband operations for Cox Communications, credits the implementation of skills-based routing as another factor in the call center's success. The center routes customer-directed sales calls to sales reps, and service calls to customer service reps. "It's difficult to handle a billing call with someone who might be having money problems, and then try to sell someone something on the next call," comments Peinado.

No part of service or sales is scripted, as Cox "wants [the rep's] personality to shine through," she adds. Cox reps don't try to cross-sell or upsell on every call. If there is an opportunity for a sale, they will offer the product. The customer service group is trained to look for key call-types that are more conducive to an upsell, and are also trained on the types of products that would be appropriate to offer to these call-types.

Reps must be trained on informal call-typing, as it is not a natural thought process for many of them, says Peinado. There are many different types of billing calls, some conducive to sales, others not. Also, there are some customer-types that one might not want to offer new services to, such as a customer who is severely past due on his or her account.

Once customer service reps get used to thinking about a call as the combination of a customer-type and a call-type, they can better understand what to offer the customer, Peinado explains. They learn to recognize the "golden combinations"—those combinations of customer-types and call-types that are very conducive to certain selling approaches and services.

Conclusion: Can You Hear the Hum and the Buzz in Your Center?

In these 15 chapters, I've described the path to peak sales performance, and have provided the methodology for you to implement your own sales improvement program. Numerous opportunities have been explored for tapping new sources of revenue. You've read about countless industry successes that reaped significant rewards for all who participated in the peak performance process. You now know how to find the revenue, what changes are necessary to mine the revenue, and how to support and sustain the new level of performance.

You have new tools, tips and best practices at your fingertips. You're primed to hear the Hum and the Buzz coming from your call center. Go for the gold! I wish you every success.

Fast-forward 18 months: You hear it! The Hum and the Buzz. Your sales are at all-time record levels. Your attrition rate is down; your absentee level is almost non-existent; and your staff is happy. Nothing seems that hard anymore. It no longer takes all your energy to sustain the performance levels. If you have not already considered it, you have started looking at your service group for peak performance potential. You have been promoted because your staff no longer really needs you. They are self-sustaining. Your staff is using their influence leadership to teach other non-technical departments how to drive results through project management. Most likely, you will be asked to assist other departments that are struggling with similar issues to launch a performance improvement system. Go inspire disciples and performance evangelists outside your organizational boundaries. Help them to discover the power of the Hum and the Buzz.

> **You have new tools, tips and best practices at your fingertips. You're primed to hear the Hum and the Buzz coming from your call center.**

Appendix

PROJECT AGREEMENT

Project Participants

Project Name	
Project Sponsor	Project Manager
Project Team Members	Date Submitted

Project Description

Business Situation	
Project Scope In Scope: Out of Scope:	
Business Objectives	
Deliverables	
Constraints	
Assumptions	

Signature denotes that this project may be viable and authorization is given to proceed with the planning stage only

Signature	Date	Signature	Date
Project Sponsor		Project Manager	

PROJECT TEAM STRUCTURE

Team Participants

Project Name	
Project Sponsor	Project Team Name
Project Manager	
Team Member, Role, Phone Number, Email Address	Estimated Time Required by Team Members

Team Description

Charter	
Administrative Guidelines	
Decision Guidelines	
Meeting Guidelines	
Estimated Duration	

WORK BREAKDOWN STRUCTURE EXAMPLE

Project: The Right Sales People

Deliverables

Recruitment strategy and tactics
- Predictive Hiring Assessment System for sales reps and supervisors
- Minimum Standards (rep, supervisor and managers)
- Deselection process
- Skills-based routing design

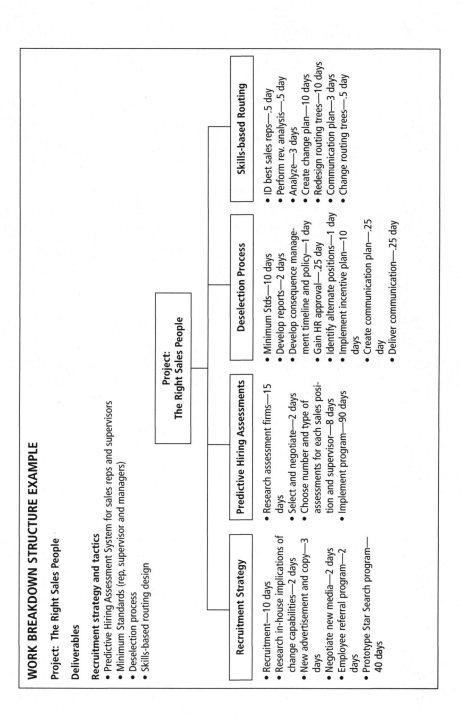

**Project:
The Right Sales People**

Recruitment Strategy	Predictive Hiring Assessments	Deselection Process	Skills-based Routing
• Recruitment—10 days • Research in-house implications of change capabilities—2 days • New advertisement and copy—3 days • Negotiate new media—2 days • Employee referral program—2 days • Prototype Star Search program—40 days	• Research assessment firms—15 days • Select and negotiate—2 days • Choose number and type of assessments for each sales position and supervisor—8 days • Implement program—90 days	• Minimum Stds—10 days • Develop reports—2 days • Develop consequence management timeline and policy—1 day • Gain HR approval—.25 day • Identify alternate positions—1 day • Implement incentive plan—10 days • Create communication plan—.25 day • Deliver communication—.25 day	• ID best sales reps—.5 day • Perform rev. analysis—.5 day • Analyze—3 days • Create change plan—10 days • Redesign routing trees—10 days • Communication plan—3 days • Change routing trees—.5 day

275

COMMUNICATION PLAN

Project					
			Project Manager		
Audience	Message	Intent	Media	Timing	Assigned to

PROJECT RISK LOG

Project Name   **Project Manager**

Risk	Possible Impact	Probability Level (low, med, high)	Impact Level (low, med, high)	Risk Level (low, med, high)	Risk Mitigation

Attach additional analysis documents as backup

PROJECT CHANGE REQUEST

Requester Section	Project Name
Requester's Name	Date Submitted
Priority ❑ Essential ❑ Important ❑ Competitive Advantage	
Proposed Change	
Reason for Change	
Implications of Not Implementing Change	
Attachments	

Project Manager Section	
Name	
Date Received	
Approved for Research ❑ Yes ❑ No	Date Approved
Comments	

PROJECT CHANGE REQUEST (continued)

Project Change Request Assessment

Change Request Number	
Analyst Name	
Date of Recommendation	
Scope Impact	
Deliverable Impact	
Work Effort Impact	
Financial Impact	
Schedule Impact	
Organizational Impact	
Research Analyst Recommendation	

	Date		Signature		Date
Approved Rejected Deferred Until					
Signature					
Project Manager			Project Sponsor		

CHANGE LOG

PROJECT NAME

#	Change Description	Date Submitted	Date Closed	☐ Approved ☐ Rejected ☐ Deferred	Impact: Schedule or Deliverable	Days Impacted	Research Hours	Change of Hours
				Total				

PROJECT ISSUE LOG

PROJECT NAME

#	Issue Name	Criticality High (H) Med (M) Low (L)	Issue Type Time (T) Schedule (S) Quality (Q)	Identifying Person	Date Issue Received	Assigned to	Date Assigned	Resolution	Date Closed

PROJECT STATUS REPORT

Project Manager	Project Sponsor
Project Team	Date

Project Name

Project Status Report for two-week period ending

Issues Requiring Management Focus

Project Timeline Task Summary	Red	Yellow	Green	Planned Start	Actual Start	Planned End

Major Tasks Accomplished

Major Tasks Planned for Next Two Weeks

PROJECT CLOSE-DOWN REPORT

Project Sponsor	Program Manager
Project Manager	**Date**
Subject: Project Close Down	

The project has been completed according to the approved Project Agreement, except for the approved changes noted below.

– List deliverables from Project Agreement
– List any approved changes
– All Issues (see attached Issues Log) have been resolved
– A Summary of "Lessons Learned" is attached

Signature	
Name	Date

283

Glossary

Accountability model. A diagram that assigns organizational accountability for a process, customer segment or business outcome. Often used when accountability must be assigned to individuals or departments outside where the work is being performed. These departments or individuals frequently control or drive the workload or quality inputs, and are held accountable for resulting costs or quality issues.

Action plan. A list of tactics or activities that the supervisor and rep believe will bring about a measurable performance improvement. For instance, if a rep's close ratio is only 20 percent, three items in the action plan might include: 1) attending a refresher class on the required dialogue points; 2) utilizing additional sales close tools; and 3) additional commitment to monitoring by the supervisor to determine other root causes.

Adverse impact. In U.S. employment law, a term used to describe a significant level of negative effect on a traditionally discriminated against group, which may be caused by certain pre-employment screening practices. Also called the *Four-Fifths Rule,* adverse impact exists if members of a protected class are selected at rates less than four-fifths (80 percent) than that of another group. If adverse impact exists, the Department of Labor's *Uniform Guidelines on Employee Selection Procedures* requires that the job-relatedness and business necessity of the assessment procedures be identified and proven.[i]

Average handling time (AHT). The sum of average talk-time plus average after-call work. Data on AHT is available from ACD reports for incoming calls, and from ERMS and Web servers for email and Web contacts. AHT may also be available from a workforce management system. AHT is an appropriate measurement for high-level purposes and for ongoing tactical planning; it is generally not recommended as a strict agent standard.[ii]

Best-of-breed. Similar to *best-in-class*, a benchmarking term used to identify organizations that outperform all others in a specified category. *Best-of-breed* concerns itself with a group (breed) of organizations that is narrower in focus than best-in-class. For example, certain call center organizations may be referred to as best-in-class when they outperform most call centers. However, best-of-breed may be used to refer to organizations that are more specialized (e.g., outbound call centers that sell or inbound call centers in the insurance industry).

Best practice. The generally accepted best demonstrated policy, procedure or method within a best-in-class or best-of-breed organization. Best-practice studies are frequently conducted within an industry sector to benchmark practices that drive performance metrics, as well as across industries to spur innovation.

Business case. Fundamentally, the justification and multiple-year projection of a project's future costs (capital and expense), revenues and business benefits.

Business outcome. Business outcome refers to final measurable business results (e.g., revenue, sales, profit, etc.), as opposed to internal process measurements (e.g., AHT, close ratio, cancellation rate).

Call-typing. The organization of calls into categories, both major and minor, for analysis. Calls are frequently further typed by call group, time of day or day of week distribution, and length of call, and tabulated by either an IVR, ACD, CSR, quality-control coordinator or supervisor. Often calls are typed by a smaller group, such as QA individuals, and then extrapolated, thereby reducing the cost of collecting the data. Root Cause Analysis is used to determine the cause of the calls or how to modify the business rules in order to improve the final business outcome.

Catalytic mechanism. A term that originated in the world of chemistry to denote the presence of a catalyst whose presence speeds up a chemical process, but is not consumed by the process. In the business world, it refers to a process, policy or practice, which, by its very nature, induces a rapid self-sustaining change in organizational behavior.

Close ratio. The ratio of closed sale calls to all calls handled, expressed as a percentage. The ratio could be a metric for an individual sales rep or for a shift, team or call group.

Consequence management. Refers to the positive and negative actions that management should exercise either to reward above-standard performance, or penalize performance that is consistently below standards, in spite of training and coaching. Rewards include recognition in a variety of formats, incentives or promotions. Penalties generally are progressive in nature, and include lack of incentives, warnings and ultimately termination of employment.

Conversion ratio. The ratio of closed sales transactions to sales-eligible calls (closeable calls), expressed as a percentage. Generally not recommended as a KPI or a performance driver since it is too difficult to track accurately on a real-time basis, and is normally extrapolated from sample call-typing. Usually, you would not use a conversion ratio as a KPI because there are many non-sales-potential calls in any call-answering group. If this is not the case, and all calls have sales potential, conversion ratio and close ratio mean the same thing and could be used as a performance driver.

Correlation analysis. Correlation analysis is concerned with the degree to which one variable is related to another; for example, whether the high or low AHT has any effect on the close ratio. Frequently performed in conjunction with regression analysis.

Customer-focused sales (CFS). A termed coined by some organizations to establish a group of strategies around first serving and then selling customers additional services or items that are targeted to meet their needs.

Linear correlation coefficient. A linear correlation coefficient is the measure of the linear relationship between two random variables. For example, the *extent* to which AHT or key script elements affect the close ratio (or net revenue per phone hour).

Correlation scattergrams. Also known as scatter diagrams. A quality tool that assesses the strength of the relationship between two variables, and is used to test and document possible cause and effect. If there is positive correlation between two variables, dots will appear on the graph as an upward slope. If there is a negative correlation, the dots will appear as a downward slope. The closer the pattern of dots to a straight line, the stronger the (linear) correlation is between the two variables.[iii]

Customer relationship management (CRM). The process of holistically developing the customer's relationship with the organization. It takes into account the customer's history, the depth and breadth of his or her business with the organization, as well as other factors. Customer relationship management generally uses sophisticated applications and database systems that include elements of data mining, contact management and enterprise resource planning, enabling agents and analysts to know and anticipate customer behavior.[iv]

A common misconception of CRM is that it primarily consists of a database or set of technology tools. While technology is an enabler, CRM involves much more (e.g., processes, organizational structure, information/data and an understanding of which customers you want to serve and how you will address the needs of different types of customers).

Cross-sell. Offering additional products or services to current customers, usually based on relationships established between the customer's profile and the attributes of customers who have already purchased the products or services being cross-sold.

Deselection. The removal of an individual from his or her current job position, be it voluntary or involuntary. An individual may also be moved into a different job within the company, but still be deselected from his or her current position.

Developmental coach. The job position responsible for assisting a rep in improving his or her individual performance. Typically, it would be the rep's immediate supervisor. Many progressive call centers have changed the team leader or supervisor title to developmental coach to emphasize the importance and focus of this aspect of the supervisory position.

Environmental assessments. A short, anonymous manual or computer-based questionnaire regarding the work environment for a work group. The assessments are created to evaluate the impact of various factors (e.g., impediments, leadership, policies, work tools, etc.) on the job performance of the workforce. Unlike an employee opinion survey, it is designed to be frequent, quick and actionable.

Goal. The point of arrival (POA). It's the quantifiable component of the performance objective. For example, in the objective "increase close ratio to 25 percent within the next 12 months," the goal is a 25 percent close ratio.

Impression management. A technique sometimes used by sales-oriented individuals to get the customer to like them, and in turn, the product(s) they're selling. Consciously or unconsciously, these individuals try to project themselves as being similar in outlook to the prospect, or sometimes, to an interviewer.

Institutionalization. The process by which a program's projects, new policies, procedures, competencies and values are accepted into the culture, becoming second-nature to the organization and providing a self-sustaining level of performance.

Interactive voice response (IVR). Systems that enable callers to use their telephone keypad (or spoken commands, if speech recognition is used) to access a company's computer system for the purpose of retrieving or updating information, conducting a business transaction or routing their call. Also referred to as voice response unit (VRU).[v]

Key performance indicator (KPI). The single, most important business outcome—usually the measure of how effectively a call center or department performs its mission. For example, if the mission is sales, the sales KPI might be: net revenue per phone hour (NRPH), or net sales units/rep/month. If the center's or department's mission is service, the service KPI might be: service inquiries/complaints as a percentage of total transactions or net first point-of-contact close. A center may have multiple KPIs, but generally only one per skill or per department.

Matrix management. An organizational structure that is permanently or temporarily created to address complex issues or projects. On an organizational chart, functional managers report to functional department heads on a straight line, but are "matrixed" through a dotted-line relationship to another department or project director. The department head with the straight line relationship typically has responsibility for formal reviews and merit increases, but the dotted-line director sets priorities and direction for projects the manager is involved in, and has input into the manager's review.

Measurement. A quantifiable unit. In call centers, this is generally *time* (e.g., handle time, after-call work time), an *input* (e.g., a call, an email, a customer), an *output* (e.g., a sales unit, a proposal, a completed problem resolution), or a *ratio* (e.g., schedule adherence percentage, absenteeism percentage, close ratio, first-call resolution percentage, reopened complaint percentage).

Performance boards. A board that shows the team performance trend line for a KPI, often accompanied by a performance ranking alongside actual results for every individual on the team. Performance boards can take the form of a physical report, a wallboard or, more commonly, a database that can be accessed by each team member. Best-practice call centers use performance ranking boards that are displayed on the rep's daily "sign-on" screen or screensaver.

Performance database. A database and related analytic software—either homegrown or off-the-shelf—comprised of extracts of other databases containing performance data, scheduling data, administrative data, payroll data and incentive plans. Database queries by reps or supervisors can be viewed on a physical report or at the desktop, and are easily exported to another spreadsheet format. Incentive programs are generally paid from this database and performance evaluations generated, making backup processes and redundancy databases crucial.

Performance driver. A previously "suspect" performance driver that has been validated to drive the business outcome KPI through statistically sound correlation and regression analysis. When used in sales call centers, a performance driver typically falls into one of three categories: 1) a skill or personality factor; 2) a sales approach or element of a script outline; or 3) any one of a few metrics that analytically has been shown to affect the corresponding KPI (e.g., net revenue per hour).

Performance driver dialogue elements. The points in a script outline that have been statistically validated to positively drive the key performance indicator (KPI).

Performance gap analysis. The process of analyzing the gap between lower performers and higher performers who perform the identical job under similar conditions. When extrapolated into final business results (profitability), the numbers are often compelling.

Performance management. The sum total of all personnel selection systems, metrics and goals, training and coaching systems, environmental conditions—including incentive plans and structural and systemic factors—which allow the individual and the business unit to perform at a given level of competency.

Performance objective. Usually stated as a quantifiable goal that must be accomplished within a given set of constraints (e.g., quality) and within a specified period of time or by a given date (e.g., increase close ratio to 25 percent within two weeks). A good objective or target generally follows the design guidelines of the S.M.A.R.T. acronym (Specific, Measurable, Attainable, Realistic and Time-bound).

Performance pyramid. A diagram that links all of the components of a company's mission with its strategies and departmental and individual performance contributions (metrics) so that all individuals can easily see how their performance affects the company's success.

Performance standard. A quantifiable acceptable level or range of performance. Performance below or outside the standard range should not be acceptable or tolerated for very long. Frequently in call centers, the standard is expressed as an acceptable range of tolerance (e.g., an AHT standard over a 30-day rolling average period might be expressed as 240-300 seconds). Times below and above that standard indicate something is wrong, which shows up in variances in other standards.

Personal best. The best measurement over a cyclical period—such as one month—achieved by an individual in any one area. Sustaining a personal best on a daily basis and surpassing it consistently to a new sustainable performance level is known as *peak individual performance.*

Point of arrival (POA). A peak performance plateau designated in the performance planning process for an individual, department or business unit.

Point of departure (POD). The current performance level from which one embarks on the path to a higher performance level.

Predictive hiring assessments. A series of tests, administered in a "hurdle fashion," which have been validated by industrial psychologists for specific jobs to predict with a high degree of certainty which individuals will perform at a high level or a low level for the specified position. These assessments generally include psychometric testing, hard-skill testing, behavior interviews and job simulations.

Project management. The process of planning, managing and controlling the course and development of a project or undertaking (e.g., implementing a new ACD or opening a new call center). Key project management terms include:

- **Scope:** The boundaries of the project, including a statement of what is and is not part of the project. "Scope creep" is when a project grows beyond what was originally approved, without formal change control, often because the scope was not clearly defined at the outset.

- **Project plan:** Listing of all tasks required to complete the project, showing (for each task) start date, completion date, resources required, the person responsible for each task and a task number.

- **Gantt chart:** Visual representation of the project plan, using bars that extend to the right of each task representing the amount of time the task requires. Sophisticated Gantt charts use arrows and symbols to indicate task dependencies, milestones, etc.

- **Milestone:** Measurable point of progress in the project plan. The milestone is listed in the project plan along with the tasks, but is present really as a marker that either has or has not been achieved. For example, "Collect responses to request for proposal."

- **Deliverables:** Completed units of work with tangible results. For example, a report could be a deliverable, as could a software module.

- **Dependency:** Relationship between tasks that makes execution of one task dependent upon execution of another. For example, "determine number of trunks needed" must be completed before "place order for trunks."

- **Critical path:** The sequence of tasks upon which the project completion date depends. In other words, a change in the duration of any of these tasks will change the project's completion date, due to dependencies among the tasks on the critical path. Tasks that are not on the critical path can be delayed without affecting the project end date.

- **Owner:** Person accountable for completion of a task.

- **Sponsor/champion:** Person in the organization with the authority and/or funds to make the project happen, or who is the project advocate to the organization's decision makers.[vi]

- **Work breakdown structure (WBS):** A tool for expressing the breadth of a project in graphic terms. Through the use of boxes, diagrammed in the format of an organizational chart, it represents the products, services and deliverables that the project will produce. By using this tool, you can describe the level of detail in which you will be reporting (e.g., costs, deliverable attainment and performance).

Proven practice. Those practices that have been shown through hard data analysis to drive either increased sales, customer loyalty or cost advantages, and thereby profitability. While "best practices" are generally derived from benchmarking top-performing companies, they are not always quantifiably proven. Proven practices, however, can come from anywhere. Even companies that perform poorly overall often have some departments or practices that have been proven quantifiably to be superior.

Regression analysis. Regression analysis concerns itself with predicting one variable from the knowledge of selected independent variables. Frequently performed in conjunction with correlation analysis.

Regrets reporting. Automated or rep-generated reporting of the time, date, conditions and reasons under which a sales rep had to decline a sale to a customer. Since declining a sale is frequently caused by structural or systemic reasons, the resulting data analysis can lead to operational changes throughout the organization that will allow reps to say "yes" to the sale and increase revenues.

Role-clarity document. A table of approved and unapproved tasks and activities for a specific job position, used to help individuals focus on areas critical to job success and performance.

Script. The words, logic or flow to be followed when handling a contact. Scripts are designed to assist reps in handling contacts. Strict definitions of script refer to detail right down to the words that reps are to use in conversations. But scripts also refer to call logic and call flows where word choice is up to the rep but call flow is suggested by the script (e.g., a technical support environment).[vii]

Script outline. An outline of the call flow with recommended dialogue for key points, designed to expedite the call while providing for quality and an improved business outcome (increased revenue or high customer loyalty).

Script points. Any of a number of validated or non-validated dialogue elements that are resident in a script outline.

Second close tools. Marketing tools (e.g., dialogue, promotions or discounts) that have been designed to assist the sales rep to close the sale after the first attempt has failed. Usually targeted at addressing an objection, product shortfall, availability or pricing issue.

Skills-based routing. Skills-based routing matches a caller's specific needs with a rep who has the best skills to handle that call on a real-time basis. The basic requirements to get started with skills-based routing include:

- Identify what differentiates the caller's needs and desires. This comes from the customer access strategy.

- Identify and define the skills required for each call-type.

- Identify and define individual rep skills.

- Prioritize rep skills, based on individual competency levels.

- Devise and program into the ACD an appropriate routing plan.

You will essentially create two "maps" when you program your ACD for skills-based routing. One will specify the types of calls to be handled, and the other will identify the skills available by rep.

In general, skills-based routing works best in environments that have small groups where multiple skills are required. It can also help to quickly integrate new reps into call handling, by sending only simple calls to them. It also has the potential to improve efficiency by matching callers with "just the right rep."

Skills-based routing has some disadvantages. Getting people in the right place at the right times can be difficult, and small specialized groups are tough to manage. Moreover, they can eliminate the efficiencies of pooling, common to conventional ACD groups, and routing and resource planning becomes more complex.[viii]

Standard deviation threshold. The standard deviation threshold ensures that the variance in the statistical performance metrics is not a result of normal fluctuations. For a sales environment, this includes seasonal fluctuations, price consciousness of the customer or a day-of-week phenomenon. Whether you should use one, two or three standard deviations, or something in between depends upon the purpose, and the quality and distribution of the data.

Structural factors. Those performance factors that are structural in nature, that is, they are components of the structure in which the workers work.

Change a structural factor in a positive way, and the performance of all workers generally will improve. Structural factors include organizational structure; for example, who is allowed to sell, what they are allowed to sell, and to whom they are allowed to sell.

Suspected performance driver. One of a large number of qualitative or quantitative purported performance drivers that, over the years, have been attributed to driving the major departmental KPI, referring to increased revenue or better service. Each of the rational suspects must be tested through correlation and regression analysis to determine if it is a true performance driver of the KPI.

Systemic factors. Those performance factors that are systemic in nature, that is, they are components of the system in which the workers work. Change a systemic factor in a positive way, and the performance of all workers generally will improve. Systemic factors include policies, procedures, computer system capabilities and response time.

Performance target. A short-term or interim performance improvement level required within a specific future point in time. It is a "checkpoint" to reassess progress, and correct action as necessary, to reach the final point of arrival (e.g., decrease cancellation rates to 5 percent by the end of the month).

Test kitchen. An ad hoc work area of the organization that is consistently dependable, which can function as a lab to test new ideas and tools (e.g., second close tools, dialogue elements), and report results with a high degree of reliability and credibility. Not to be confused with a "pilot program," which is performed prior to a rollout, the test kitchen does not attempt to refine a concept, only to quickly validate whether the concept has merit.

Upsell. A suggestive selling technique of offering more expensive products or additional services to customers during the sales decision-making process. In the case of an established customer, the offer is usually based on relationships established between the customer's profile and the attributes of customers who have already purchased the products or services being upsold.[ix] In the case of a service call, the upsell may also be the extension of a plan or increase in current usage rate.

Up-training. A term used to describe any new skills training initiated subsequent to new-hire training. Usually a budget (e.g., for time off phones, rep development, training materials and trainer) is developed for up-training so that tenured reps keep current and fresh on advanced skills and product knowledge.

Value prospectus. A one-page visual representation of a company's product costs and sale price, compared with the product cost and sale price of a selected product from a different industry with which sales reps may have experience. It is used to help sales reps understand the value proposition for a product or service they may not use personally, but that they're trying to sell. Generally useful when the perceived sale price of the company's product is high relative to the earning power of the sales rep.

i   U.S. Department of Labor Testing Guide, Uniform Guidelines on Employee Selection Procedures. 1978

ii Excerpt from *ICMI's Call Center Management Dictionary*

iii Excerpt from *ICMI's Call Center Management Dictionary*

iv Excerpt from *ICMI's Call Center Management Dictionary*

v   Excerpted from *ICMI's Call Center Management Dictionary*

vi Excerpted and adapted from *ICMI's Call Center Management Dictionary*

vii Excerpted from *ICMI's Call Center Management Dictionary*

viii Excerpted from *ICMI's Call Center Management Dictionary*

ix Excerpted and paraphrased from *ICMI's Call Center Management Dictionary*

Bibliography

Preface

i   Cleveland, Brad and Mayben, Julia. *Call Center Management On Fast Forward,* Call Center Press, ICMI Inc. 1997.

ii   Greenberg, H. and Greenberg, J. "The Personality of a Top Salesman," *Nation's Business,* December 1983.

iii   Schwartz, A.L. "Recruiting and Selection of Salespeople" (1983), in *Sales Managers Handbook.* Dow Jones-Irwin.

Chapter 1

i   Mapes, James. *Quantum Leap Thinking,* Dove Audio Inc. 1996.

ii   Interview with Dr. Wendell Williams Ph.D., Managing Director, ScientificSelection.com. December 2003.

iii   Performix Technologies' presentation, ICCM Conference & Exposition. August 2003.

iv   Zona Research, quoted in ICMI Industry Stats online. May 2001.

Chapter 2

i   Joachimsthaler, Eric. *Harvard Business Review on Brand Management,* Harvard Business School Press. 1999.

ii   Zaccaro, Stephan J. *The Nature of Organizational Leadership: Understanding the Performance Imperatives Confronting Today's Leaders,* Josey-Bass Inc. 2001.

Chapter 3

i   The Standish Group. *The CHAOS Report.* 1994.

Chapter 5

i   Portland Research Group study, quoted on destinationCRM.com. April 2004.

Chapter 6

i Furnham, A. *Personality at Work: The role of individual differences in the workplace*, London: Rutledge. 1992.

ii Interview with Williams, Dr. Wendell, ScientificSelection.com.

iii Fazzini, D., Hogan, R. and Raskin, R. "The Dark Side of Charisma," in *Measures of Leadership*, Leadership Library of America Inc. 1990.

Chapter 7

i Williams, Dr. Wendell. "Shiny-toed Selling: Salespeople Who Ignore the Shoe," Electronic Recruiting Exchange (www.erexchange.com). October 2003.

ii Williams, Dr. Wendell. "Why good Salespeople Don't Make Good Sales Managers," Electronic Recruiting Exchange (www.erexchange.com). November 2003.

iii Williams, Dr. Wendell. "Shiny-toed Selling: Salespeople Who Ignore the Shoe," Electronic Recruiting Exchange (www.erexchange.com). October 2003.

iv Interview with Dr. Wendell Williams Ph.D., Managing Director, ScientificSelection.com.

v *National Employers Survey*, Bureau of the Census. 1997. Cited by Capelli, Peter and Wilk, Steffanie. "Understanding the Determinants of Employer Use of Selection Methods," *Personnel Psychology*, Vol 56. 2003.

vi Barrick, M. R. and Mount, M.K. "The Big Five Personality Dimensions and Job Performance: A Meta Analysis," *Personnel Psychology*, Vol. 44. 1991.

vii Dr. Wendell Williams Ph.D.. ScientificSelection.com. 1999.

viii Administrative Office of the U.S. Courts' Bureau of Justice Statistics Civil Rights Complaints Report. 1990-1998

ix Gallup Organization. "U.S. Employment Engagement Index" (ongoing study). 2004.

Chapter 9

i   Falvey, J. "The Benefits of Working with the Best Workers," *Wall Street Journal.* May 1981.

ii *ICMI's Call Center Monitoring Study II Final Report,* ICMI Inc. 2002.

Chapter 11

i   Study by the American Compensation Association. Cited in *Call Center Management Review,* ICMI Inc. April 2001.

ii Graham, Dr. Gerald H. *The 1993 National Study of the Changing Workforce,* Wichita State University. 1991.

Chapter 12

i   Cleveland, Brad. *ICMI's Call Center Management Dictionary,* Call Center Press, ICMI Inc. 2003.

Index

71
Performance objective(s) 60, 62, 75
Performance pyramid 80
Performance review 10
Performance standards 16, 18, 53
Performance, individual 7, 15, 31, 66, 147, 241
Performance, individual's potential 144
Performance, integrated database 218
Performance, job 66-68, 70, 100
Performance, peak individual performance 62
Performance, peak performance methodology 20
Performance, peak performance path 18
Performance, rep performance factors 4
Performance, rep performance improvements 47
Performance, sales 1, 4, 6-8, 10-12, 14, 16, 18, 20, 24, 26, 28, 30, 32, 34, 36, 38, 40, 43-46, 48, 50, 52-54, 59-60, 62, 64, 66, 68, 70, 72, 74, 76, 79-82, 84, 86, 88, 90, 93, 94-103
Performance, setting S.M.A.R.T. (Specific, Measurable, Attainable, Realistic, Time-bound) objectives 62
Performance, stellar sales strategies 251-252
Performance-ranking feedback 157, 163
Performance-related attrition 121
Performix 221, 222
Perry, Sam 5-6
Personal Best Incentive Plan 192-195
Personality attributes 63, 100
Personality factors 101
Personality profile 264
Personality tests 108, 115
Personality traits 66, 80, 100
Pike Place Fish Market 262
Point of arrival (POA) 98
Positive reinforcement 143, 152, 154, 161, 173
Presentation(s) 45, 48-51, 53-54
Prioritization quadrant 242-243
Product value 129, 131
Project agreement(s) 18, 236
Project management 235-243, 252, 270
Project Management Forum, The 19
Project management organization 237
Project manager(s) 18, 29, 53, 236, 237,

238, 243
Project plan document 236
Project prioritization 241
Project software 236
Project team 236, 239, 249
Projects, tracking 235, 237, 239, 241, 243
Promus Group 5
Psychological Bulletin 108
Psychometric testing 264
Quality 8-9, 11, 25, 38, 62-63, 67, 74, 76, 118, 124, 132, 135, 157, 159-160, 172-173, 177-178, 188-190, 209, 214-215, 256-257
Quality measure(s) 74
Quantifiable data 18, 20, 28-29, 48
Quantifiable goal(s) 62
Quantifiable metrics 81
Quantification of escalation call-types 150-151
Quizzes 149, 150, 152, 180
Recognition 89-90, 124, 154-155, 163, 172, 185-186, 197-198, 206-211, 214, 221
Recognition, programs 89, 211
Recognition, top incentives 207
Reconfirmations 26-27
Recruiting (see also Assessments, Hiring) 87, 238, 256-257, 259
Recruiting process 116-117, 257, 259
Recruiting, best practices 124
Recruiting, bonuses 124
Recruiting, sales 19
Refresher training 131, 138, 148-149, 151-152, 173
Regression analysis 138
Regression analysis 60-61, 63, 65, 68-72, 80-81, 90
Regrets reporting 228
Report-tracking statistics 220
Resource requirements 50
Retention 139, 178, 206, 219, 241
Retry studies 26
Return on investment (ROI), back-of-envelope ROI exercise 34
Revenue generating units (RGU) 262-263
Revenue improvements 20, 54
Revenue management 13-14, 16, 24-25, 31
Revenue opportunities 3-5, 7-9, 11, 13,

How to Reach the Author

Do you have any comments, problems, solutions, results or opinions to discuss or share with the author? You can reach Mary Murcott at:

Telephone: 972-998-6734

Email: murcott@performancetransformations.biz

Web site: www.performancetransformations.biz

About the Author

Mary Murcott is founder and president of Performance Transformations Inc., a consulting firm based in Dallas, which provides speaking, consulting, management workshops and executive coaching services. She is an innovative strategic business transformation executive with more than 20 years' experience in designing service delivery platforms, developing global distribution channel strategies and leading high-performance teams in attaining best-in-class technology, service, sales and economics.

Mary has been instrumental in driving change and performance turnaround in leading-edge companies, including American Express, DHL, Budget Rent-a-Car, Ryder TRS and Cox Communications. She has proven extremely successful at directing start-up operations, consolidations and turn-around situations.

With her unique perspective on organizational performance and her ability to leverage technological innovation, combined with her leadership, project management and performance management expertise, Mary has repeatedly proven successful in driving significant improvements in enterprise-level performance.

Mary is a builder of award-winning customer contact centers. Her projects have received numerous awards from *Teleprofessional Magazine*, as well as the American Express' Chairman's Award and Call Center Network Group's "Call Center of the Year" award.

A highly sought-after speaker, Mary has delivered keynote speeches at industry conferences around the world.

Mary is the former CIO and SVP Worldwide Reservation Services for Budget Group Inc. She received her B.A. in Philosophy from Creighton University.

How to Reach the Publisher

We would love to hear from you! How could this book be improved? Has it been helpful? No comments are off limits! You can reach us at:

Mailing Address: Call Center Press, a division of ICMI, Inc.
P.O. Box 6177
Annapolis, MD 21401

Telephone: 410-267-0700, 800-672-6177

Fax: 410-267-0962

Email: icmi@icmi.com

Web site: www.icmi.com

About Incoming Calls Management Institute

ICMI Inc. is a global leader in call center consulting, training, publications and membership services. ICMI's mission is to help call centers (contact centers, help desks, customer care, support centers) achieve operational excellence and superior business results. Through the dedication and experience of its team, uncompromised objectivity and results-oriented vision, ICMI has earned a reputation as the industry's most trusted resource for:

- Consulting
- Seminars
- Publications
- Management Tools
- Conferences and Networking Events
- Professional Membership

Based in Annapolis, Maryland, ICMI was established in 1985 and was first to develop and deliver management training customized for call centers. Through constant innovation and research, ICMI's training has become the industry's gold standard, and is recommended by 99.3% of those managers who have experienced its value first-hand. Over the years, ICMI has become the industry's leading provider of membership services with an impressive line-up of call center management resources, including instant access to prominent research, expert advice and career development tools, and a networking forum that spans more than 40 countries worldwide. ICMI is not associated with, owned or subsidized by any industry supplier—its only source of funding is from those who use its services. For more information about ICMI, visit www.icmi.com, or call 800-672-6177 (410-267-0700).

Order Form

QTY.	Item	Member Price	Price	Total
	Driving Peak Sales Performance in Call Centers**	**$33.96**	$39.95	
	Call Center Management On Fast Forward: Succeeding In Today's Dynamic Inbound Environment**	**$23.76**	$34.95	
	Call Center Technology Demystified: The No-Nonsense Guide to Bridging Customer Contact Technology, Operations and Strategy**	**$33.96**	$39.95	
	ICMI's Call Center Management Dictionary: The Essential Reference for Contact Center, Help Desk and Customer Care Professionals**	**$21.21**	$24.95	
	ICMI's Pocket Guide to Call Center Management Terms*	**$5.12**	$5.95	
	ICMI Handbook and Study Guide Series Module 1: People Management*** Module 2: Operations Management*** Module 3: Customer Relationship Management*** Module 4: Leadership and Business Management***	**$169.15 ea.**	$199.00 ea.	
	Topical Books: **The Best of *Call Center Management Review*** Call Center Recruiting and New Hire Training* Call Center Forecasting and Scheduling* Call Center Agent Motivation and Compensation* Call Center Agent Retention and Turnover*	**$14.41 ea.**	$16.95 ea.	
	Forms Books Call Center Sample Monitoring Forms** Call Center Sample Customer Satisfaction Forms Book**	**$42.46 ea.**	$49.95 ea.	
	Software QueueView: A Staffing Calculator—CD ROM* Easy StartTM Call Center Scheduler Software—CD-ROM*	**$41.65** **$254.15**	$49.95 $299.00	
	Call Center Humor: The Best of *Call Center Management Review* Volume 3*	**$8.45**	$9.95	
	The Call Centertainment Book*	**$7.61**	$8.95	
	Shipping & Handling @ $5.00 per US shipment, plus .50¢ per* item, $1.00 per** item and $2.00 per*** item. Additional charges apply to shipments outside the US.			
	Tax (5% MD residents, 7% GST Canadian residents)			
	TOTAL (US dollars)			

Please contact us for quantity discounts
For more information on our products, please visit **www.icmi.com**

❏ Please send me a free issue of *Call Center Management Review* (ICMI's journal for members) and information on ICMI's publications, services and membership.

Please ship my order and/or information to:

Name _____

Title _____

Industry_____

Company_____

Address_____

City_____State _____Postal Code _____

Telephone (   )_____

Fax (   )_____

Email_____

Method of Payment (if applicable)

❏ Check enclosed (Make payable to ICMI Inc.; U.S. Dollars only)

❏ Charge to: ❏ American Express   ❏ MasterCard   ❏ Visa

Account No._____

Expiration Date _____

Name on Card _____

Fax order to:	410-267-0962
call us at:	800-672-6177 or 410-267-0700
order online at:	www.icmi.com
or mail order to:	ICMI Inc.
	P.O. Box 6177, Annapolis, MD 21401